THE SCARECROW AUTHOR BIBLIOGRAPHIES

EZRA POUND:
a bibliography of secondary works

compiled by
Beatrice Ricks

The Scarecrow Author Bibliographies,
No. 74

The Scarecrow Press, Inc.
Metuchen, N.J., & London
1986

Library of Congress Cataloging-in-Publication Data

Ricks, Beatrice.
  Ezra Pound, a bibliography of secondary works.

  (The Scarecrow author bibliogaphies ; no. 74)
  Bibliography: p.
  Includes indexes.
  1. Pound, Ezra, 1885-1972--Bibliography.
I. Title.   II. Series.
Z8709.3.R53   1986   [PS3531.082]   016.811'52   85-26140
ISBN 0-8108-1862-0

Dedicated to the Staff of the
Ward Edwards Library
of
Central Missouri State University

PREFACE

Ezra Pound was chosen as the subject of this bibliography because he was very controversial during and after the Second World War. War arouses emotions, both political and personal, which are sometimes long lasting, and which often influence opinion as to the quality of a work, or character of a poet.

Despite the pain inflicted by the war, Ezra Pound's poetic influence awakened our love of poetry. History provides a record of the past, but poetry helps us to feel the emotions of those involved, and thus perhaps helps us to cope more efficiently with our own world and our own times.

B. R.

CONTENTS

ABBREVIATIONS AND PUBLICATIONS

ABnG	Amsterdamer Beitrage zur neueren Germanistik
Accent	Accent
ACF	Annali di Ca'Foscari
Agenda	Agenda
AI	American Imago: A Psychoanalytic Journal for Culture, Science and the Arts
AION-SG	Annali Istituto Universitario Orientale, Napoli Sezione Germanica
AJES	The Aligarh Journal of English Studies
Akzente	Akzente
AL	American Literature: A Journal of Literary History, Criticism and Bibliography
AmerDialog	American Dialogue
AmLS	American Literary Scholarship: An Annual
AmMerc	American Mercury
AmP	American Poetry
AmQ	American Quarterly
AmS	American Studies
AmsT	Amerikastudien/American Studies
Analyst	Analyst
AN&Q	American Notes & Queries (New Haven, Conn.)
AnRS	Annual Reports of Studies (Kyoto, Japan)
Antaeus	Antaeus
AntigR	Antigonish Review
Approdo	L'Approdo Letterario (Rome)
APR	American Poetry Review
AQ	American Quarterly
AR	The Antioch Review
ArAA	Arbeiten aus Anglistik und Amerikanistik
Archiv	Archiv für das Studium der neueren Sprachen und Literaturen
Arion	Arion (University of Texas)
ArionNS	Boston University
ArQ	Arizona Quarterly

ArtInt	Art International
AsSt	Asian Student
Atenea	Atenea
AtlM	Atlantic Monthly
ATQ	American Transcendental Quarterly
AUB-LG	Analele Universitatii, Limbi Germanice [formerly AUB]
Audit	Audit
AUMLA	Journal of the Australasian Universities' Language and Literature Association
Aut-Aut	Aut-Aut
AWR	The Anglo-Welsh Review (Pembroke Dock, Wales)
BA	Books Abroad
B&B	Books and Bookmen
Bachelor	The Bachelor (Wabash College, Crawfordsville, Ind.)
BColl	Book Collector
BJA	British Journal of Aesthetics (London)
BLM	Bonniers Litterära Magasin (Stockholm)
BNM	Book News Monthly
BNYPL	Bulletin of the New York Public Library
Booklist	Booklist
Bookman	Bookman
BookW	Bookweek
Borghese	Borghese
Boundary	Boundary I
BRH	Bulletin of Research in the Humanities
BRMMLA	Bulletin of the Rocky Mountain Modern Lang. Assn.
Brotéria	Brotéria
BSA	Bibliographical Society of America
BSAP	(See PBSA)
BSNotes	Browning Society Notes
BSUF	Ball State University Forum
BUJ	Boston University Journal
BuR	Bucknell Review
BUSE	Boston University Studies in English
CahiersdlH	Cahiers de l'Herne
CalcR	Calcutta Review
CamJ	Cambridge Journal
CaM	The Carleton Miscellany
CamQ	Cambridge Quarterly
CamR	Cambridge Review
CanForum	Canadian Forum
CanL	Canadian Literature
CanMusicJ	Canadian Music Journal
CaSE	Carnegie Studies in English
CathW	Catholic World

Cave	Cave
CdA	Camp de l'Arpa: Revista de Literatura
CdS	Cahiers du Sud
CE	College English
CEA	CEA Critic
CentR	The Centennial Review (Michigan State U.)
CHA	Cuadernos Hispanoamericanos (Madrid)
ChC	Chinese Culture
Chelsea	Chelsea
ChR	ChicagoR
ChrC	Christian Century
CimR	Cimarron Review (Oklahoma State U.)
Civ/n	Civ/n (Montreal)
CJ	Classical Journal
CJIS	Canadian Journal of Irish Studies (Vancouver)
CL	Comparative Literature
CLAJ	College Language Assn. Journal (Morgan State U., Baltimore)
CLit	Contemporary Literature (U. of Wisconsin, Madison)
CLS	Comparative Literature Studies
CollL	College Literature (Westchester State Coll.)
Coloquio	Coloquio
ColQ	Colorado Quarterly
Commentary	Commentary
CompLit	Comparative Literature
ConL	Contemporary Literature (Supersedes WSCL)
ConnR	Connecticut Review
ConP	Contemporary Poetry: A Journal of Poetry Criticism
ContempI	Contemporary Issues
ContP	Contemporary Poetry: A Journal of Poetry Criticism
CP	Classical Philology
ConP	Concerning Poetry (West. Wash. State Coll.)
Conv	Convivium (Barcelona)
ConvLit	Convorbiri literare (Jassy, Romania)
CRAS	The Centennial Review of Arts and Sciences (Michigan State U.)
Cresset	Cresset
CRevAS	Canadian Review of American Studies
Criterion	Criterion
Critic	Critic
Criticism	Criticism (Wayne State U.)
CritP	Critique: Revue Generale des Publication Francaises et Etrangeres (Paris)

CritQ	Critical Quarterly
Cronica	Cronica
Cronos	Cronos
CSMM	Christian Science Monitor Magazine
CurBio	Current Biography
Cw	Commonweal

DagensN	Dagens Nyheter
Delo	Delo (Belgrade)
DenQR	Denver Quarterly Review
Diagonale	Diagonale
Dial	Dialoghi
DilR	Diliman Review
Direction	Direction
DoshL	Doshisha Literature (Kyoto)
DQ	Denver Quarterly
DQR	Dutch Quarterly Review of Anglo-American Letters
DR	Dalhousie Review
Drama	Drama, The Quarterly Theatre Review
DramC	Drama Critique
DRund	Deutsch Rundschau
DSARDS	Dante Studies with the Annual Report of the Dante Society
DubM	Dublin Magazine
DubR	Dublin Review
DurhamUJ	Durham University Journal
DWB	Dietsche Warande en Belfort

E&S	Essays and Studies by Members of the English Association
Edda	Edda
Egoist	Egoist
EH	Eastern Horizons (Hong Kong)
EIC	Essays in Criticism
EIE	English Institute Essays
EigoS	Eigo Seinen [The Rising Generation] (Tokyo)
EJ	English Journal
ELH	English Literary History
ELN	English Language Notes (Univ. of Colorado, Boulder, Colorado)
ELWIU	Essays in Literature (Western Ill. Univ.)
EM	English Miscellany
EmoryUQ	Emory University Quarterly
Encounter	Encounter (London)
English	English
EngQ	English Quarterly
EngRec	English Record
EngRev	English Review
Epoch	Epoch (Cornell U.)
ES	English Studies

ESA	English Studies in Africa: A Journal of the Humanities (Johannesburg, South Africa)
ESPSL	O Estado de São Paulo, Suplemento Literário
Esquire	Esquire
Estaciones	Estaciones
Estafeta Literaria	Estafeta Literaria
Europa-Kurier	Europa-Kurier
Europe	Europe: Revue Litteraire Mensuelle
European	European
Evening Bulletin	Evening Bulletin
EvR	Evergreen Review
EWR	East-West Review (Doshisha U., Kyoto, Japan)
Expl	Explicator
Fantasy	Fantasy: A Literary Quarterly
FarP	Far Point
FDP	Four Decades of Poetry, 1890-1930
FH	Frankfurter Hefte
FlaRev	Florida Review
FLe	La Fiera Letteraria
FN	Filologičeskie Nauki
Forum	Forum (São Paulo)
ForumH	Forum (Houston)
Freeman	Freeman
Furioso	Furioso
FurmanMag	Furman Magazine
FurmS	Furman Studies (Furman U., Greenville, S.C.)
Gakujutsu Kenkyu Nempo	Gakujutsu Kenkyu Nempo
Galleria	Galleria (Italy)
GaR	Georgia Review
Genre	Genre (U. of Illinois at Chicago Circle)
Germanisch-Romanische	Germanisch-Romanische Monatsschrift, NS
GQ	German Quarterly
GR	Germanic Review
Greyfriar	Greyfriar: Siena Studies in Literature (Siena College, NY)
GRM	Germanisch-Romanische Monatsschrift
HA	Harvard Advocate
HAB	Humanities Association Bulletin/La Revue de l'Association des Humanites [Formerly: Humanities Association Bulletin (Canada)]
H&H	Hound and Horn
HAR	Hamilton Alumni Review

HarpB	Harper's Bazar
HarperW	Harper's Weekly
HINL	History of Ideas Newsletter
HJAS	Harvard Journal of Asiatic Studies
HLB	Harvard Library Bulletin
Hollins Critic	Hollins Critic
Horizon	Horizon
HSELL	Hiroshima Studies in English Language and Literature (Hiroshima, Japan)
HSL	University of Hartford Studies in Literature: A Journal of Interdisciplinary Criticism
HudR	The Hudson Review
Humanities	Humanities
Humanist	Humanist
HumR	Humane Review

Idea	Idea (Itlay)
IE	Interdisciplinary Essays
IJAS	Indian Journal of American Studies
Il Borghese	Il Borghese
Il Caffe	Il Caffe
Il Mare	Il Mare
Il Merle Giallo	Il Merle Giallo
Il Ponte	Il Ponte; Rivista mensile di politica e letteratura
Il Secolo d'Italia	Il Secolo d'Italia (Rome)
Il Tempo	Il Tempo
Imagi	Imagi
IM	Il Mondo
Indep	Independent
IndianLit	Indian Literature (New Delhi)
Intro	Intro
IowaR	Iowa Review (U. of Iowa, Iowa City)
IQt	Italian Quarterly
Ish	Ishmael
Isis	Isis
Irish Writing	Irish Writing
Italian Qt	Italian Quarterly
Izraz	Izraz: Časopis za Književnu i Umjetničku Kritiku (Sarajevo, Yugoslavia)

JA	Jahrbuch für Amerikastudien
JAAC	Journal of Aesthetics and Art Criticism
JAE	Journal of Aesthetic Education
JAmS	Journal of American Studies
JBeSt	John Berryman Studies
JEGP	Journal of English and Germanic Philology

JHS	Journal of Historical Studies
JJQ	James Joyce Quarterly
JML	Journal of Modern Literature
JoP	Journal of Politics
JPC	Journal of Popular Culture
JQ	Journalism Quarterly
Jubilee	Jubilee
KAL	Kyushu American Literature (Fukuoka, Japan)
KBAA	Kieler Beiträge zur Anglistik und Amerikanistik
KN	Kwartalnik Neofilologiczny (Warsaw)
KompH	Komparatistische Hefte (Formerly: Mainzer Komparatistische Hefte)
KR	Kenyon Review
KuL	Kunst und Literatur
KyR	Kentucky Review
L&I	Literature and Ideology (Montreal)
Landfall	Landfall
LC	Library Chronicle
LCUT	Library Chronicle of the University of Texas
LE&W	Literature East and West
Left Review	Left Review
Let	Letteratura
LetM	Letterature Moderne (Milan)
Lettere Italiane	Lettere Italiane
L'Europeo	L'Europeo
LGJ	Lost Generation Journal
LHR	Lock Haven Review (Lock Haven State College, Pa.)
LHY	Literary Half-Yearly
LibJ	Library Journal
Life	Life
Listener	Listener
L'Italia	L'Italia
LitD	Literary Digest
LitHY	Literary Half-Yearly (Mysore)
LitRev	Little Review
LitRNYEP	Literary Review, New York Evening Post
LJGG	Literaturwissenschaftliches Jahrbuch im Auftrage der Görres-Gesellschaft
LMS	Letopis Matice Srpske (Novi Sad)
LonM	London Magazine
LonMer	The London Mercury
LonSpec	London Spectator
Look	Look
Luc	Luceafărul (Bucharest)

LugR	Lugano Review
LWU	Literatur in Wissenschaft und Unterricht
Mainstream	Mainstream
MalahR	Malahat Review: An International Quarterly of Life and Letters (Victoria, British Columbia)
MalR	Malahat Review
M &M	Masses & Mainstream
MarkhamR	Markham Review
Martin	Martinella
MASJ	Midcontinent American Studies Journal (U. of Kansas, Lawrence)
MassR	Massachusetts Review
MdF	Mercure de France
Meanjin	Meanjin (U. of Melbourne)
MELUS	MELUS
Merkur	Merkur (Stuttgart)
Metrop	Metropolitan
MFS	Modern Fiction Studies
MGSL	Minas Gerais, Suplemento Literário
Midst	Midstream
MidwQ	Midwest Quarterly (Pittsburg, Kansas)
MinnR	Minnesota Review
MJSS	Montclair Journal of Social and Behavioral Sciences (Montclair State College, NJ)
MLN	Modern Language Notes
MLQ	Modern Language Quarterly
MLS	Modern Language Studies
MMN	Marianne Moore Newsletter
ModA	Modern Age (Chicago)
ModAmerG	Modern American Guide
ModR	Modern Review (Calcutta)
MoOc	Modern Occasions
Mosaic	Mosaic: A Journal for the Interdisciplinary Study of Literature
MP	Modern Philology
MPS	Modern Poetry Studies
MQ	Midwest Quarterly (Pittsburg, Kansas)
MQR	Michigan Quarterly Review
MR	Massachusetts Review
MSE	Massachusetts Studies in English
MSpr	Moderna Språk (Stockholm, Sweden)
NA	Nuova Antologia (Roma)
N &Q	Notes and Queries
NAR	North American Review
Nation	Nation
NatlR	National Review

Nazione	Nazione (Firenze)
NC	Nuova Corrente
NConL	Notes on Contemporary Literature
NDEJ	Notre Dame English Journal
NDH	Neue Deutsche Hefte
NDQ	North Dakota Quarterly
NE	Nueva Estafeta
NEQ	New England Quarterly
New Democracy	New Democracy
NEW	New English Weekly
NewF	New Freeman
NewSt	New Statesman
Nimbus	Nimbus
Ninepence	Ninepence
NL	Nouvelles Littéraires
NLB	Newberry Library Bulletin
NLH	New Literary History: A Journal of Theory and Interpretation (Charlottesville, VA)
NMAL	Notes on Modern American Literature
NMQ	New Mexico Quarterly
NOR	New Orleans Review
Novite	Novite
NR	New Republic
NR de DM	Nouvelle Revue des Deux Mondes
NS	Die Neueren Sprachen
NS&N	New Statesman and Nation
NSt	New Statesman
NWR	Northwest Review
NY	New Yorker
NYRB	New York Review of Books
NYT	New York Times
NYTBR	New York Times Book Review
NZZ	Neue Zürcher Zeitung (Zürich)
Obs	Observer
Occ	Occident (Berkeley, Calif.)
Oggi	Oggi (Milan)
OhR	The Ohio Review
OL	Orbis Litterarum: International Review of Literary Studies
OLR	Oxford Literary Review
OperaN	Opera News
OSA	Ohio State Argo
OT	Oakland Tribune
Outlook	Outlook
Paideuma	Paideuma: A Journal Devoted to Ezra Pound Scholarship
PaG	Pennsylvania Gazette
PaR	Pennsylvania Review
P&R	Philosophy and Rhetoric

Paragone	Paragone: Rivista Mensile di Arte Figurativa e Letteratura
ParisR	Paris Review
PBA	Proceedings of the British Academy
PBSA	Papers of the Bibliographical Society of America
Person	Personalist
Perspective	Perspective: A Magazine of Modern Literature
Plamen	Plamen (Praha)
Playboy	Playboy
PLL	Papers on Language and Literature (So. Ill. U.)
PM	PM Newspaper, Inc.
PMASAL	Papers of the Michigan Academy of Science, Arts, and Letters
PMLA	Publications of the Modern Language Association of America
PNR	PN Review
PoetA	Poetry Australia (New South Wales)
Poetica	Poetica (Tokyo)
Poet Lore	Poet Lore
Poetry	Poetry
PoetryN	Poetry Nation (Manchester, England)
PoundN	Pound Newsletter
PQ	Philological Quarterly
PR	Partisan Review
Prose	Prose
Prospects	Prospects: Annual of American Cultural Studies
Prospetti	Prospetti
PrR	Princeton Review
PrSch	Prairie Schooner
PsyToday	Psychology Today
PubW	Publisher's Weekly
PULC	Princeton University Library Chronicle
Purpose	Purpose
PUSA	Perspectives USA
QLS	Quarterly Journal of Speech
QL	La Quinzaine Littéraire (Paris)
QQ	Queen's Quarterly
QRL	Quarterly Review of Literature
Quadrant	Quadrant: An Australian Bi-Monthly
RAA	Revue Anglo-Américaine
RA&A	Recherches Anglaises et Américaines
RadioT	Radio Times
RALS	Resources for American Literary Studies
RBA	Revista de Bellas Artes
RdE	Rivista di Estetica (U. di Padova)
REL	Review of English Literature

Rendezvous	Rendezvous: Journal of Arts and Letters (Idaho State U)
Reporter	Reporter
RES	Review of English Studies
Review	Review: A Magazine of Poetry and Criticism
RevR	Review of Reviews
RGB	Revue Générale Belge (Brussels)
RL	Revista de Literatura
RLC	Revue de Littérature Comparée
RLM	Revue des Lettres Modernes
RLMC	Rivista di Letterature Moderne e Comparate (Florence, Italy)
RLV	Revue des langues vivantes (Bruxelles)
RN	Revue nouvelle
RNL	Review of National Literatures
RO	Revista de Occidente
RomLit	România literară (Bucharest)
RomN	Romance Notes (U. of North Carolina)
RPol	Review of Politics
RR	Romantic Review
RS	Research Studies (Pullman, WA)
RutgersRev	Rutgers Review
SA	Studi Americani (Roma)
Sal	Salmagundi
SAQ	South Atlantic Quarterly
SatRL	Saturday Review of Literature
SAVL	Studien zur Allgemeinen und Vergleichenden Literaturwissenschaft
SBHC	Studies in Browning and His Circle: A Journal of Criticism, History, and Bibliography
Sch&Soc	School and Society
SCR	South Carolina Review (Clemson U)
Scrutiny	Scrutiny
SCSML	Smith College Studies in Modern Languages
Secolul	Secolul
SEL	Studies in English Literature (Tokyo)
SELit	Studies in English Literature (English Literary Society of Japan, U. of Tokyo)
SELL	Studies in English Literature and Language (Kyushu U., Fukuoka, Japan)
Shan	Shantih: Journal of International Writing and Art
Shen	Shenandoah
SHR	Southern Humanities Review
SIR	Studies in Romanticism
SN	Studia Neophilologica: A Journal of

	Germanic and Romance Languages and Literature
SoR	Southern Review (Louisiana State U)
SoRA	Southern Review: Literary and Inter-disciplinary Essays (Adelaide, Australia)
Sou	Sou'wester
Southerly	Southerly
SP	Studies in Philology
SPe	Lo Spettatore Italiano
Spect	Spectator (London)
Spectrum	Spectrum
Spirit	Spirit: A Magazine of Poetry
SR	Sewanee Review
Sreaua	Sreaua
SSMLN	Society for the Study of Midwestern Literature Newsletter (Michigan St. U., East Lansing)
Stagione	Stagione
Stand	Standpunte
StAR	StAR (St. Andrews Review, St. Andrews Presbyterian College)
StHum	Studies in the Humanities (Indiana U. of Pennsylvania)
Stony Brook	Stony Brook
Streven	Streven (Amsterdam)
Sumac	Sumac
SUS	Studi Urbinati di Storia, Filosofia e Letteratura
SWR	Southwest Review
SXX	Secolul XX (Bucharest)
TamR	Tamarack Review
T&T	Time and Tide
TC	Twentieth Century (Melbourne, Australia)
TCL	Twentieth Century Literature: A Scholarly and Critical Journal. (Hofstra U., Hempstead, NY)
Tel Quel	Tel Quel (Paris)
Tempo	Tempo (Rome)
TexQT	Texas Quarterly
Thought	Thought
ThQ	This Quarter (Paris)
Threshold	Threshold
Time	Time Magazine
TkR	Tamkang Review
TLS	Times Literary Supplement (London)
Today	Today
Topic	Topic: A Journal of the Liberal Arts
Townsend	Townsend

Townsman	Townsman
Trace	Trace
Transition	Transition
TriQ	Tri-Quarterly (Evanston, Ill.)
TSE	Tulane Studies in English
TSEN	T. S. Eliot Newsletter
TSER	T. S. Eliot Review
TSLL	Texas Studies in Language and Literature
TUSAS	Twayne United States Author Series
Tyro	Tyro
UDQ	University of Denver Quarterly
UES	UNISA English Studies: A Journal of the Department of English
UKCR	University of Kansas City Review
UMPAW	University of Minneapolis Pamphlets on American Writers
Universidad	Universidad de Mexico
Unser Tsait	Unser Tsait
UPortR	University of Portland Review
UR	University Review (Kansas City, MO)
UTQ	University of Toronto Quarterly
UWR	University of Windsor Review
Vanity Fair	Vanity Fair
Veltro	Veltro (Rome)
Verri	Il Verri
VLit	Voprosy Literature
Voices	Voices
Vort	Vort
VQR	Virginia Quarterly Review
VR	Viata Romaneasca (Bucharest)
VWQ	Virginia Woolf Quarterly (Calif. State U., San Diego)
WAL	Western American Literature
WASAL	Wisconsin Academy of Sciences, Arts, and Letters
WCR	West Coast Review
WCWN	William Carlos Williams Newsletter
WHR	Western Humanities Review
World	World Magazine
WR	Western Review (U. of Kansas, Lawrence)
WSCL	Wisconsin Studies in Contemporary Literature
WuW	Welt und Wort
WWR	Walt Whitman Review
WZ	Wort in der Zeit (Vienna)
XRev	X, A Quarterly Review

YCGL	Yearbook of Comparative and General Literature
YeA	Yeats Annual
YER	Yeats-Eliot Review
YES	Yearbook of English Studies
YFS	Yale French Studies
YLG	Yale Library Gazette
YLM	Yale Literary Magazine
YPR	Yale Poetry Review
YR	Yale Review
YSE	Yale Studies in English
YULG	Yale University Library Gazette
Zivot	Zivot: Casopis za Knjizevnost i Kulturu

I. BIOGRAPHY

1 Ackroyd, Peter. Ezra Pound and His World. New York: Charles Scribner, 1980.

2 Auden, W. H., et al. Ezra Pound at Seventy. Norfolk, Conn.: New Directions, 1956.

3 Baker, Carlos. "Pound in Venice," VQR, 50, #4 (Autumn, 1974), 597-605.

4 Banta, R. E. "Ezra Pound Among the Hoosiers," Wabash Bulletin, 49 (December, 1953), 11-13.

5 Berryman, John. "The Poetry of Ezra Pound," Partisan Review, 16, #4 (April, 1949), 377-394.

6 _____. "A Tribute," Agenda, Special Issue in Honor of Ezra Pound's Eightieth Birthday, IV, ii (October-November, 1965), 27-28.

7 Bibesco, H. "Lunch with Uncle Ez," AtlM, 240, #2 (August, 1977), 55-58.

8 Bottome, Phyllis. "Ezra Pound," From the Life. London: Faber & Faber, Ltd., 1944, pp. 70-82.

9 _____. "Ezra Pound--Happy Exile," This Week (December 1, 1935), 10-11.

10 Bowers, Faubion, and Carroll F. Terrell. "Memoir within Memoirs," Paideuma, 2, #1 (Spring, 1973), 49-66.

11 Boyd, Ernest L. "Ezra Pound at Wabash College," JML, 4 (September, 1974), 43-54.

12 Bradbury, Malcolm. "Pound of Flesh," NSt, 7 (August, 1970), 156-157.

13 Braidwood, John, et al. "Ezra Pound: A Commemorative Symposium," Paideuma, 3 (Winter, 1974), 151-168.

14 Brown, John L. "A Troubadour at Hamilton," Hamilton Literary Mag, 62 (November, 1932), 53-63.

15 Cann, Louise Beghard. "With the Pounds in Paris," Pound
    Newsletter, 8 (October, 1955), 24–27.

16 Capellan, Angel. "Ezra Pound (1885–1972), Estudio biografico,"
    RO, 12, #132 (March, 1974), 309–342.

17 Capote, Truman, and Richard Avedon. "Observations on Ezra
    Pound," Esquire, 52 (September, 1959), 74–76.

18 Carruth, Hayden. "On a Picture of Ezra Pound," Poetry, 110,
    #2 (May, 1967), 103–105.

19 Clark, William Bedford, "'Ez sez': Pound's 'Pithy Promulga-
    tions,'" AntiochRev, 37 (Fall, 1979), 420–427.

20 Connolly, Cyril. "The Break-Through in Modern Verse," LonM,
    n.s., 1 (June, 1961), 27–40.

21 Cory, Daniel. "Ezra Pound: A Memoir," Encounter, 30, #5
    (May, 1968), 30–39; repr., in Ezra Pound: A Critical Anthology.
    J. P. Sullivan, ed. Baltimore, MD., 1970, pp. 374–376.

22 Cournos, John. Autobiography. New York: G. P. Putnam's
    Sons, 1935, passim.

23 Cowley, Edmund. "Fox in Flight," Furioso, 6 (Spring, 1951),
    7–10.

24 Dahlberg, Edward, and Herbert Read. "On T. S. Eliot and
    Ezra Pound," Truth Is More Sacred: A Critical Exchange on
    Modern Literature. New York: Horizon Pr., 1961, pp. 169–222.

25 Darrach, Brad. "Poetry and Poison," Review of Ezra Pound:
    The Last Rower by C. David Heymann. Time, 107 (March 8,
    1976), pp. 74, 75, 77.

26 Davenport, Guy. "Ezra Pound, 1885–1972," Arion, n. s., 1
    (1973), 188–196.

27 De Rachewiltz, Mary. Discretions: A Memoir by Ezra Pound's
    Daughter. London: Faber & Faber, 1971; Boston: Little
    Brown, 1971.

28 _____. "Ezra Pound at Eighty," Esquire, 65 (April, 1966),
    114–116, 178–180.

29 Deutsch, Babette. "The Teacher," YLM, 126 (December, 1958),
    v, 10; repr., in A Casebook on Ezra Pound. Wm. Van O'Connor
    and Edward Stone, eds. New York: Crowell, 1959, pp. 151–152.

30 Devlin, Vianney M. "In Memoriam--Ezra Pound," Greyfriar, 13
    (1972), 42–44.

31 Diesendorf, Margaret. "A Lume Spento: Ezra Pound (1885-1972)," Poetry Australia, 46 (1972), 4-5.

32 Doob, Eveline Bates. "Some Notes on Ezra Pound," Paideuma, 8 (1979), 69-78.

33 Doob, Leonard W., ed. "Ezra Pound Speaking," Radio Speeches of World War II. Westport, Conn.: Greenwood Pr., 1978.

34 Doody, M. A. "Elegy for Ezra Pound," AWR, 22 (Spring, 1973), 194-196.

35 Doolittle, Hilda [H. D.] An End to Torment: A Memoir of Ezra Pound by H. D. Norman Holmes Pearson and Michael King, eds. Foreword by Michael King. New York: New Directions Pub. Co., 1979.

36 Duncan, Ronald. "Pull Down Thy Vanity: A Visit to Ezra Pound," Sunday Times (February 11, 1962), p. 33, cols. 2-5.

37 Eastman, Barbara. "The 90th Birthday Symposium," Paideuma, 4, #2 & 3, (Fall and Winter, 1975), 519-523.

38 Edwards, John Hamilton. "A Critical Biography of Ezra Pound: 1885-1922," Diss. University of California, Berkeley, 1952.

39 Enright, D. J. "Dialect and Analect: A Life of Ezra Pound," Man Is an Onion: Reviews and Essays. The Library Press, U. S.; Distr. by Open Court Pub. Co., LaSalle, Ill., 1973, pp. 123-127.

40 Evans, Luther H. "A Letter from the Librarian of Congress," and "A Reply," SatRL, 32 (July 2, 1949), 20-23.

41 Fiedler, Leslie. "Traitor or Laureate: The Two Trials of the Poet," New Approaches to Ezra Pound. Eva Hesse, ed. Berkeley and Los Angeles: University of California, 1969, pp. 365-377.

42 Foote, Edward. "A Note on Ezra Pound," Prose, 7 (Fall, 1973), 71-78.

43 Ford, Ford Madox. It Was the Nightingale. New York: Farrar, Straus & Giroux; Octagon Books, 1975, pp. 203-205, passim.

44 Gallup, Donald Clifford. T. S. Eliot and Ezra Pound: Collaborators in Letters. New Haven, Conn.: Henry W. Wenning, 1970.

45 Gatter, Carl, and Noel Stock. "Ezra Pound's Pennsylvania," Poetry Australia, 46 (Spring, 1973), 5-36.

46 Geddes, Virgil. "A Visit to Ezra Pound," Paideuma, 7 (1924), 281-286.

47 Ginsberg, Allen. "Allen Verbatim," Paideuma, 3, #2 (Fall, 1974), 253-273.

48 _____. "The Death of Ezra Pound," Allen Verbatim: Lectures on Poetry, Politics, Consciousness. Gordon Ball, ed. New York: McGraw-Hill, 1974, pp. 179-187, passim.

49 Goacher, Denis. "Pictures of Ezra Pound," Nimbus, 3, #4 (1956), 24-32.

50 Goodwin, K. L. The Influence of Ezra Pound. London: Oxford U. P.; New York: Oxford, 1966.

51 Gordon, David. "Meeting E. P., and Then ...," Paideuma, 3, #3 (Winter, 1974), 343-360.

52 Grover, Philip, ed. Ezra Pound: The London Years, 1908-1920. New York: AMS Press, 1978.

53 Guthrie, Ramon. "Ezra Pound in Paris and Elsewhere," Nation, 185, #16 (November 16, 1957), 345.

    H. D. [See Doolittle, Hilda]

54 Hall, Donald. "Fragments of Ezra Pound," and "The Paris Review Interviews with T. S. Eliot and Ezra Pound," Remembering Poets: Reminiscences and Reflections: Dylan Thomas, Robert Frost, T. S. Eliot, Ezra Pound. New York: Harper & Row, 1978, pp. 111-194, 201-244.

55 _____. "Pound's Death," Goatfoot Milktongue Twinbird: Interviews, Essays, and Notes on Poetry, 1970-1976. Ann Arbor: University of Michigan Pr., 1978, pp. 55-56.

56 Herzinger, Kim. "The Night Pound Ate the Tulips: An Evening at Ernest Rhys's," JML, 8, #1 (1980), 153-155.

57 Heymann, C. David. Ezra Pound, the Last Rower: A Political Profile. New York: Viking Pr., 1976.

58 Homberger, Eric. "A Glimpse of Pound in 1912 by Arundel del Re," Paideuma, 3, #1 (Spring, 1974), 85-88.

59 Hutchins, Patricia. "Ezra Pound as Journalist," TC, 167 (January, 1960), 39-48.

60 _____. Ezra Pound's Kensington: An Exploration, 1885-1913. London: Faber & Faber; Chicago: Regnery, 1965.

61 _____. "Yeats and Pound in England," TexQ, 4 (Autumn, 1961), 203-216.

62 _____. "Young Pound in London, Friends and Acquaintances," ConnR, 7 (1974), 86-93.

63 Iwasaki, Ryozo. "Pound Yuku," EigoS, 118 (1972), 624-625.

64 Kappel, Andrew J. "What Ezra Pound Says We Owe to Edward VIII, Duke of Windsor," JML, 9, #2 (May, 1982), 313-315.

65 Kazin, Alfred. Contemporaries. Boston: Little, Brown, 1962.

66 _____. "The Youngest Man Who Ever Was," Reporter, 21 (August 20, 1959), 43-46.

67 Kenner, Hugh. "D[orothy], P[ound] Remembered," Paideuma, 2, #3 (Winter, 1973), 485-493.

68 _____. "Ezra Pound and Money," Cf., #6, pp. 50-55.

69 _____. "Incurious Biography," NR, 163 (October 17, 1970), 30-32.

70 _____. "In Memoriam: Ezra Pound," SatRL, 55 (December 12, 1972), 30.

71 Knox, Bryant. "Allen Upward and Ezra Pound," Paideuma, 3 (Spring, 1974), 71-83; cf., A. D. Moody, "Pound's Allen Upward," Paideuma, 4, #1 (Spring, 1975), 55-70.

72 Lawrence, D. H. The Collected Letters of D. H. Lawrence. New York: Viking Pr., 1962, passim.

73 _____. Lawrence in Love: Letters to Louie Burrows. James T. Boulton, ed. University of Nottingham Pr., 1968, pp. 147-148, 165-166, passim.

74 Lewis, Wyndham. "Ezra: The Portrait of a Personality," QRL, 5, #2 (November 2, 1949), 136-144.

75 Livi, Grazia. "The Poet Speaks," Paideuma, 8 (1979), 243-247; Natalie Harris, trans., "Vi Parla Ezra Pound," Epoca (March 24, 1963).

76 Lottman, Herbert R. "The Silences of Ezra Pound," TexQ, 10, #4 (Winter, 1967), 105-128.

77 Lowell, Robert. "A Tribute," Cf., #6, p. 22.

78 McAlmon, Robert. Being Geniuses Together, 1920-1930. Rev.

with Supp. Chapters by Kay Boyle. Garden City, N.Y.: Doubleday, 1968, pp. 31-33, 99-101, 178-179, passim.

79 _____. McAlmon and the Lost Generation. Robert E. Knoll, ed. Lincoln: U. of Nebraska Pr., 1962. [Reprint of articles from books by Robert McAlmon.]

80 McCormick, John. "George Santayana and Ezra Pound," AL, 54, #3 (October, 1982), 413-433.

81 McCracken, Van. "Ezra Pound: The London Years," LGJ, 6, #3 (Winter, 1981), 12-14.

82 MacNaughton, William. "Pound, a Brief Memoir: 'Chi Lavora, Ora,'" Paideuma, 3, #3 (Winter, 1974), 319-324.

83 Maia, Joao. "Na Morte de Ezra Pound," Broteria, 95 (1972), 555-558.

84 Meacham, Harry. "I Remember Ezra," StAR, 1, #1 (Fall-Winter, 1970), 21-24.

85 Monroe, Harriet. "Ezra Pound," Poetry, 26 (May, 1925), 90-91.

86 _____. A Poet's Life: Seventy Years in a Changing World. New York: Macmillan, 1938, passim.

87 Montale, Eugenio. "Uncle Ez," IQ, 16, #64 (1973), 23-29; trans. of "Uncle Ez," Corriere della sera, Milan, 1953.

88 Montgomery, Marion. "Ezra Pound's Search for Family," GaR, 22 (Winter, 1968), 429-436.

89 _____. "Homage to Ezra Pound," UDQ, 3 (Winter, 1969), 1-17.

90 Moore, Marianne. "A Note," Cf., #6, p. 22.

91 Mullins, Eustace. "Ezra and America," Sou'w, 3-5 (1970), Special EP No.

92 _____. This Difficult Individual, Ezra Pound. New York: Fleet Pub. Corp., 1961.

93 Norman, Charles. Ezra Pound. New York: Macmillan, 1960; rev. ed., New York: Minerva Pr., 1960; London: 1969.

94 _____. The Magic-Maker: E. E. Cummings. New York: Macmillan, 1958, passim.

95 Olson, Charles. "Encounter with Ezra Pound," Antaeus, 17 (January, 1975), 72-92.

96 Oppen, George. "Pound in the U.S.A., 1969," Sagetrieb, 1,
    #1 (Spring, 1982), 119.

97 Palandri, Angela Jung. "Homage to a Confucian Poet,"
    Paideuma, 3, #3 (Winter, 1974), 301-311; TkR, 5, #1 (1974),
    129-142.

98 Patmore, Brigit. "Ezra Pound in England," TQ, 7, #3 (Au-
    tumn, 1964), 69-81.

99 _____. My Friends When Young: The Memoirs of Brigit
    Patmore. Ed. with Introduction by Derek Patmore. London:
    Heinemann, 1968.

100 Pearce, Donald. "A Wreath for Ezra Pound: 1885-1972,"
    Shenandoah, 24, #3 (Spring, 1973), 3-14.

101 Pearlman, Daniel D. "Ezra Pound: America's Wandering Jew,"
    Paideuma, 9 (1980), 461-480.

102 Peel, Robert. "The Poet as Artist and Citizen," CSMM (De-
    cember 9, 1950), 7.

103 Pellizzi, Camillo. "Ezra Pound, uomo difficile," Il Tempo,
    (Rome: March, 1953), 3; translation: "Ezra Pound: A Dif-
    ficult Man," Civ/n (Montreal), #4, pp. 20-22.

104 Pinck, Dan. "A Visit with Ezra Pound," Reporter, 10, 3
    (February 2, 1954), 40-43.

105 Rader, James E., ed. "A Pound of Flesh," Wabash College
    Review, 6 (Spring, 1959), 5-10.

106 _____. "Ship in the Night," The Bachelor, 50 (May 9,
    1958), 7-10.

107 Rattray, David. "Weekend with Ezra Pound," Nation, 185,
    #16 (November 16, 1957), 343-349; Reply by D. R. Wang, 185
    [inside cover], (December 28, 1957); repr., in A Casebook on
    Ezra Pound, Cf., #29, pp. 104-117.

108 Reck, Michael. "A Conversation between Ezra Pound and Allen
    Ginsberg," EvergreenRev, 12 (June, 1968), 27-29, 84-86.

109 _____. Ezra Pound: A Close-up. London: 1967; New
    York: McGraw-Hill, 1967.

110 Redman, Tim. "The Repatriation of Pound, 1939-1942: A
    View from the Archives," Paideuma, 8 (1979), 447-457.

111 Regnery, Henry. "Eliot, Pound, and Lewis: A Creative
    Friendship," ModA, 16, #2 (Spring, 1972), 146-160.

112   Roche, Denis. "Pour Ezra Pound," Tel Quel (Paris), No. 2
      (Autumn, 1962), 17-24.

113   Rogers, William D. "Ezra Pound and the Law," NR, 140 (June
      1, 1959), 20-21; Reply: Weyl, Nathaniel. "Pound and US
      Treason Law," NR, 140, #25 (June 22, 1959), 3, 22-23.

114   Russell, Peter. Ezra Pound: A Collection of Essays to be
      Presented to Ezra Pound on His 65th Birthday. London:
      Peter Neville, 1950; and under title An Examination of Ezra
      Pound: A Collection of Essays. New York: New Directions,
      1950.

115   _____. "Ezra Pound: The Last Years," MHRev, 29 (July,
      1974), 11-44.

116   _____. "The Youth of Ezra Pound," SoR, II, #2 (Spring,
      1966), 443-452.

117   Savery, Pancho. "Lie Quiet, Ezra Pound," Epoch (Cornell U.),
      22 (1973), 364-365.

118   Schaffner, Perdita. "Merano, 1962," Paideuma, 4, #2-3 (Fall-
      Winter, 1975), 513-518.

119   Schultz, Robert. "A Detailed Chronology of Ezra Pound's
      London Years, 1908-1920; Part One: 1908-1914; Part Two:
      1915-1920," Paideuma, 11, #3 (Winter, 1982), 456-472; 12,
      #2-3 (Fall-Winter, 1983), 357-373.

120   Sheldon, Michael. "Allen Upward: Some Biographical Notes,"
      Agenda, 16, iii-iv (1978-79), 108-121.

121   Simpson, Louis A. Three on the Tower: The Lives and
      Works of Ezra Pound, T. S. Eliot, and William Carlos Williams.
      New York: Wm. Morrow, 1975.

122   Slocum, John J. "Remembering Ezra Pound," YULG, 57, #1-2
      (October, 1982), 52-65.

123   Stern, Richard. "A Memory or Two of Mr. Pound," Paideuma,
      1, #2 (Winter, 1972), 215-219.

124   Stock, Noel. "Danger: Biographers at Work," XRev, 2
      (August, 1961), 144-149.

125   _____, ed. Ezra Pound: Perspectives--Essays in Honor of
      His Eightieth Birthday. Chicago: Henry Regnery, 1965.

126   _____. Ezra Pound's Pennsylvania. Toledo, Ohio: Friends
      of the Univ. of Toledo Libraries, 1976.

127 _____. The Life of Ezra Pound. New York; London: Routledge & Kegan Paul, 1970; New York: Pantheon Books [First American Edition], 1970; expanded edition, North Point Pr., 1982.

128 _____. "A Scholar's View--A Poet's Life and Content," Agenda, I, #11 (June, 1960), 1-2.

129 Sullivan, John Patrick, "An Afternoon with Ezra," Paideuma, 7 (Spring-Fall, 1978), 283-286.

130 Tanselle, G. Thomas. "Ezra Pound and a Story of Floyd Dell's," N&Q, 8 (September, 1961), 350-352.

131 _____. "The Lawrence Gomme Imprint," PBSA, 61 (Third Qt., 1967), 225-240.

132 Taylor, James, ed. "Ezra Pound Birthday Issue, October 30, 1970," Sou'wester (So. Ill. U.), #35 (October 30, 1970), 3-5.

133 Terrell, Carroll. "Ezra Pound," Paideuma, 3, #3 (Winter, 1974), 363-379.

134 _____. "Memoir within Memoirs," Paideuma, 2, #1 (Spring, 1973), 49-51.

135 Thayer, Mary Dixon. "Ezra Pound's Father Tells How Son Went to London with a Shilling and Found Fame," Philadelphia Evening Bulletin (February 20, 1928), p. 12.

136 Thomas, Edward. Letters from Edward Thomas to Gordon Bottomley. Edited with Introduction by George Thomas. London: Oxford U. Pr., 1968, pp. 185, 187, 197.

137 Thompson, Francis J. "Ezra in Dublin," UTQ, 21 (October, 1951), 64-67.

138 Thompson, Harold W. Body, Boots, and Britches: Folk Tales, Ballads and Speeches from Country New York. New York: Dover Pubs., c1939, 1962, pp. 11, 12, 85.

139 Torrey, E. Fuller. "The Protection of Ezra Pound," Psychlogy Today, 15, #1 (November, 1981), 57-66.

140 Uberti, Riccardo M. degli. "Ezra Pound and Ubaldo degli Uberti: History of a Friendship," IQ, 64 (1973), 95-107.

141 Wallace, Emily Mitchell. "Afterword: 'Grampaw'--Thaddeus Coleman Pound," WCWN, 2, i (Spring, 1976), 5-6. [Facts about Pound's grandfather.]

142 _____. "Penn's Poet Friends," Pennsylvania Gazette, 71
(February, 1973), 35.

143 _____. "Pound and Williams at the University of Pennsylvania," Pennsylvania Rev. (Spring, 1967), i, 41-53.

144 Whigham, Peter. "Ezra Pound and Catullus," Cf., #125,
pp. 62-77.

145 _____. "Four from Martial for Ezra Pound's Eightieth
Birthday," Cf., #6, p. 29.

146 _____. "Pound in the Classroom," Cf., #6, pp. 62-68.

147 Whittemore, Reed. "Ezra Pound, 1884-1972," NR, 167, #18,
Issue, 3018 (November 11, 1972), 28.

148 Wieners, John. "Ezra Pound at the Spoleto Festival, 1965,"
Cf., #6, pp. 68-69.

149 Wigginton, Waller B. "A Homer Pound Letter," Rendezvous,
4, #2 (Winter, 1969), 27-29.

150 _____. "The Pounds at Hailey," Cf., #149, pp. 31-68.

151 Wilhelm, James J. "Ezra Pound's New York, 1887-1908: A
Recreation," Paideuma, 12, #1 (Spring, 1983), 55-87.

152 _____. "The Wadsworths, the Westons, and the Farewell of
1911," Paideuma, 12, #2-3 (Fall-Wntr, 1983), 305-347.

153 Williams, William Carlos. "A Letter from William Carlos Williams
to Norman Holmes Pearson Concerning Ezra Pound's Father and
Grandfather," WCWN, 2, 1 (Spring, 1976), 4-5.

154 _____. "Some Notes toward an Autobiography," Poetry, 74
(May, 1949), 94-111.

155 _____. "Something for a Biography," General Magazine and
History Chronicle, 50 (Summer, 1948), 211-213.

156 Yoder, Jonathan. "Pound as Odysseus, the Prisoner Psychot-
ic," Rendezvous, 8, 1 (Summer, 1973), 1-11.

THE BOLLINGEN AWARD

157 Adams, Leonie, Secretary to the Fellows in American Letters.

"Statement of Procedure of the Jury for the Bollingen Award,"
Cf., #195, pp. 21-23.

158   Agnoletti, Enriques E.   "Il Caso Ezra Pound," Il Ponto (Italy),
      (October, 1949), 1327.

159   Ames, Alfred C.   "The Case of Ezra Pound," SatRL, 29, #11
      (March 16, 1946), 34.

160   Auden, W. H.   "The Question of the Pound Award," PR, 16,
      #5 (May, 1949), 512-513; repr., #371, 54-56.

161   Barrett, William.   "A Prize for Ezra Pound," PR, 16, #4 (April,
      1949), 344-345; 16, #5 (May-July, 1949), 512-522.

162   Benet, William Rose.   "Ezra Pound," NR, 121, #16 (October 17,
      1949), 4.

163   Berryman, John.   "A Tribute," Agenda, Cf., #6, 27-28.

164   Blish, James.   "The Pound Scandal," SR, 67, #4 (October-
      December, 1959), 703-706.

165   Brooks, Cleanth.   "Letter to the Editor," SatRL, 32, #44
      (October 29, 1949), 24.

166   Burt, Struthers.   "Pro Bollingen Bosh," SatRL, 32, #35
      (August 27, 1949), 21-23.

167   Canby, Henry Seidel.   "Ezra Pound," SatRL, 28, #50 (Decem-
      ber 15, 1945), 10.

168   Carruth, Hayden.   "The Anti-Poet All Told," Poetry, 74, #5
      (August, 1949), 274-285.

169   _____.   "The Bollingen Award: What Is It?" Poetry, 74
      (June, 1949), 154-156.

170   _____.   "A Few Notes on the Recent Essays of Mr. Hillyer,"
      Poetry, 74, #5 (August, 1949), 283-285.

171   Childs, Harwood Lawrence, and John B. Whitton, eds.
      Propaganda by Short Wave.   Princeton: 1951, pp. 153-180.

172   Corrigan, Robert A.   "Ezra Pound and the Bollingen Prize
      Controversy," MASJ, 8, #2 (Fall, 1967), 43-57.

173   _____.   "Ezra Pound and the Bollingen Prize Controversy,"
      The Forties: Fiction, Poetry, Drama.   Deland, Fla.:   Everett/
      Edwards, 1969, pp. 287-295.

174 _____. "'What's My Line': Bennett Cerf, Ezra Pound and
    the 'American Poet,'" AQ, 24 (March, 1972), 101-113.

175 Cousins, Norman, and Harrison Smith. "The Destruction of
    Art for Art's Sake," SatRL, 33, #14 (April 8, 1950), 22-23.

176 _____, and _____. "Ezra Pound and the Bollingen Award,"
    SatRL, 32 (June 11, 1949), 20-21.

177 _____, and _____. "More on Pound," SatRL, 32, #31
    (July 30, 1949), 22.

178 Cowley, Malcolm. "The Battle Over Ezra Pound," NR, 121
    (October 3, 1949), 17-20.

179 Cummings, Annette. "The Case of Ezra Pound," SatRL, 29,
    #11 (March 16, 1946), 34-35.

180 Davidson, Gustav. "Cancellation of Prizes Protested," NYT
    (August 29, 1949), p. 16, col. 7.

181 _____. "Poet Protests Award to Pound," NYT (March 3,
    1949), p. 24, col. 6.

182 Davis, Earle. "Ezra Pound, Traitor and Poet," Kansas Maga-
    zine [annual], 1951; repr., in A Casebook on Ezra Pound,
    Cf., #29, pp. 78-86.

183 Davis, Robert Gorham. John Dos Passos. Minneapolis: U. of
    Minn. Pr., 1962, passim.

184 _____. "The New Criticism and the Democratic Tradition,"
    AmerScholar, 19 (Winter, 1949-50), 9-19.

185 _____. "The Pound Award," PR, 16, #5 (April, 1949),
    513-515.

186 Deutsch, Babette. "Odi et Amo," PR, 16 (June, 1949), 668-
    670.

187 Diggins, John P. "The Arcadian Political Vision: Ezra Pound
    and John Horne Burns," Mussolini and Fascism: The View
    from America. Princeton U. Pr., 1972, pp. 240-269ff.

188 Dougherty, James P. "The Aesthetic and the Intellectual
    Analyses of Literature," JAAC, 22 (1964), 315-324.

189 Elliott, Robert C. "Moral Evil and Literary Value: The Case
    of Ezra Pound," Ohio State Argo (Spring, 1951), 27-36.

190 "Ezra Pound and the Bollingen Award," SatRL, 32 (June 11,

1949), 20; (June 25, 1949), 26; (July 2, 1949), 24-26; September 27, 1949), 22.

191   "Ezra Pound Awarded Bollingen Prize for Poetry," PubW, 155 (March 5, 1949), 1162-1163.

192   "Ezra Pound Crowned," LitD, 96 (January 14, 1928), 24-25.

193   Fitzgerald, Robert. "Further Comment on the Pound Award," Cf., #185, pp. 765-766.

194   Franzen, Erich. "T. S. Eliot und die Masken Ezra Pounds," Die Wandlung, 4 (August, 1949), 593-604.

195   "Further Remarks on the Pound Award," Cf., #160, pp. 666-670.

196   Gordon, David. "Zuk and Ez at St. Liz," Paideuma, 7, #3 (Winter, 1978), 581-584.

197   H. S. and N. C. "A Reply to Mr. Evans," SatRL, 32, #27 (July 2, 1949), 22-23.

198   Harnwell, Anna Jane. "The Case of Ezra Pound," Cf., #159, #11 (March 16, 1946), 32-33.

199   Hillyer, Robert. "The Case of Ezra Pound," Cf., #159, #11, p. 34.

200   _____. "Poetry's New Priesthood," SatRL, 32, #25 (June 18, 1949), 7-9, 38.

201   _____. "Treason's Strange Fruit: The Case of Ezra Pound and the Bollingen Award," SatRL, 32 (June 11, 1949), 9-11, 28.

202   Hopkins, Harry L. "The Case of Ezra Pound," Cf., #159 (March 16, 1946), 34.

203   Hoult, Thomas Ford. "More About the Pound Award," Cf., #160, #5 (1949), 767-768.

204   Howe, Irving. "The Question of the Pound Award," PR, Cf., #160, #5 (May, 1949), 516-517.

205   Huett, Richard. "Non-Sequitur," Cf., #160, #5 (1949), 671-672.

206   Hynes, Sam. "The Case of Ezra Pound," Cw, 63 (1955), 251-254.

207   James, Roberta. "The Case of Ezra Pound," SatRL, 29, #11 (March 16, 1946), 35.

208 Kapp, Jack. "The Case of Ezra Pound," Cf., #207, pp. 33-34.

209 Koch, Adrienne, and W. M. Lowry. "Evaluating the Pound
     Award," NYT (February 24, 1949), p. 22, col. 7.

210 Library of Congress. "Annex IV to the Statement: The An-
     nouncement of the Award: Library of Congress Press Release
     No. 542, February 20, 1949; repr., in The Case Against the
     Saturday Review, Cf., #215, pp. 29-38.

211 Loftus, Beverly J. G. "Ezra Pound and the Bollingen Prize:
     The Controversy in Periodicals," JQ, 39 (Summer, 1962),
     347-354.

212 Louchheim, Aline B. "The State and Art," NYT (September 4,
     1959), p. 8, cols. 1-3. Cf., also #352.

213 MacDonald, Dwight. "Homage to Twelve Judges," Politics
     (Winter, 1949); repr., in Memoirs of a Revolutionist. New
     York: Farrar, Straus & Cudahy, 1957; Meridian Bks., Inc.,
     1958; repr., Cf., #29, pp. 46-48.

214 McGuire, William. "The Bollingen Foundation: Ezra Pound and
     the Prize in Poetry," QJLC, 40, #1 (Winter, 1983), 16-25.

215 Meredith, William. "Letter of Protest," The Case Against The
     Saturday Review of Literature. Poetry [Modern Poetry Assn.].
     Chicago: 1949, pp. 63-64. [Cf., #210]

216 Miller, Noland. "The Case of Ezra Pound," Cf., #159, p. 34.

217 Musselman, M. M. "The Case of Ezra Pound," Cf., #159,
     p. 35.

218 Norman, Charles. The Case of Ezra Pound. New York: The
     Bodley Pr., 1948; Funk & Wagnalls, 1968.

219 O'Connor, William Van. [Letter], Cf., #215, pp. 64-67.

220 O'Grady, Desmond. "Ezra Pound: A Personal Memoir,"
     Agenda, 17, #3-4; 18, #1 (Autumn-Wntr-Spring., 1979-80),
     285-299.

221 Olson, Paul A. "The Bollingen Controversy Ten Years After:
     Criticism and Content," Prairie Schooner, 33 (Fall, 1959),
     225-229.

222 Orwell, George. "The Question of the Pound Award," PR, 16
     (May, 1949), 517-518; repr., in A Casebook on Ezra Pound,
     Cf., #29, pp. 60-61.

223 Reit, Seymour V. "The Case of Ezra Pound," SatRL, 29, #11
     (March 16, 1946), 34.

224 Ringer, Gordon. "More about the Pound Award," PR, 16, #7
     (1949), 766-767.

225 Rosten, Norman. "The Case Against Ezra Pound," Cf., #159,
     p. 32.

226 Ruggeri, Cosimo. "Inveco del capestro il premio 'Bollingen,'"
     Momenta-Sera (February 2, 1949).

227 Shapiro, Karl. "Letter to the Editor," The Baltimore Sun,
     (February 25, 1949), 16.

228 _____. "More about the Pound Award," PR, 16, #7 (1949),
     764.

229 _____. "The Question of the Pound Award," PR, 16, #5
     (April, 1949), 518-519.

230 Sheerin, J. B. "The Pound Affair," Catholic World, 169
     (August, 1949), 322-323.

231 Sillen, Samuel. "A Prize for Ezra Pound," M&M, 2 (April,
     1949), 3-6. Cf., also, #1178.

232 Smith, Harrison. "End of Controversy," Sat RL, 32 (Septem-
     ber 3, 1949), 23.

233 _____. "Lock, Stock, and Barrel," SatRL, 33 (March 4,
     1950), 24.

234 _____, and Norman Cousins. "A Reply to Mr. Evans,"
     SatRL, 32, #27 (July 2, 1949), 22-23.

235 Squires, Radcliffe. "Ambassador of Culture," Allen Tate: A
     Literary Biography. New York: Pegasus (A Division of Bobbs-
     Merrill Co.), 1971, pp. 184-189.

236 Struthers, Burt. "Pro Bollingen Bosh," SatRL, 32, #35
     (August 27, 1949), 21-23.

237 Tate, Allen. "Annex I to the Statement: A Personal State-
     ment on Fascism by Allen Tate," The Case Against the Satur-
     day Review, Cf., #215, pp. 19-21.

238 _____. "Ezra Pound," Collected Essays. Denver: Allan
     Swallow, 1959, pp. 364-371, 532-536, passim.

239 _____. "Ezra Pound," An Examination of Ezra Pound.
     Rev. and Enl. Peter Russell, ed., Cf., #114, pp. 66-72.

240 _____. "Ezra Pound and the Bollingen Prize," Essays of Four Decades. Chicago: Swallow Pr., 1959, 1968, pp. 509-513.

241 _____. "Ezra Pound," The Forlorn Demon. Chicago: H. Regnery, 1953, pp. 156-160.

242 _____. "Ezra Pound," Ezra Pound: Perspectives. Noel Stock, ed., Cf., #125, pp. 86-89.

243 _____. "Ezra Pound and the Bollingen Prize," The Man of Letters in the Modern World. London: 1936; Meridian Bks., 1957, pp. 264-267.

244 _____. "Further Remarks on the Pound Award," PartisanRev, 16 (June, 1949), 666-668.

245 _____. "Poetry and Politics," NR, 75 (August 2, 1933), 308-311.

246 _____. "The Question of the Pound Award," PartisanRev, 5 (April, 1949), 520.

247 Tichenor, George H. "This Man Is a Traitor," PM (August 15, 1943), 3-5.

248 Van Doren, Mark. Letter [to Harrison Smith, Publisher of SatRL], May 26, 1949, Cf., #215, p. 62.

249 Viereck, Peter. "My Kind of Poetry," SatRL, 32 (August 27, 1949), 7-8, 35-36.

250 _____. "Pure Poetry, Impure Politics, and Ezra Pound," Commentary, 12 (April, 1951), 340-346; "Pure Poetry, Impure Politics: The Implications of Ezra Pound and the Bollingen Controversy," Dream and Responsibility: Four Test Cases of the Tension Between Poetry and Society. Washington, D.C., 1953, pp. 1-22.

251 _____. "Symbols: Hiss and Pound," Cw, 55 (March 28, 1952), 607-608.

252 Weissman, David L. "Ezra Pound," NR, 121, #16 (October 17, 1949), 4.

253 Wenning, Henry W. T. S. Eliot and Ezra Pound. New Haven: C. A. Stonehill, Inc., 1970.

254 West, Ray. "Excerpts from a Journal," Western Review, 14 (Winter, 1950), 82, 151-159; repr., Item #29, pp. 67-73.

255 Weyl, Nathaniel. "The Bollingen Award," Cf., #29, pp. 17-18.

256 Winters, Yvor. "Letter to Editors of Saturday Review of Lit-
     erature," in The Case Against the Saturday Review, Cf., #215,
     pp. 69-71.

257 Woodfin, Henry A., Jr. "More about the Pound Award," PR,
     16, #7 (July, 1949), 764-765.

258 Young, Gordon. "The Case of Ezra Pound," SatRL, 29, #11
     (March 16, 1946), 35.

259 Young, Thomas Daniel. "The Little Houses against the Great,"
     SR, 88 (Spring, 1980), 320-330.

THE CASE OF EZRA POUND AND HIS
CONFINEMENT AT ST. ELIZABETH'S

260 Aiken, Conrad. Reviewer's ABC: Collected Criticism of Con-
     rad Aiken from 1916 to the Present. New York: Meridian,
     1958.

261 Allen, Robert L. "The Cage," Esquire (February, 1958);
     repr., Cf., #29.

262 Alvarez, A. "Ezra Pound: Craft and Morals," Stewards of
     Excellence: Studies in Modern English and American Poets.
     New York: Gordian Pr., 1971, pp. 48-72; repr., in Ezra
     Pound: Perspectives: Essays in Honor of His Eightieth
     Birthday. Noel Stock, ed., Cf., #125.

263 _____. "The Wretched Poet Who Lived in the House of
     Bedlam," SatRL, 53 (July 18, 1970), 27-39.

264 Arnold, Thurman. Fair Fights and Foul: A Dissenting Law-
     yer's Life. New York: Harcourt, Brace & World, 1965, pp.
     236-242.

265 "An Artist Confined," Life Magazine, 40 (February 6, 1956),
     30; repr., Cf., #291, pp. 121-122.

266 Barry, Iris. "Ezra Pound in London," Ezra Pound: Dichtung
     und Prosa. Eva Hesse, ed. Frankfurt: Athenaum, 1967,
     pp. 389-397.

267 Bayes, Ronald H. "Who Sprung Ezra? Continued Specula-
     tion," UPortR, 20, i (1968), 47-48.

268 Benet, William Rose. "The Case of Ezra Pound," SatRL, 26,
     #10 (March 6, 1943), 20-21.

269 _____. "Phoenix Nest," SatRL, 32 (July 23, 1949), 28.

270 Bishop, Elizabeth. "Visits to St. Elizabeth's," NC, #5-6 (1956), 28-34.

271 Blish, James. "The Pound Scandal," Cf., #164.

272 Bonfante, Jordan. "An Aging Genius in Exile," Life, 56 (March 27, 1964), 43-44, 46, 48.

273 Booth, Marcella Spann. "Through the Smoke Hole: Ezra Pound's Last Year at St. Elizabeth's," Paideuma, 3, #3 (Winter, 1974), 329-334.

274 Bosha, Francis J. "Faulkner, Pound, and the P.P.P.," Paideuma, 8 (1979), 249-256. [P.P.P., People-to-People Program]

275 Bradbury, Malcolm. "A Visit to Ezra Pound," TC, 159 (June, 1956), 604-606.

276 Breit, Harvey. "Birthday," NYTBR, 61, #39 (September 23, 1956), 8.

277 Bridson, D. G. "Ezra Pound's 'Four Steps,'" SoR, 13 (Autumn, 1977), 862-871.

278 Brooks, Cleanth. Letter to Editor of Saturday Review of Literature, (October 4, 1949), in The Case Against The Saturday Review, Cf., #215, pp. 68-69.

279 "Brought Back to Face Treason Charges," NYT (November 19, 1945), p. 12, col. 3.

280 Brown, Peter. "Revalued Pound," NSt, 86 (December 14, 1973), 904.

281 Canby, H. S. "Ezra Pound," SatRL, 28, #50, Cf., #167, p. 10.

282 Carruth, Hayden. "The Anti-Poet All Told," Poetry, 74, #5 (August, 1949), 274-282; repr., in The Case Against The Saturday Review, Cf., #215, pp. 46-55.

283 The Case Against The Saturday Review of Literature. Chicago: Poetry, [Pub.], Cf., #215.

284 Cerf, Bennett. "The Case of Ezra Pound," SatRL, 29, #6 (February 9, 1946), 26-27.

285 _____. "The Case of Ezra Pound," SatRL, 29, #11 (March 16, 1946), 32-36, 49-53.

286 Chilanti, Felice. "Ezra Pound Among the Seditious in the
     1940's," Paideuma, 6 (Fall, 1977), 235-250.

287 Cohane, J. J., Jr. "Poet without a Country: Reply," Com-
     monweal, 41 (November 10, 1944), 101.

288 Connolly, Cyril. "Ezra Pound: 1, 2, 3," The Evening Colon-
     nade. New York; London: Harcourt, Brace, Jovanovich,
     1973, pp. 217-221, 222-225, 226-228.

289 Cornell, Julien. "Letter to Bennett Cerf," (May 10, 1946),
     The Trial of Ezra Pound. New York: John Day Co., 1966,
     p. 115.

290 _____. "Letter to the Editor," SatRL, 31 (October 2,
     1948), p. 21.

291 _____. The Trial of Ezra Pound: A Documented Account
     of the Treason Case by the Defendant's Lawyer. New York:
     John Day Co.,; London: Faber, 1967.

292 Corrigan, Robert A. "Ezra Pound and the Italian Ministry for
     Popular Culture," Journal of Popular Culture, 15, #4 (Spring,
     1972), 767-781.

293 _____. "Literature and Politics: The Case of Ezra Pound
     Reconsidered," American Character and Culture in a Changing
     World. John A. Hague, ed. Westport, CT, 1964, pp. 81-98;
     see also: Prospects, 2 (1976), 463-482.

294 Cowley, Malcolm. "A Literary Odyssey of the 1920's," Exile's
     Return. New York: Viking Pr., 1934, 1959, pp. 119-124,
     passim.

295 _____. "Fox in Flight," Furioso, 6 (Spring, 1951), 7-10.

296 Cruvant, Bernard A. [Letter] "From Pound's Psychiatrist,"
     SatRL, 32, #10 (October 1, 1949), 22.

297 Cummings, E. E. "Re: Ezra Pound: I--Ezra Pound: II:
     New York," E. E. Cummings: A Miscellany Revised. Ed. with
     Introduction and Notes by George J. Firmage. Foreword by
     E. E. Cummings. New York: October House, Inc., 1965,
     pp. 312, 313-315.

298 Davenport, Guy. "Il Vecchio," StAR, 1, #1 (Fall-Winter,
     1970), 19-20.

299 Davis, Clyde Brion. "The Case of Ezra Pound," SatRL, 29,
     #11 (March 16, 1946), 33.

300 Delehanty, Elizabeth. "Day with Ezra Pound," NY, 16 (April 13, 1940), 76-77.

301 Deutsch, Albert. "Ezra Pound, Turncoat Poet, Seeks Release from Federal Mental Hospital," PM (January 25, 1947), 1, 24.

302 _____. "Pound Gets 'Unsound Mind' Verdict," PM (February 14, 1946), p. 7.

303 Dickey, R. P. "Ezra Pound," Sou'wester (So. Ill. U.) (October 30, 1970), 129.

304 Drummond, John. "Accusato non condannato," Paese Sera, 6 (June 16, 1954), 3.

305 _____. "I Passatempi dell' ambasciatore," Il Borghese, 7, 3 (Milano: January 21, 1955), 111.

306 _____. "Il Caso di Ezra Pound," Fiera Lettaria, 16 (April 17, 1949).

307 _____. "Il Dissenziente," Il Borghese, 49 (December 9, 1955), 882-883.

308 _____. "Pound's Lire," TLS (July 14, 1972), 819.

309 _____. "La verita sul caso Pound," FLe, 1 (January 7, 1951), 1.

310 Dudek, Louis. "Visit to Ezra Pound," Contemporary Verse (Summer, 1950), 20-23.

311 _____. "Why Is Ezra Pound Being Held in St. Elizabeth's Hospital, Washington, D.C.?" Civ/n, #4 (1953), 19.

312 [Editors of Hudson Review]. "Comment," HudR, 2, #3 (Autumn, 1949), 325-326; repr., in The Case Against The Saturday Review, Cf., #215, pp. 43-45.

313 Enriques Agnoletti, E. "Il Caso Ezra Pound," Il Ponte (Italy), (October, 1949), p. 1327.

314 Evans, David W. "Ezra Pound as Prison Poet," UKCR, 23 (Spring, 1957), 215-220.

315 Feldman, David. "Ezra Pound: A Poet in a Cage," Paideuma, 10, #2 (Fall, 1981), 361-365.

316 Feuchtwanger, Lion. "'Should Ezra Pound Be Shot?'-Five Writers Indict Him as a Traitor," New Masses (December 25, 1945), 5-6.

317 Fleming, William. "A Lone Ant from a Broken Ant-hill,"
     Meanjin, 4 (Melbourne), 1954.

318 _____. "The Melbourne Vortex," Paideuma, 3, #3 (Winter,
     1974), 325-328; also in AntigR, 9 (Spring, 1972), 74-77.

319 _____. "Prometheus Unbound: The Case of Ezra Pound,"
     TCAus, 16 (1962), 208-213.

320 Friar, Kimon. "Politics and Some Poets," NR, 127 (July 7,
     1952), 17-18.

321 Frost, Robert. "Statement of Robert Frost," United States of
     America, vs. Ezra Pound, Defendant. Criminal No. 76028;
     repr., in A Casebook on Ezra Pound. Wm. Van O'Connor and
     Edward Stone, eds. Cf., #29, pp. 135-138.

322 Gannett, Lewis. [Letter] New York Herald Tribune, repr.,
     in SatRL, Cf., #284, pp. 26-27.

323 Garrison, Omar. "Ezra Pound's Italian Friends Campaign for
     His Release," The Mirror [Los Angeles], (April 21, 1954).

324 Giovannini, Giovanni. "The Strange Case of Ezra Pound,"
     New Times (Melbourne), 21 (August 26, 1955), 194-196.

325 Glicksberg, Charles I. "Ezra Pound and the Fascist Complex,"
     SAQ, 45 (July, 1947), 349-358.

326 _____. "Ezra Pound and the Commitment to Fascism," The
     Literature of Commitment. Bucknell U. Pr., Lewisburg, PA,
     1977, pp. 100-110.

327 Gold, Michael. "A Bourgeois Hamlet of Our Time," New
     Masses, 11, #2 (April 10, 1934), 28-30.

328 _____. [Open Letter to Ezra Pound], New Masses (Septem-
     bor, 1931), repr., New Masses (December 25, 1945).

329 Gordon, Arthur. "Intruder in the South," Look (February 19,
     1957), 27-31.

330 Graham, John F. "Letter to the Editor," Paideuma, 4, #1
     (Spring, 1975), 200-203. [Comment on C. F. Terrell's article
     on Pound at St. Elizabeth's, Cf., #133.]

331 Haley, Martin. "Is Ezra Pound, Modern Don Quixote, Really
     Mad?" Advocate (Melbourne), (September 13, 1951), 9.

332 Heymann, C. David. "The Case of Ezra Pound," Shantih:
     Journal of International Writing & Art (Brooklyn, New York),
     3, #4 (1977), 48-52.

333 Holder, Alan. "Prisoner Ezra Pound," VQR, 44 (Spring, 1968), 337-341.

334 Homberger, Eric. "Pound and the Ostriches," CambridgeRev, 89 (November 4, 1967), 70-72; repr., in Ezra Pound: A Critical Anthology. J. P. Sullivan, ed. Baltimore, Md., 1970, pp. 350-353.

335 Howe, Irving. "The Case of Ezra Pound," The Critical Point: On Literature and Culture. New York: Horizon Pr., 1973, pp. 109-120.

336 _____. "The Return of the Case of Ezra Pound," World, 1, #9 (October 24, 1972), 20-24.

337 Humphries, Rolphe. "Poets, Traitors and Patriots," NR, 109, #22 (November 29, 1943), 748.

338 Hutchens, John K. "Round Two," New York Times (March 31, 1946), Section 7, 36.

339 Kavka, Jerome. "Ezra Pound's Sanity: The Agony of Public Disclosure," Paideuma, 4, #2 and 3 (Fall-Winter, 1975), 527-529.

340 Kenner, Hugh. "Ezra Pound on Visitors Day," NYT (November 19, 1972), 6.

341 Kimpel, Ben D., and T. C. Duncan Eaves. "More on Pound's Prison Experience," AL, 53, #3 (November, 1981), 469-476.

342 Knoll, Robert E. "Ezra Pound at St. Elizabeth's," PrS, 47 (Spring, 1973), 1-13.

343 Kutler, Stanley I. "'This Notorious Patient'--The Asylum of Ezra Pound," The American Inquisition: Justice and Injustice in the Cold War. New York: Hill & Wang of Farrar, Straus & Giroux, 1982, pp. 59-88.

344 Laughlin, James. "Letter to T. S. Eliot," Humanities Research Center, University of Texas, (December 23, 1945); (February 15, 1946).

345 Lawson, John Howard. "Inner Conflict and Proletarian Art--A Reply to Michael Gold," New Masses (April 17, 1934), p. 29.

346 LaZebnik, Jack. "The Case of Ezra Pound," NR, 136 (April 1, 1957), 17-20.

347 "Letters: The Case for Pound," LonM, 3, #4 (New Series), (July, 1963), 68-74. Cf., Conquest, Robert, "Letters," #2098.

348   "Letters to the Editor," SatRL, 32 (June 25, 1949), 26-27;
      (July 9, 1949), 23-25; (July 16, 1949), 21-22; (July 23, 1949),
      22-23; (July 30, 1949), 23-24; (August 27, 1949), 21-23;
      (September 3, 1949), 26; (September 24, 1949), 27; (October
      1, 1949), 22.

349   Lewis, Anthony. "U.S. Asked to End Pound Indictment:
      Court Told Poet's Insanity Is Incurable; Wife Would Take Him
      Back to Italy," NYT (Tuesday, April 15, 1958); repr., in A
      Casebook for Ezra Pound, Cf., O'Connor and Stone, eds.,
      #29, pp. 132-134.

350   "Liberare Pound," in "Copialettere," Il Tempo, March 12, 1954;
      (report of Boris de Rachewiltz's reply to attack on Pound in
      "Una Storia d'Italia ed alcuni canti mazisti," by F. Fortini).

351   Lottman, Herbert R. "The Silences of Ezra Pound," Cf., #76,
      pp. 105-110.

352   Louchheim, Aline B. "The State of Art," Cf., #212, p. 8,
      cols. 1-3.

353   McCabe, Victoria. "Pound," [poem], Sou'wester (October 30,
      1970), pp. 133-134.

354   MacDonald, Dwight. "Homage to Twelve Judges," Cf., #213,
      pp. 46-48.

355   McGrory, Mary. "Ezra Pound Still Sees Mad World Out of
      Step," Washington Star, April 30, 1958; repr., in A Casebook
      on Ezra Pound, Cf., O'Connor and Stone, eds., #29, pp. 144-
      148.

356   McKenzie, Donald. "T(h)inker Pound and Other Italian
      Legends," The Left, 1 (Summer-Autumn, 1931), 48-52.

357   MacShane, Frank, et al. "Letters: The Case for Pound,"
      LonM, 3 (July, 1963), pp. 68-74.

358   Marshall, Margaret. "The Saturday Review Unfair to Litera-
      ture," Nation, 169 (December 17, 1949), 598-599.

359   Matthiessen, F. O. [Response to Isidor Schneider], New
      Masses (December 25, 1945), p. 6.

360   Mayfield, John S. The Black Badge of Treason: An Account
      of Ezra Pound. Washington, D.C., Park Book Shop, 1944.

361   Meacham, Harry M. The Caged Panther: Ezra Pound at Saint
      Elizabeth's. New York: Twayne Pubs., 1967.

362 _____. "I Remember Ezra," Cf., #84, pp. 21-24.

363 Meyers, Jeffrey. "Shrinking Pound," Spectator (April 28, 1984), 25-26.

364 Mizener, Arthur. The Saddest Story: A Biography of Ford Madox Ford. New York; Cleveland: The World Pub. Co., 1971, passim.

365 Mullins, Eustace Clarence. This Difficult Individual: Ezra Pound. Cf., #92.

366 Neame, Alan. "Speech and Penalty," European, 10 (February, 1958), 351-360.

367 _____. "Typing Under the Bed," and "Neame Is Nuts," Agenda, 17, #3-4, and 18, #1 (Aut-Wntr-Spr., 1979-80), 194-196, 196-197.

368 Norman, Charles. "The Case for or against Ezra Pound," PM Newspaper, 6 (November 25, 1945), 12-17.

369 _____. "Pound in St. Elizabeth's," and "The Trial," Ezra Pound. Cf., #93, pp. 418-435; 436-458.

370 O'Connor, William Van, and Edward Stone, eds. A Casebook on Ezra Pound. Cf., #29.

371 Odlin, Reno. "Pound at St. Elizabeth's," AntigR, 51 (Autumn, 1982), 39-48.

372 Olmstead, Edwin G. "Usher Burdick and Ezra Pound," NDQ, 28 (Summer, 1960), 66-68.

373 Olson, Charles. Charles Olson and Ezra Pound: An Encounter at St. Elizabeth's by Charles Olson. Catherine Seelye, ed. New York: Grossman Pubs., 1975.

374 _____. "This is Yeats Speaking," PR, 13 (Winter, 1946), 139-142. Cf., #373, pp. 27-31.

375 Patchen, Kenneth. "Ezra Pound's Guilt," Renascence, 2 (February, 1946), 3-4.

376 Pearson, R. M. "Poet in a Cage," LGJ, 1, i (May, 1973), 26-29.

377 Pegler, Westbrook. "As Pegler Sees It," New York Journal-American (April 15, 1955).

378 _____. "Cult Lowdown: Ezra Pound Mystery," Boston Evening American (April 15, 1955).

379 _____. "History of the Case of Ezra Pound," San Francisco Call-Bulletin (September 16, 1955), 32.

380 Pepper, Bill. "It Happened in Italy," Rome Daily American (June 17, 1954).

381 "Pound Awaits Treason Trial," NYT (November 25, 1945), p. 7, col. 3.

382 "Pound Foolish," Newsweek, 27, No. 8 (February 25, 1946), 29; repr., in A Casebook on Ezra Pound, Cf., #29, p. 23.

383 Raddatz, Fritz J. "Poetischer Materialist. Zum Tode [Poetic Materialist. On the Death of] Ezra Pound," Merkur, 26, #296 (December, 1972), 1224-1232.

384 Reck, Michael. "Letter to the Editor," Paideuma, 3, #3 (Winter, 1974), 419-420.

385 Reinhold, Robert. "Ezra Pound Is Focus of New Dispute," NYT (July 5, 1972), Sec. 1, p. 29.

386 Rosenfeld, Paul. "The Case of Ezra Pound," AmMercury, 58 (January, 1944), 98-102.

387 Rovere, Richard. "The Contraries of Ezra Pound," Opinions and Speculations. New York: Harcourt, Brace & World, 1962, pp. 204-222.

388 _____. "The Question of Ezra Pound," Esquire, 48 (September, 1957), 66-80.

389 Russell, Francis. "Poet in the Madhouse," Observer (London), (March 1, 1953), 10.

390 Scarfoglio, Carlo. "Il caso Ezra Pound," Paeso Sera, 6 (June 16, 1954), 3.

391 Schneider, Isidor. "Should Ezra Pound Be Shot?" New Masses, 57, #11 (December 11, 1945), 5.

392 _____. "Traitor or Holy Idiot," New Masses, 57, #11 (December 11, 1945), 13.

393 Scott, Tom. "The Poet as Scapegoat," Agenda, 7, #2 (Spring, 1969), 49-58.

394 "The Seeker," Time, 46 (December 10, 1945), 22.

395 Shapiro, Karl. Beyond Criticism. Lincoln: University of Nebraska, 1953, pp. 1-6.

396 Sherman, William David. "The Case of Ezra Pound: A Documentary Play," AWR, 19 (Autumn, 1970), 85-108.

397 Shirer, William L. "The American Radio Traitors," Harper's Mag, 187 (October, 1943), 397-404.

398 Sieber, H. A., and Rudd Fleming. "The Case of Ezra Pound: A Cause Célèbre Is Ended," Washington Post & Times Herald (July 6, 1958), E-7.

399 _____, ed. The Medical, Legal, Literary and Political Status of Ezra Weston [Loomis] Pound, Selected Facts and Comments. Washington: The Library of Congress Legislative Reference Service, March 31, 1958; revised April 14, 1958.

400 Smith, Harrison. "Strange Paradox," SatRL, 35 (February 9, 1952), 20.

401 Spingarn, Natalie Davis. "St. Elizabeths, pace-setter for Mental Hospitals," Harpers (January, 1956), 58-63.

402 Stock, Noel. Poet in Exile: Ezra Pound. Manchester, 1964; New York: Barnes & Noble, 1964.

403 _____. "Why Is Ezra Pound Imprisoned?" New Times, Melbourne (March 9, 1956).

404 Szasz, Thomas S. "Politics and Mental Health: Some Remarks Apropos of the Case of Mr. Ezra Pound," American Journal of Psychiatry, 115 (1958), 508-511.

405 _____. "Politics and Psychiatry: The Case of Mr. Ezra Pound," Law, Liberty, and Psychiatry: An Inquiry Into the Social Uses of Mental Health Practices. New York: Macmillan, 1963, p. 228; Collier Books, 1968, pp. 199-211.

406 Terrell, Carroll F. "St. Elizabeths," Cf., #133.

407 Torrey, E. Fuller. The Death of Psychiatry. Radnor, Pennsylvania: Chilton Book Co., 1974, p. 81.

408 _____. The Roots of Treason: Ezra Pound and the Secret of St. Elizabeth's. New York: McGraw-Hill Book Co., 1984. Rev. by Jeffrey Meyers, "Shrinking Pound," Spectator (April 28, 1984), 25-26.

409 "Treason," Time, 46, #24 (December 10, 1945), 22; repr., Cf., #370, pp. 19-20.

410 Untermeyer, Louis. Letter to Charles Norman, October 8, 1945, Van Pelt Library, University of Pennsylvania; published

in [Charles Norman], "Ezra Pound," PM (November 15, 1945), 17.

411   Varney, H. L. "Mental Health, Fact and Fiction," AmMercury, 84 (April, 1957), 11-12.

412   "Vatican Radio Appeal for Pound Circulated," Paris Herald Tribune, (June 8, 1954).

413   Viator. "El Poeta Loco," La Universidad del Zulia, 2, #61 (May 6, 1958), 4.

414   Walton, Edna Lou. "Should Ezra Pound Be Shot?--Five Writers Indict Him as Traitor," New Masses (December 25, 1945), 5-6.

415   Watts, Harold H. "Philosopher at Bay," Cronos, 2 (March, 1948), 1-16.

416   "Wertham Assails Ezra Pound [Insanity] Ruling," NYT, (November 27, 1949), p. 33, col. 1, (I).

417   Wertham, Frederic. "For Ezra Pound's Release," SatRL, 34 (April 7, 1951), 22.

418   _____. "The Road to Rapallo: A Psychiatric Study," American Journal of Psychotherapy," 3 (1949), 585-600; survey of press comments, replies, and rejoinders appears in American Journal of Psychotherapy, 4, #1, pp. 123-140, and 4, #2, pp. 320-322.

419   Weyl, Nathaniel. "Pound and US Treason Law," NR, 140, #25 (June 22, 1959), 3, 22-23.

420   _____. "The Strange Case of Ezra Pound," Treason: The Story of Disloyalty and Betrayal in American History. Washington, D.C.: Public Affairs Pr., 1950; Cf., #370, pp. 5-18.

421   "What the Pound Case Means," Nation, 186, #16 (April 19, 1958), 335; repr., Cf., #370, pp. 130-131.

422   "Why Is Ezra Pound Being Held in St. Elizabeth's Hospital, Washington, D.C.?" Civ/n, No. 4 (Montreal: 1953), 19.

423   Williams, William Carlos. "Ezra Pound at St. Elizabeth's," The Autobiography of William Carlos Williams. New York: Random House, 1948, pp. 335-344; repr., in The William Carlos Williams Reader. New York: New Directions, 1966, pp. 308-318.

424   _____. "Poets and Critics Size up Pound as an Artist and as a Man," PM (November 25, 1945).

425 Wood, Lewis. "Pound Awaits Treason Trial," NYT (November
     25, 1945), Sec. 4, p. 7.

426 "Your Witness: Ezra Pound," Scholastic, 48 (April 29, 1946),
     20.

II. POETRY AND PROSE WORKS

CANTOS

427   Abiru, Shin. "Ezura Paundo no Kanto," [The Cantos of Ezra Pound], Shiho (Poetical Methods), #2 (1934), pp. 47-53.

428   Adams, Stephen Jon. "Are the Cantos a Fugue?" UTQ, 45 (Fall, 1975), 67-74.

429   _____. "Ezra Pound and Music," DAI, 37, #1 (Toronto: 1974), 7746.

430   _____. "The Soundscape of the Cantos: Some Ideas of Music in the Poetry of Ezra Pound," HAB, 28 (Spring, 1977), 177-181.

431   Alexander, Michael. "On Rereading the Cantos," Agenda, 4, #2 (October-November, 1965), 4-10.

432   _____. The Poetic Achievement of Ezra Pound. Berkeley: California U. Pr., 1979.

433   Amdur, Alice Steiner. "The Cantos," The Poetry of Ezra Pound. Cambridge, Mass., 1936; reissued, Russell & Russell, 1966.

434   Axelrod, Steven Gould. Robert Lowell, Life and Art. Princeton, New Jersey: Princeton U. Pr., 1978, pp. 74-75, 122-123, passim.

435   Baar, Ron. "Ezra Pound: Poet as Historian," AL, 42, #4 (January, 1971), 531-543.

436   Bachinger, Katrina. "A Make/Made Dialectic as a Key to Pound's Cantos," The Servant of the Muse: A Garland for Peter Russell on His Sixtieth Birthday. James Hogg, ed. Salzburg: Inst. für Anglistik & Amerikanistik, U. of Salzburg, 1981, VIII, pp. 207-224.

437   Bacigalupo, Massimo. "'Absolute' Timelessness: The Case of the Middle Cantos," The Forméd Trace: The Later Poetry of Ezra Pound. New York: Columbia U. Pr., 1980, pp. 52-100.

438 _____. "Ezra Pound's Canto 106: A Late Mythologem,"
IQ, 16, #64 (1973), 77-93.

439 _____. "The Poet at War: Ezra Pound's Suppressed
Italian Cantos," SAQ, 83, #1 (Winter, 1984), 69-79.

440 _____. "Sofocle e la danza tragica: Le Franchinie di
Pound," Paragone, 334 (1976), 60-70.

441 _____. "Un tardo mitologema: Il canto 106 di Ezra
Pound," Verri, Ser. 6, #1 (1976), 36-65.

442 Balagot, Thelma C. "A Guide to Ezra Pound's Cantos (VI),"
Analyst, 3 (December, 1953), 1-9, 10.

443 Banerjee, R. D. K. "Formality and Intimacy in the Cantos of
Ezra Pound," IJAS, 2, #2 (December, 1972), 2-11.

444 Barker, George. "Mr. Pound's New Cantos," Criterion, 14
(July, 1935), 649-651.

445 Baumann, Walter. "But to Affirm the Gold Thread in the Pattern (116/797): An Examination of Canto 116," Paideuma, 12,
2/3 (Fall-Winter, 1983), 199-221.

446 _____. "Pound and Layamon's Brut," JEGP, 68 (April,
1969), 265-276.

447 _____. The Rose in the Steel Dust: An Examination of
the Cantos of Ezra Pound. Francke Verlag, Bern, 1967; Coral
Gables, Florida: U. of Miami Pr., 1970.

448 _____. "The Structure of Canto IV," Cf., #52, pp. 117-
137.

449 Bell, Ian F. A. "'Speaking in Figures': The Mechanical
Thomas Jefferson of Canto 31," Ezra Pound: Tactics for
Reading. Ian F. A. Bell, ed. London: Vision Pr.; Totowa,
NJ: Barnes & Noble, 1982, pp. 148-186.

450 Berezin, Charles. "Poetry and Politics in Ezra Pound," PR,
48, #2 (1981), 262-279.

451 Bergonzi, Bernard. "From Imagism to Fascism," TLS (September 24, 1976), 1195-1196.

452 Bernstein, Michael André. "Distinguendum est inter et inter:
A Defense of Calliope," Paideuma, 12, 2/3 (Fall-Wntr., 1983),
269-274.

453 _____. Ezra Pound and the Modern Verse Epic. Diss.,
Oxford U., 1975.

454 _____. "Identification and Its Vicissitudes: The Narrative
Structure of Ezra Pound's Cantos," YR, 69 (Summer, 1980),
540-556.

455 _____. "Myths and Logos in Ezra Pound: The Splitting of
the Realms," Paideuma, 8 (1979), 543-548.

456 _____. The Tale of the Tribe: Ezra Pound and the Modern
Verse Epic. Princeton: Princeton U. Pr., 1980.

457 Bishop, John Peale. "The Talk of Ezra Pound," Nation, 151
(December 21, 1940), 637-639.

458 Bishop, Philip E. "Avatars of the Avant-Garde: Pound,
Brecht, and Modern Culture," DAI, 43, #8 (Wisconsin: 1982),
2657A.

459 Blackmur, R. P. "An Adjunct to the Muses' Diadem: A Note
on Ezra Pound," Poetry, 68, #6 (September, 1946), 338-347.

460 Blamires, David. "The Ordered World: The Anathemata of
David Jones," Agenda, 5 (Spring-Summer, 1967), 101-111.

461 Blish, James. "The Rituals of Ezra Pound," SR, 58 (Spring,
1950), 185-226.

462 Bodenheim, Maxwell. "Isolation of Carved Metal," Dial, 72
(January, 1922), 87-91.

463 Bogan, Louise. "The Cantos," NY, 16 (November 9, 1940),
76-78.

464 _____. "The Cantos," NY, 24 (October 30, 1948), 107-109.

465 _____. "Pound's Later Cantos," Selected Criticism: Prose,
Poetry. Noonday: 1955, pp. 178-183.

466 Bornotcin, Daniel. "The Poet as Historian. Researching the
Malatesta Cantos," Paideuma, 10, #2 (Fall, 1981), 283-291.

467 Bornstein, George. "The Forest of His Mind: Mauberley and
The Cantos," The Postromantic Consciousness of Ezra Pound.
(English Literary Studies), Victoria: U. of Victoria, 1977,
pp. 60-72.

468 _____. "Yeats's 'Those Dancing Days Are Gone' and
Pound's 'Canto 23,'" YeA, #2 (1983), 93-95.

469 Bosha, Francis J. "Canto LXXXIV: Pound's 'Henriot,'"
Paideuma, 4, #1 (Spring, 1975), 99-100.

470 _____. "Pound's References to Borah and Stalin in Canto 84," Paideuma, 11, #2 (Fall, 1982), 284-286.

471 Bottrall, Ronald. "XXX Cantos of Ezra Pound," Scrutiny, 2 (September, 1933), 112-122.

472 _____. "XXX Cantos," Determinations: Critical Essays. F. R. Leavis, ed. London: Chatto & Windus, 1934, pp. 179-198.

473 _____. "XXX Cantos of Ezra Pound: An Incursion into Poetics," Ezra Pound: A Critical Anthology. J. P. Sullivan, ed. Baltimore, Md., 1970, pp. 133-143.

474 Bradford, Curtis B. Yeats at Work. Carbondale & Edwardsville: Southern Ill. U. Pr., 1965, p. 174. [Canto LXXXIII].

475 Bridson, D. G. "A Draft of XXX Cantos," New English Weekly, 3 (October 5, 1933), 593-595.

476 _____. "Italian Painting in the Cantos," Agenda, 17, #3-4 (Aut-Wintr-Spring, 1979-80), 210-217.

477 Brooker, Peter. A Student's Guide to the Selected Poems of Ezra Pound. London: Faber & Faber, 1979.

478 Brooke-Rose, Christine. "Ezra Pound: Piers Plowman in the Modern Waste Land," REL, 2, #2 (April, 1961), 74-88.

479 _____. "'Lay me by Aurelie': An Examination of Pound's Use of Historical and Semi-Historical Sources," Cf., #125, pp. 242-279.

480 _____. A Structural Analysis of Pound's Usura Canto: Jakobson's Method Extended and Applied to Free Verse. The Hague: Mouton, 1976.

481 _____. A ZBC of Ezra Pound. Berkeley and Los Angeles: U. of California Pr., 1971.

482 Brooks, David Gordon. "A Critical-Textual Study of Cantos I-XVI of Ezra Pound," DAI, 43, #3 (U. of Toronto: 1982), 796A.

483 Bunting, Basil. "Mr. Ezra Pound," New English Weekly, 1 (May 26, 1932), 137-138.

484 _____. "On the Fly-leaf of Pound's Cantos," Agenda, 4 (October-November, 1965), 28.

485 Burchardi, Johannis. "Extract from Diarium," Paideuma, 4, #1 (Spring, 1975), 107-110.

486   Burns, Gerald. "Intellectual Slither in the Cantos," SWR, 59
      (Winter, 1974), 76-84.

487   Bush, Ronald L. "The Genesis of Ezra Pound's Cantos," DAI,
      36, #3 (Princeton: 1974), 1499A; repr., by Princeton U. Pr.,
      1976.

488   Butterick, George. "On Maximus IV, V, VI," WCR, 4, #4
      (April, 1970), 3-6.

489   Campbell, K. T. S. "The Purification of Poetry--A Note on
      the Poetics of Ezra Pound's Cantos," BJA, 8 (1968), 124-137.

490   Cantrell, Carol Helmstetter. "Obscurity, Clarity, and Sim-
      plicity in the Cantos of Ezra Pound," MQ, 23, #4 (1982),
      402-410.

491   _____. "Quotidian to Divine: Some Notes on Canto 81,"
      Paideuma, 12, #1 (Spring, 1983), 11-20.

492   Carne-Ross, D. S. "The Cantos as Epic," Cf., #114, pp.
      134-153.

493   _____. "Ezra Pound," TLS (April 13, 1973), 420-421.

494   _____. "The Music of a Lost Dynasty: Pound in the Class-
      room," BUJ, 21, #1 (Winter, 1972), 25-41; Instaurations: Es-
      says in and out of Literature. Berkeley: U. of Calif. Pr.,
      1979, pp. 193-217.

495   Casillo, Robert. "Plastic Demons: The Scapegoating Process
      in Ezra Pound," Criticism, 24, #4 (Fall, 1984), 355-382.

496   Cayley, John. "'New Mountains': Some Light on the Chinese
      in Pound's Cantos," Agenda, 20, #3-4 (1982-83), 122-158.

497   Chace, William M. "The Canto as Cento: A Reading of Canto
      33," Paideuma, 1 (Spring-Summer, 1972), 89-100.

498   Cheadle, Brian. "The Rhythm of a Canto: A Reading of
      Canto 81," ESA, 23 (1980), 103-116.

499   Childs, John Steven. "Larvatus Prodeo: Semiotic Aspects of
      the Ideogram in Pound's Cantos," Paideuma, 9 (Fall, 1980),
      289-307.

500   _____. "Modernist Form: Pound's Style in a Draft of XXX
      Cantos," DAI, 44, #6 (Arkansas: 1983), 1787A.

501   Clark, Thomas. "The Formal Structure of Pound's Cantos,"
      EWR, #1 (1964), 97-144.

502   Connolly, Cyril. "A Short Commentary," Agenda, 8 (Autumn-
      Winter, 1970), 44-46.

503   Cook, Albert S. "Die Einheit des Selbstbewusstseins in den
      Cantos," Ezra Pound: 22 Versuche über einen Dichter. Eva
      Hesse, ed. Frankfurt: Athenaum, 1967, pp. 254-262;
      Cf., #41, pp. 349-364.

504   _____. Prisms: Studies in Modern Literature. Blooming-
      ton: Indiana U. Pr., 1967, pp. 93-98, 176-187.

505   Cookson, William. "Donald Davie on Ezra Pound," Agenda, 14,
      #3 (1976), 87-88.

506   _____. "Ezra Pound and Myth: A Reader's Guide to Canto
      II," Agenda, 15, #2 (1977), 87-92.

507   _____. "A Few Notes on 'Drafts and Fragments,'" Agenda,
      8, #3-4 (Autumn-Winter, 1970), 5-6; 47-49; UES, 15, #2
      (1977), 46.

508   _____. "Paradise of Just Rulers," T&T, 41, #21 (May 21,
      1960), 584-585.

509   _____. "Some Notes on Hugh MacDiarmid," Agenda, 5, #4
      (Aut-Wint., 1967-68), 35-41.

510   _____. "Some Notes on Rock-Drill and Thrones," Agenda,
      4, (October-November, 1965), 30-37.

511   Cooney, Douglas L. "Ezra Pound: A Study of His Prosody,"
      Sou'wester, (Special Pound No.), (October 30, 1970), 100-117.

512   Cory, Daniel. "Second Thoughts on Ezra Pound," Encounter,
      37, #4 (October, 1971), 86-92.

513   Cowan, James C. "The Classical Figure as Archetype in
      Pound's Cantos, I-XXX," TCL, 6, #1 (April, 1960), 25-32.

514   Cowley, Malcolm. "Pound Reweighed," A Many-Windowed House:
      Collected Essays on American Writers and American Writing.
      Henry Dan Piper, ed. Carbondale: S. Ill. U. Pr., 1970, pp.
      178-190; [a shorter version in Reporter, 24, #5 (March 2,
      1961), 35-40.]

515   Cox, Kenneth. "New Things Seen," Agenda, 8, #3-4 (Autumn-
      Winter, 1970), 38-39.

516   Culver, Michael. "The Art of Henry Strater: An Examination
      of the Illustrations for Pound's A Draft of XVI Cantos,"
      Paideuma, 12, #2-3, (Fall-Wntr., 1983), 447-478.

517 Cunard, Nancy. "Ezra Pound: XXX Cantos," These Were the
     Hours: Memories of My Hours Press, Reanville and Paris.
     Ed., & Foreword by Hugh Ford. Carbondale & Edwardsville:
     So. Ill. U. Pr., 1969, pp. 123-132.

518 D'Agostino, Nemi. "The Cantos," Italian Images of Ezra Pound:
     Twelve Critical Essays. Angela Jung and Guido Palandri, eds.
     & tr. Taipei, Taiwan: Mei Ya, 1979, pp. 37-54.

519 _____. "The Cantos," Ezra Pound. Rome: Edizioni di
     Storia e Letteratura, 1960, pp. 151-171.

520 _____. "Sulle origini dei Cantos," NC, #5-6 (January-
     June, 1956), 92-104.

521 Davenport, Guy. Cities on Hills: A Study of I-XXX of Ezra
     Pound's Cantos. Ann Arbor, Michigan: UMI Research Pr.,
     1983.

522 _____. "A Collation of Two Texts of the Cantos," Pound
     Newsletter, #6 (April, 1955), 5-13.

523 _____. "Ezra Pound's Radiant Gists: A Reading of Cantos
     II and IV," WSCL, 3, #2 (Spring-Summer, 1962), 50-64.

524 _____. "The House that Jack Built," Salmagundi, 43
     (1979), 140-155.

525 _____. "Persephone's Ezra," Arion, 7 (Summer, 1967),
     164-199; repr., #41, pp. 143-173.

526 _____. "A Reading of I-XXX of the Cantos of Ezra Pound,"
     Diss., Harvard U., 1961.

527 _____. "Thrones [A Portion of the Cantos], Audit, I, #1
     (February 22, 1960), 15-16.

528 Davidsen, Carol. "The Cantos and Culture," ConnR, 8, #2
     (April, 1975), 55-62.

529 Davie, Donald. "Adrian Stokes and Pound's Cantos," TC, 160
     (November, 1956), 419-436.

530 _____. "The Cantos: Towards a Pedestrian Reading,"
     Paideuma, 1, #1 (Spring-Summer, 1972), 55-62.

531 _____. "Cypress Versus Rock-Slide: An Appreciation of
     Canto 110," Agenda, 8, #3-4 (Autumn-Winter, 1970), 19-26.

532 _____. Ezra Pound: Poet as Sculptor. London: 1965;
     New York: Oxford U. Pr., 1964.

533 _____. "'Form' and 'Concept' in Pound's Cantos," Irish
Writing, 36 (Autumn, 1956), 160-173.

534 _____. "Ideas in The Cantos," and "Rhythms in The Cantos," Ezra Pound. Frank Kermode, ed. New York: Viking
Pr., 1976, pp. 62-76, 77-98.

535 _____. "On Thrones: Cantos 96-109," Paris Review, 28
(Summer-Fall, 1962), 49; repr., in Critics on Ezra Pound.
E. San Juan, Jr., ed. Coral Gables, Florida: U. of Miami
Pr., 1972, pp. 95-96.

536 _____. "The Poet as Sculptor," Cf., #41, pp. 198-214.

537 _____. "Sicily in the Cantos," Paideuma, 6, #1 (Spring,
1977), 101-107.

538 _____. "The Significance of The Cantos," CamR, 94, #2214
(June 8, 1973), 165-166.

539 Davis, Earle. "The Man in The Cantos," Vision Fugitive:
Ezra Pound and Economics. Lawrence: U. of Kansas Pr.,
1968, pp. 1-16.

540 Davis, Helen Kathryn. "Fugue, Fresco, and Ideogram:
Structures in Pound's Cantos," DAI, 43, #7 (Utah: 1982),
2347A.

541 Davis, Kay. "Fugue and Canto LXIII," Paideuma, 11, #1
(Spring-Summer, 1982), 15-38.

542 _____. "An Index to Canto References in Paideuma,"
Paideuma, 8 (1979), 317-324.

543 _____. "Ring Composition, Subject Rhyme, and Canto VII,"
Paideuma, 11, #3 (Winter, 1982), 429-439.

544 Deane, Hugh. "Ezra Pound's Chinese Translucencies," EH,
20, #4 (April, 1981), 39-41.

545 De Bedts, Ruth. "The Ideogrammatic Method in The Cantos
of Ezra Pound," FlaR, 2 (Spring, 1958), 30-39.

546 Decavalles, Anthony M. "A Guide to Ezra Pound's Cantos
(X)," Analyst, 11 (July, 1956), 1-18.

547 Dekker, George. The Cantos of Ezra Pound: A Critical
Study. London: Routledge, 1963; New York: Barnes &
Noble, 1963.

548 _____. "Poetic Motive and Strategy in The Cantos," Cf.,
Critics on Ezra Pound. E. San Juan, ed., #535, pp. 84-88.

549 _____. Sailing After Knowledge: The Cantos of Ezra
Pound. London: Routledge; New York: Barnes & Noble,
1963.

550 Demetz, Peter. "Marginalien: Ezra Pound's Pisaner Gesange,"
Merkur, 12 (January, 1958), 97-100.

551 Demott, Robert. "Ezra Pound and Charles Bowlker: Note on
Canto LI," Paideuma, 1, #2 (Winter, 1972), 187-198.

552 de Nagy, N. Christoph. Ezra Pound's Poetics and Literary
Tradition: The Critical Decade. Bern: Francke Verlag, 1966.

553 _____. The Poetry of Ezra Pound: The Pre-Imagist Stage.
Bern: Francke Verlag, 1960.

554 _____. "Pound and Browning," Cf., #503, pp. 231-251.

555 D'Epiro, Peter Francis. "Canto 74: New Light on Lucifer,"
Paideuma, 10, #2 (Fall, 1981), 297-301.

556 _____. "A Touch of Rhetoric: Ezra Pound's Malatesta
Cantos," DAI, 42, #6 (Yale: 1981), 2673A.

557 _____. A Touch of Rhetoric: Ezra Pound's Malatesta
Cantos. Ann Arbor, Mich.: UMI Research Pr., 1983.

558 de Rachewiltz, Boris. "Pagan and Magic Elements in Ezra
Pound's Works," Cf., #41, pp. 174-197.

559 de Rachewiltz, Mary. "Traduzione Integrale," Arion, 6, #2
(Summer, 1967), 208-215.

560 _____. "Nota introduttiva al Canto 51 di Ezra Pound,"
L'Approdo Letterario (Rome), 38 (1967), 51-54.

561 Deutsch, Babette. "Chinese to Cleanthes," NY Herald
Tribune (December 15, 1940), 17.

562 _____. "Ezra Pound's Sparks of Knowledge," NY Herald
Tribune, (March 26, 1933), 4.

563 _____. "Odi et Amo," Cf., #186, pp. 668-670.

564 _____. "Poetry versus Politics," NY Herald Tribune
(August 22, 1948), 7.

565 _____. "Pound Rises Again," NY Herald Tribune (March 13,
1938), 13. (Review: Fifth Decade of Cantos).

566 _____. "Speech and Song," Poetry in Our Time: A

Critical Survey of Poetry in the English-Speaking World, 1900-
1960. 2nd ed., Rev. & Enl. Doubleday, 1963, pp. 133-145.

567 _____. "With Seven League Boots," [Eleven New Cantos]
NY Herald Tribune (November 25, 1934), 18.

568 Dickey, R. P. "Introduction to the Esthetic and Philosophy
of the Cantos," Sou'wester (Ezra Pound Birthday Issue),
(October 30, 1970), 21-35.

569 Dilligan, Robert J., James W. Parins, and Todd K. Bender.
A Concordance to Ezra Pound's Cantos. New York: Garland
Pub. Co., 1981.

570 Dillon, George. "A Note on the Obvious," Poetry, 68 (September, 1946), 322-325.

571 Dodsworth, Martin. "The Marshall Plan," NSt, 84 (July 28,
1972), 129.

572 Donoghue, Denis. "Ezra Pound's School Book," LugR, 1, #3-4
(1965), 133-146; The Ordinary Universe: Soundings in Modern
Literature. New York: Macmillan, 1968, pp. 291-308.

573 Doria, Charles. "Pound, Olson, and the Classical Tradition,"
Boundary, 2, #2 (Fall-Winter, 1973), 127-143.

574 Driscoll, John. "Canto LX and Ezra Pound's Use of Histoire
générale de la Chine," SN, 50 (1978), 215-232.

575 _____. The China Cantos of Ezra Pound. Uppsala:
Almqvist & Wiksell, 1983. (AUUSAU 46). [Cantos 52-61:
Sources in Chinese literature].

576 Drummond, John. "La verità sul caso Pound," FLe, #1, 1
(January 7, 1951), 1.

577 Duclos, Jacques. "Cantos," RLV, 31, #1 (1955), 70-72.

578 Dudek, Louis. "Exotic Reference in the Cantos of Ezra
Pound," AntigR, 11 (1972), 55-66; IJAS, 2, #2 (1972), 30-39.

579 Duffey, Bernard I. "The Experimental Lyric in Modern
Poetry: Eliot, Pound, Williams," JML, 3 (July, 1974), 1085-
1103.

580 Durant, Alan. Ezra Pound, Identity in Crisis: A Fundamen-
tal Reassessment of the Poet and His Work. New Jersey:
Barnes & Noble, 1981; Sussex: The Harvester Pr., 1981.

581 Eastman, Barbara C. Ezra Pound's Cantos: The Story of the

Text, 1948-1975. Introduction by Hugh Kenner. Orono:
Maine National Poetry Foundation, U. of Maine, 1979.

582 _____. "The Gap in The Cantos: 72 and 73," Paideuma,
8 (1979), 415-427; Agenda, 17, #3-4, and 18, #1 (Aut-Wntr-
Spr., 1979-1980), pp. 142-156.

583 _____. "Unlocking The Cantos with Mauberley's Key,"
DQR, 9, #2 (1979), 82-100.

584 Eaves, T. C. Duncan, and Ben D. Kimpel. "The Birth of a
Nation: A Note on Pound's Canto XIX," PQ, 62, #3 (Summer,
1983), 417-418.

585 Eder, Doris L. "Review: The Cantos of Ezra Pound: The
Lyric Mode by Eugene Nasser," Paideuma, 5, #1 (1976),
195-197.

586 Edwards, John Hamilton. The Cantos of Ezra Pound. New
York: New Directions, 1948.

587 _____. "Poet or Pooh-Bah?" KR, 14, #4 (Autumn, 1953),
684-689.

588 _____, and William V. Vasse. Annotated Index to the
Cantos of Ezra Pound: Cantos I-LXXXIV. Berkeley: U. of
Calif. Pr., 1957.

589 Eisenhauer, Robert G. "'Jeweler's Company': Topaz, Half-
Light, and Bounding-Lines in The Cantos," Paideuma, 9
(1979), 249-270.

590 Eliot, T. S. After Strange Gods: A Primer of Modern Heresy.
New York: Harcourt, Brace & Co., 1934, pp. 44-47.

591 _____. "The Method of Mr. Pound," Athenaeum, 4,669
(October 24, 1919), 1065-1066.

592 _____. "A Note on Ezra Pound," Today, 4, #19, (September, 1918), 3-9.

593 Elizondo, Salvador. "Il miglior fabbro: La poesia de Ezra
Pound anterior a los Cantos," Estaciones, 5 (August, 1960),
3-15.

594 Elliott, Angela Pantaleone. "Light as Image in Ezra Pound's
Cantos," DAI, 39 (Drew U: 1978), 2234A-35A.

595 _____. "Lucifer's Fall in Pound's Canto LXXIV," Paideuma,
8 (1979), 59-60.

596 Elliott, George P. "Poet of Many Voices," The Carleton Mis-
     cellany, 2 (Summer, 1961), 79-103; repr., in Ezra Pound: A
     Collection of Critical Essays. Walter Sutton, ed. Englewood
     Cliffs, N.J.: Prentice-Hall, 1963, pp. 152-162.

597 Ellmann, Maud. "Floating the Pound: The Circulation of the
     Subject in Pound's The Cantos," OLR, 3, #3 (1979), 16-27.

598 Ellman, Richard. "Ez and Old Billyum," KR, 28, #4 (Septem-
     ber, 1966), 470-495.

599 Emerson, Dorothy. "Poetry Corner: Ezra Pound," Scholastic,
     24 (May 12, 1934), 10.

600 Emery, Clark. Ideas into Action: A Study of Pound's Cantos.
     Coral Gables, Fl: U. of Miami Pr., 1958.

601 Espey, John J. "Addenda," Analyst (Northwestern U.), III
     (December, 1953), 10-11.

602 _____. "Note by John Espey," Paideuma, 4, #1 (1975),
     181-185, 187.

603 _____. "Sidelights from the Italian and German Cantos,"
     Paideuma, 8 (1979), 297-299.

604 Fang, Achilles. "Aspects of the Cantos: Notes on China and
     the Cantos," Pound Newsletter, 9 (January, 1956), 3-5.

605 _____, et al. "A Guide to Ezra Pound's Cantos I-VIII:
     Addenda," Analyst (Northwestern), VI (January, 1955).
     (Entire Issue).

606 Feldman, A. Bronson. "The Critical Canons of Ezra Pound,"
     Poet Lore, 57 (Summer, 1953), 226-246.

607 Fender, Stephen. "Ezra Pound and the Words off the Page:
     Historical Allusions in Some American Long Poems," YES, 8
     (1978), 95-108.

608 Fink, Jon-Stephen. "Ezekial Ton and Isaih Ounce (E. P.
     Perspective)," St. Andrew's Rev, 3, #4 (1976), 31-35.

609 Fitts, Dudley. "Music Fit for the Odea," H&H, 4 (January-
     March, 1931), 278-289.

610 _____. "Pound and the Cantos," SatRL, 8 (December 26,
     1931), 416.

611 Fitzgerald, Edward J. "Eleven New Cantos," American Poetry
     Journal (March, 1935), 23.

612 Fitzgerald, Robert. "Gloom and Gold in Ezra Pound," En-
     counter, 7 (July, 1956), 16-22.

613 _____. "Mr. Pound's Good Governors," Accent, 1 (Winter,
     1941), 121-122.

614 _____. "A Note on Ezra Pound, 1928-1956," KR, 18, #4
     (Autumn, 1956), 505-518.

615 _____. "Notes on Ezra Pound, 1928-1956," NC, Nos. 5-6
     (January-June, 1956), 35-57.

616 _____. "What Thou Lovest Well Remains," NR, 119 (August
     16, 1948), 21-23.

617 Fleming, William. "Ezra Pound's 'Thrones': Its Place in the
     Cantos," TC (Australia), (Autumn, 1961), 252-259.

618 Fletcher, John Gould. "The Neglected Assessment," Criterion,
     8 (April, 1929), 513-524.

619 Flint, R. W. "Pound and Modern Poetry," HudR, 8, #1
     (Spring, 1955), 134-135.

620 Flory, Wendy Stallard. "Alexander Del Mar: Some Additional
     Sources," Paideuma, 4, #2-3 (Fall-Winter, 1975), 325-327.

621 _____. Ezra Pound and The Cantos: A Record of a Strug-
     gle. New Haven; London: Yale U. Pr., 1980.

622 _____. "Pound's Blake and Blake's Dante: 'The Circle of
     the Lustful' and Canto 20," Paideuma, 6 (Fall, 1977), 155-165.

623 Foster, John L. "Pound's Revision of Cantos I-III," MP, 63
     (August 1, 1948), Sec. 7, p. 14.

624 Frankenberg, Lloyd. "Ezra Pound and His Magnum Opus,"
     NYT (August 1, 1948), Sec. 7, p. 14.

625 Freudenheim, Richard Jesse. "Ezra Pound: Canto 85," DAI,
     39, #2 (Calif., Berkeley: 1977), 871A.

626 Friar, Kimon, and John Malcolm Brinnin. "The Cantos,"
     Modern Poetry, American and British. New York: Appleton-
     Century-Crofts, 1951, pp. 525-531.

627 Frohock, W. M. "Ezra Pound: Images of Revolt," Strangers
     to This Ground: Cultural Diversity in Contemporary American
     Writing. Dallas: Southern Methodist U. Pr., 1961, pp. 111-
     131.

628   _____. "The Revolt of Ezra Pound," SWR, 44 (Summer,
       1959), 190-199.

629   Fuller, Dorothy V. "Ezra Pound and the Cantos," ArQ, 8,
       #4 (Winter, 1952), 361-362.

630   Furia, Philip. "Pound and Blake on Hell," Paideuma, 10, #3
       (Winter, 1981), 599-601.

631   _____. Pound's Cantos Declassified. University Park, Pa.:
       Pa. State U. Pr., 1984.

632   Fussell, Edwin. "Dante and Pound's Cantos," JML, I, 1
       (1970), 75-87.

633   _____. "The Waste Land and The Cantos," Lucifer in
       Harness: American Meter, Metaphor, and Diction. Princeton:
       Princeton U. Pr., 1973, pp. 80-88.

634   Galigani, Giuseppe. "Montis Pascuorum," YLM, 126, #5
       (December, 1958), 18-23.

635   Gall, Sally M. "Pound and the Modern Melic Tradition: To-
       wards a Demystification of 'Absolute Rhythm,'" Paideuma, 8
       (1979), 35-47.

636   Géfin, Laszlo. "Ideagram: The History of a Poetic Method,"
       DAI, 40 (McGill U.: 1979), 3299A.

637   Gibbs, Alonzo. "The Sports Department," Voices, 173
       (September-December, 1960), 38-41.

638   Giovannini, Giovanni. Ezra Pound and Dante. Nijmegen,
       Utrecht, Netherlands: Dekker and Van de Vegt, 1961.

639   Glenn, Edgar M. "Addenda," Analyst (Northwestern U.),
       No. 2 (July, 1953), 8-9.

640   _____. "Association and the Cantos of Ezra Pound," DAI,
       15 (Stanford: 1955), 1853-54. [Cf., Pound Newsletter, 8
       (October, 1955), 28.]

641   _____. "A Guide to Canto I of Ezra Pound (Revised and
       Enlarged)," Analyst, 8, #4 (June, 1955). [Entire Issue.]

642   _____. "A Guide to Ezra Pound's Cantos (I-IV)," Analyst,
       1 (March, 1953), 1-7.

643   _____. "Pound and Ovid," Paideuma, 10, #3 (Winter,
       1981), 625-634.

644 Goacher, Denis. "Ezra Pound's Cantos," Listener, 68 (September 6, 1962), 357-358.

645 _____. Reading the Cantos. New York: Random House, 1966.

646 Goodspeed, George. "Corrections and a Clarification," The Month at Goodspeed's, 33 (January-February, 1962), 98-99.

647 Goodwin, K. L. "Ezra Pound: The Formal Structure of the Later Cantos," Australasian Universities Language and Literature Association: Proceedings and Papers of the Thirteenth Congress Held at Monash University, August 12-18, 1970. J. R. Ellis, ed. Melbourne: AULLA and Monash U., 1971, pp. 154-156.

648 _____. "The Structure of Pound's Later Cantos," SoRA, 4, #4 (1971), 300-307.

649 Gordon, David M. "'Confucius, Philosophe': An Introduction to the Chinese Cantos 52-61," Paideuma, 5, #3 (Winter, 1976), 387-403.

650 _____. "Corpus Juris and Canto XCIV," Paideuma, 11, #2 (Fall, 1982), 313-324.

651 _____. "Edward Coke: The Azalea Is Grown," Paideuma, 4, #2 & 3 (Fall-Winter, 1975), 223-229.

652 _____. "A Place for Buddhism in Canto 99," Paideuma, 5, #2 (Fall, 1976), 275-278.

653 _____. "Pound's Use of the Sacred Edict in Canto 98," Paideuma, 4, #1 (Spring, 1975), 121-168.

654 _____. "The Sacred Edict: Thought Built on Sagetrieb," Paideuma, 3, #2 (Fall, 1975), 169-190.

655 _____. "The Sources of Canto LIII," Paideuma, 5, #1 (Spring-Summer, 1976), 123-152.

656 Graham, Robin. "Will and Sensibility in the Cantos," ESA, 21 (1978), 87-97.

657 Gregory, Horace. "The Search for a Frontier," NR, 75 (July 26, 1933), 292-294.

658 Grigsby, Gordan Kay. "The Modern Long Poem: Studies in Thematic Form," DA, 21 (Wisconsin: 1960), 622-623.

659 _____. "Newspeak in Pound's Cantos," SAQ, 62, #1 (Winter, 1962), 51-56.

660   Grigson, Goeffrey. "Aspects of Modern Poetry," NS&N, 8
      (December 15, 1934), 899.

661   _____. "The Methodism of Ezra Pound," New Verse, #5
      (October, 1933), 17-22.

662   Gross, Harvey. "The Cantos of Ezra Pound," The Contrived
      Corridor: History and Fatality in Modern Literature. Ann
      Arbor: Michigan U. Pr., 1971, pp. 100-123.

663   _____. "Pound's Cantos and the Idea of History," BuR, 9,
      #1 (March, 1960), 14-31.

664   Gugelberger, Georg M. "By No Means an Orderly Dantescan
      Rising," IQ, 64 (1973), 31-48.

665   Guiliani, Alfredo. "Le ragioni metriche de Ezra Pound," NC,
      5-6 (January-June, 1956), 105-110.

666   Haberstroh, Patricia Boyle. "The Two Worlds of the Cantos,"
      DAI, 38, #9 (Bryn Mawr: 1977), 5461A.

667   Halawatsch, Wolfhard. "Ezra Pound's Weg sum Licht: Eine
      Interpretation von Canto XV," NS, 18 (November, 1969), 551-
      557.

668   Hall, Donald. "The Art of Poetry V," ParisR, 7, #28 (Summer-
      Fall, 1962), 22-51.

669   _____. "The Cantos in England," NS&N, 59 (March 12,
      1960), 368.

670   Hall, Ian Roger. "Murdering the Time: A Study of Temporal
      Order in Selected Works of Henry Thoreau, Nathaniel Haw-
      thorne, T. S. Eliot, and Ezra Pound," DAI, 36, #9 (Kent
      State: 1975), 6099A.

671   Halperen, Max. "How to Read a Canto," The Twenties: Fic-
      tion, Poetry, Drama. Warren French, ed. Deland, Florida:
      Everett/Edwards, Inc., 1975, pp. 335-350.

672   _____. "Old Men and New Tools: The Chinese Cantos of
      Pound," Trace, 52 (Spring, 1964), 1-8.

673   _____. "The Structural Reading of The Cantos of Ezra
      Pound," DA, 20 (Florida St., 1960), #4659.

674   Hankins, John E. "Notes and Queries," Paideuma, 2, #1
      (Spring, 1973), 141-145.

675   _____. "Notes and Queries," Paideuma, 3, #1 (Spring,
      1974), 135-137.

676 Harmon, William. <u>Time in Ezra Pound's Work</u>. Chapel Hill: U.
     of North Carolina Pr., 1977.

677 _____. "Visions of Perfection: Some Recurrent Figures in
     the Poems of Eliot and Pound," Yeat-EliotRev, 5, #1 (1978),
     18-20.

678 Harper, Michael F. "Truth and Calliope: Ezra Pound's
     <u>Malatesta</u>," PMLA, 96, #1 (January, 1981), 86-103.

679 Harrison, John. <u>The Reactionaries: Yeats, Pound, Eliot,
     Lawrence: A Study of the Anti-Democratic Intelligentsia</u>.
     New York: Schocken, 1967.

680 Hartley, Anthony. "<u>The Cantos</u> of Ezra Pound," Spectator
     (July 23, 1954), 124-126.

681 Helmling, Steven. "Del Mar Material in <u>Canto 97</u>: Further
     Annotations," Paideuma, 5, #1 (Spring, 1976), 53-57.

682 _____. "Pound, Del Mar, and Canto 97," UES, 15, #2
     (1977), 26-34.

683 Hénault, Marie, ed. <u>Studies in the Cantos</u>. Columbus, Ohio:
     Charles E. Merrill Pub. Co., 1971.

684 Heppenstall, Rayner. "Poetry," New English Weekly, 7
     (April 18, 1935), 10.

685 Herdeck, Donald Elmer. "The Golden Bitch: A Study of
     Ezra Pound's 'Anti-Semitism' and 'Fascism' as Affecting Struc-
     ture, Theme, and Imagery in <u>The Cantos</u>," DAI, 29, #10
     (Penn. U: 1968), 3613A.

686 Hesse, Eva. "Answers to Queries on <u>Canto 38</u>; and Letters to
     the Editor," Paideuma, 5, #2 (Fall, 1976), 345-352.

687 _____. "Answers to Queries and Letters to the Editor,"
     Paideuma, 5, #3 (Winter, 1976), 493-500.

688 _____. "Baedeker zu einer Kontinent: Ein Versuch über
     die Cantos von Ezra Pound," Akzente, 11 (1964), 79-95.

689 _____. "Books Behind <u>The Cantos</u>, Part One: <u>Cantos I-
     XXX</u>," Paideuma, 1 (Winter, 1972), 137-151.

690 _____, ed. "Canto XIII übertragen von Eva Hesse," Merkur,
     #87 (September, 1963), 833-836.

691 _____. "Franco Sacchetti in <u>Canto 22/106:110</u>," Paideuma,
     5, #3 (Winter, 1976), 413-414.

692 _____. "Frobenius as Rainmaker," Paideuma, 1, #1 (Spring-Summer, 1972), 85-88.

693 _____. "'Kadzu, Arachidi, Acero' in Canto XCVII/683: A Matter of Coherence," Paideuma, 8 (1979), 53-54.

694 _____. "Klages in Canto LXXV/450: A Positive Identification," Paideuma, 10, #2 (Fall, 1981), 295-296.

695 _____. "Margarethe von Taufers," Paideuma, 2, #3 (Winter, 1973), 497-502.

696 _____. "Notes and Queries," Paideuma, 3, #3 (Winter, 1974), 413-416.

697 _____. "A Redefinition of the Problem of mo in Canto LXXIV/430 in the Light of Its Source," Paideuma, 8 (1979), 407-408.

698 _____. "Smaragdos, Chrysolihos ... Reflexionen zu Canto VII," Jahresring (Stuttgart), 62/63, pp. 90-109.

699 Heyen, William. "John Berryman: A Memoir and an Interview," OhR, 15, #2 (Winter, 1974), 46-65.

700 Highet, Gilbert. "Beer-Bottle on the Pediment," Horizon, 3, #13 (January, 1961), 116-118.

701 Hildesheimer, Wolfgang. "Die Wirklichkeit der Reaktionäre: Uber [The Reality of the Reactionary: About] T. S. Eliot und Ezra Pound," Merkur, 28 (July, 1974), 630-647.

702 Hlawatsch, Wolfhard. "Ezra Pounds Weg zum Light: Eine Interpretation von Canto XV," NS, 18 (1969), 551-557.

703 Hoffa, William W. "Ezra Pound and George Antheil: Vorticist Music and the Cantos," AL, 44 (March, 1972), 52-73.

704 Hoffman, Daniel. "Poetry: After Modernism," Harvard Guide to Contemporary American Writing. Daniel Hoffman, ed. Cambridge, Mass.; London: Belknap Pr., 1979, pp. 439-453.

705 Holaday, Woon-Ping Chin. "Ezra Pound's Use of Moyriac de Mailla's Histoire generale de la Chine: A Source Study of the Chinese History Cantos," DAI, 38 (Toledo: 1977), 2789A.

706 Holder, Alan. "The Lesson of the Master: Ezra Pound and Henry James," AL, 35, #1 (March, 1963), 71-79.

707 _____. "Three Voyagers in Search of Europe: A Study of Henry James, Ezra Pound, and T. S. Eliot," DA, 26, #3 (Columbia: 1965), 1646-47.

708 _____. Three Voyagers in Search of Europe: A Study of
Henry James, Ezra Pound, and T. S. Eliot. Philadelphia: U.
of Pa. Pr., 1966.

709 Hopes, David Brendan. "Turbulent Form: The Vortex in The
Cantos of Ezra Pound," DAI, 41, #6 (Syracuse: 1980), 2612A.

710 Horrocks, R. J. "Mosaic: A Study of Juxtaposition in literature, as an Approach to Pound's Cantos and Similar Modern
Poems," Diss. U. of Auckland, New Zealand, 1976.

711 Houston, John Porter. "The Cantos," French Symbolism and
the Modernist Movement: A Study of Poetic Structures. London; Baton Rouge: La. St. U. Pr., 1980, pp. 166-172.

712 Hugen, Dorothy Jean. "Ezra Pound's Use in Canto XXIV of
Luchino Dal Campo's Viaggio a Gerusalemme," DAI, 40, #4 (Los
Angeles: 1979), 2091A.

713 _____. "... Small Birds of Cypress," Paideuma, 3, #2 (Fall,
1974), 229-238.

714 Hughes, Robert. "Amarili," Paideuma, 2, #1 (Spring, 1973),
39.

715 Hynes, Samuel. "Pound and the Prose Tradition," YR, 51
(June, 1962), 532-546.

716 Ismail, Jamila. "News of the Universe: Muan Bpo and The
Cantos," Agenda, 9, #2-3 (Spring-Summer, 1971), 70-87.

717 Iwasaki, Ryozo. "The Cantos e no approach," EigoS, 119
(1973), 2-4.

718 Jackson, Thomas. "The Adventures of Messire Wrong-Head,"
ELH, 32 (June, 1965), 238-255.

710 Jarrell, Randall. "Five Poets," YR, 46 (September, 1956),
103-106.

720 _____. "Poets: Old, New and Aging," NR, 103 (December
9, 1940), 798-800.

721 Jenner, E. A. B. "Some Notes on the Poetry and Technique
of the Later Cantos of Ezra Pound," Cave, 3 (February,
1973), 67-69.

722 John, Roland. "A Note on the Meaning of the Cantos,"
Agenda, 17, #3-4; 18, #1 (Aut-Wntr-Spr., 1979-80), 257-263.

723 Joyce, James. "From James Joyce," The Cantos of Ezra Pound:

Some Testimonials. New York: Farrar & Rinehart, Inc., 1933, pp. 12-13.

724 Juhasz, Suzanne. "Metaphor in The Cantos of Ezra Pound," Metaphor and the Poetry of Williams, Pound, and Stevens. Lewisburg: Bucknell U. Pr., 1974. pp. 75-131, passim.

725 Kappel, Andrew J. "Napoleon and Talleyrand in The Cantos," Paideuma, 11, #1 (Spring-Summer, 1982), 55-78.

726 Kearns, George. "Guide to Ezra Pound's Selected Cantos," DAI, 42, #1 (Boston U: 1976), 210A.

727 _____. Guide to Ezra Pound's Selected Cantos. New Brunswick, NJ: Rutgers U. Pr., 1980.

728 Keith, Nobuko T. "Ezra Pound's Relationship with Fenollosa and the Japanese Noh Plays," MarkhamR, 3 (1972), 21-27.

729 Kenner, Hugh. "Art in a Closed Field," VQR, 38 (Autumn, 1962), 597-613.

730 _____. "Blood for the Ghosts," TexQt, 10, #4 (Winter, 1967), 67-79.

731 _____. "The Broken Mirrors and the Mirror of Memory," Cf., #771, pp. 3-32.

732 _____. "The Cantos-1," and "Cantos-2," The Pound Era. Berkeley, LA. & London: U. of Calif. Pr., 1971, pp. 349-381, 414-436.

733 _____. "Drafts and Fragments and the Structure of the Cantos," Agenda, 8, #3-4 (Autumn-Wntr., 1970), 7-19.

734 _____. "Gold in the Gloom," Poetry, 81, #2 (November, 1952), 127-132.

735 _____. "More on the Seven Lakes Canto," Paideuma, 2, #1 (Spring, 1973), 43-46.

736 _____. "Motz El Son," StBr, 3/4 (Fall, 1969), 371-377.

737 _____. "Plea for Metrics," Poetry, 86, #1 (April, 1955), 41-45.

738 _____. The Poetry of Ezra Pound. London: Faber & Faber; New York: New Directions, 1951, pp. 185-304.

739 _____. "Pound's Cantos, I," Expl, 11 (December, 1952), Item 20.

740 _____. "Pound on Going and on Ending," Spectrum, 15
(May, 1973), 55-59.

741 _____. "Prophets of Renaissance," HudR, 3 (Fall, 1950),
474-478.

742 _____. "The Rose in the Steel Dust," HudR, 3 (Spring,
1950), 66-124.

743 _____. "Schema for XXX Cantos," Paideuma, 2 (Fall,
1973), 201.

744 Kenny, Herbert A. "Pound's Cantos: The Failure of an
Epic," Critic, 19 (June-July, 1961), 9-10, 72.

745 Kimpel, Ben, and T. C. Duncan Eaves. "American History
in Rock-Drill and Thrones," Paideuma, 9 (1980), 417-439.

746 _____ and _____. "Ezra Pound's Use of Sources and
Illustrated by His Use of Nineteenth-Century French History,"
MP, 80 (1982-83), 35-52.

747 _____ and _____. "A Note to Ezra Pound's Canto 85,"
ELN, 17 (June, 1980), 292-293.

748 _____ and _____. "Pound's Canto LXXX," Expl, 41, #3
(Spring, 1983), 43-44.

749 _____ and _____. "Pound's 'Ideogrammatic Method,' as
Illustrated in Canto 99," AL, 51 (May, 1979), 205-237.

750 _____ and _____. "Pound's Research for the Malatesta
Cantos," Paideuma, 11, #3 (Winter, 1982), 406-419.

751 _____ and _____. "Pound's Use of Sienese Manuscripts
for Cantos 42 and 43," Paideuma, 8 (1979), 513-518.

752 _____ and _____. "Some Curious 'Facts' in Ezra Pound's
Cantos," ELH, 50, #3 (Fall, 1983), 627-635.

753 _____ and _____. "The Source of Canto L," Paideuma,
8 (1979), 81-93.

754 _____ and _____. "The Sources of Cantos 42 and 43,"
Paideuma, 6 (Winter, 1977), 333-358.

755 _____ and _____. "The Sources of the Leopoldine
Cantos," Paideuma, 7 (Spring and Fall, 1978), 249-277.

756 _____ and _____. "Two Notes on Ezra Pound's Cantos,"
MP, 78 (February, 1981), 285-288.

757   King, George T. "Janequin's 'Song of the Birds' in Pound's
      Canto 75," UES, 15, #2 (1977), 31-34.

758   Knight, Robert. "Thomas Jefferson in Canto 31," Paideuma,
      5, #1 (Spring-Summer, 1976), 79-94.

759   Kodama, Sinehide. "The Eight Scenes of Sho-Sho," Paideuma,
      6 (Fall, 1977), 131-145.

760   Kohli, Raj K. " 'Epic of the West': Some Observations on
      American History and the Cantos," IJAS, 2, #2 (December,
      1972), 40-54.

761   Koppenfels, Werner von. "Ezra Pound: Der Modernist als
      Elegike," Archiv, 212, #2 (1975), 280-302.

762   Korg, Jacob. "Jacob Epstein's Rock Drill and the Cantos,"
      Paideuma, 4 (Fall-Winter, 1975), 301-313.

763   Kostelanetz, Richard. "Ezra Pound: The Cantos," Cw, 96
      (July 28, 1972), 410-411, 413.

764   _____. "Impounding Pound's Milestone," The Old Poetries
      and the New. Ann Arbor: U. of Michigan Pr., 1981, pp.
      48-51.

765   Kwan-Terry, John. "Pound and the Limits of Prosody: Some
      Notes on the Cantos," SELit (Eng. No.), (1979), 95-113.

766   Landini, Richard G. "Confucianism and The Cantos of Ezra
      Pound," Topic, 6 (Fall, 1966), 30-42.

767   _____. "A Guide to the Economic Thought in Ezra Pound's
      Cantos," DA, 24, #2 (Fla.: 1959), 747.

768   _____. "Vorticism and The Cantos of Ezra Pound," WHR,
      14 (Spring, 1960), 173-181.

769   Lauber, John. "Pound's Cantos: A Fascist Epic," JAmS, 12
      (April, 1978), 3-21. Reply: D. Murray, JAmS, 13 (April,
      1979), 109-113.

770   Law, Richard. "The Seventh Canto Initial," Paideuma, 8
      (1979), 411.

771   Leary, Lewis, ed. Motive and Method in The Cantos of Ezra
      Pound. New York: Columbia U. Pr., 1954; 1961.

772   _____. "Pound-Wise, Penny Foolish," Paideuma, 1, #2
      (Winter, 1972), 153-159.

773 Leavis, Frank R. "Ezra Pound," Ezra Pound: A Collection of
     Critical Essays. Walter Sutton, ed. Englewood Cliffs, NJ:
     Prentice-Hall, Inc., 1963, pp. 26-40.

774 _____. "Ezra Pound," New Bearings in English Poetry: A
     Study of the Contemporary Situation. Ann Arbor: U. of
     Michigan Pr., 1960, pp. 133-157.

775 Leibowitz, Herbert. "The Muse and the News," HudR, 22
     (Autumn, 1969), 501-502.

776 Lennig, Arthur George. "An Analysis of the Cantos of Ezra
     Pound," DA, 22 (Wisconsin: 1961), 1179-80.

777 Levi, Peter. "Pound and the Classics," Agenda, 4, 2
     (October-November, 1965), 42-45.

778 Lewis, Wyndham. "Ezra Pound, Etc.," Time and Western Man.
     Boston: Beacon Pr., 1957, pp. 38-48.

779 Libera, Sharon Mayer. "Casting His Gods Back into the Nous:
     Two Neoplationists and the Cantos of Ezra Pound," Paideuma,
     2, #3 (Winter, 1973), 355-377.

780 _____. Ezra Pound's Paradise: A Study of Neoplatonism
     in the Cantos. Diss. Harvard U., 1972.

781 Logue, Christopher, and Alan Neame, assisted by Jared
     Shlaes. "Commentary: The Sixth Canto of Ezra Pound,"
     Merlin, I, #2 (Autumn, 1952), 104-109.

782 MacDiarmid, Hugh. "The Esemplastic Power," Agenda, 8,
     #3-4 (Autumn-Winter, 1970), 27-30.

783 McDowell, Colin. "'The Toys ... at Auxerre': Canto 77,"
     Paideuma, 12, #1 (Spring, 1983), 21-30.

784 McNaughton, William. "Ezra Pound's Meters and Rhythms,"
     PMLA, 78, #1 (March, 1963), 136-146.

785 _____. "The 1976 'Summer at Brunnenburg': Reading the
     Cantos," Paideuma, 5, #3 (Winter, 1976), 457-460.

786 _____. "A Note on the Main Form in The Cantos,"
     Paideuma, 6, #2 (Fall, 1977), 147-152.

787 MacNeice, Louis. Modern Poetry: A Personal Essay. Oxford:
     Clarendon Pr., 1968, pp. 162ff.

788 Madge, Charles. "Pound's Odyssey," NS&N, 40 (September
     30, 1959), 328-329.

789 Malkoff, Karl. Escape from the Self: A Study in Contemporary
     American Poetry and Poetics. New York: Columbia Pr., 1977,
     pp. 48-64, passim.

790 Mandanis, Alice Subley. "Pound and Longinus: The Didactic
     Element in The Cantos," DAI, 32 (Catholic U. of America:
     1970), 2095A.

791 Manganaris-Decavailes, Anthony. "A Guide to Ezra Pound's
     Cantos (X)," Analyst, 11 (July, 1956), 1-18.

792 Mangum, Geoff. "A Note on Canto LXXIX: Cimbica, Sacred
     Puma of the Baja Peninsula," Paideuma, 9 (1980), 323-326.

793 Martin, B. K. "Ezra Pound and T. E. Lawrence: 74/444:472,"
     Paideuma, 6 (Fall, 1977), 167-173. [Canto 74]

794 Materer, Timothy. "H. D., serenitas, and Canto LXIII,"
     Paideuma, 12, #2-3 (Fall-Winter, 1983), 275-280.

795 _____. "Henry Gaudier's 'Three Ninas,'" Paideuma, 4
     (Fall-Winter, 1975), 323-324. [Canto 107]

796 _____. "A Reading of 'From Canto CXV,'" Paideuma, 2,
     #2 (Fall, 1973), 205-207.

797 Mayo, Robert. "A Guide to Ezra Pound's Cantos (VIII),"
     Analyst, 5, (October, 1954). [Entire issue].

798 _____. "A Guide to Ezra Pound's Cantos (XI)," Analyst,
     13 (July, 1957), 1-4.

799 _____, and Sybil Wuletich. "A Guide to Ezra Pound's
     Cantos (IX)," Analyst, 7 (April, 1955), [Entire issue].

800 Merchant, Moelwyn. "The Coke Cantos," Agenda, 17, #3-4 &
     18, #1 (Aut-Wntr-Spr., 1979-80), 76-85.

801 Michaels, Walter B. "Lincoln Steffens and Pound," Paideuma,
     2, #2 (Fall, 1973), 209-210.

802 Miller, James Edwin. "An Epic Is a Poem Containing History:
     Ezra Pound's 'Cantos,'" The American Quest for a Supreme
     Fiction. Chicago: U. of Chicago Pr., 1979, pp. 68-98.

803 Miller, Vincent. "Pound's Battle with Time," YR, 66, #2
     (December, 1976), 193-208.

804 Millett, Fred B. "Ezra Pound and The Cantos," AL, 25, #4
     (January, 1954), 517-519.

805 Miner, Earl. "Ezra Pound," The Japanese Tradition in British and American Literature. Princeton: Princeton U. Pr., 1958.

806 Miyake, Akiko. "Between Confucius and Eleusis: Ezra Pound's Assimilation of Chinese Culture and Writing the Cantos I-LXXI," DAI, 31 (Duke: 1971), 5416A-17A.

807 _____. "The Greek-Egyptian Mysteries in Pound's 'The Little Review Calendar' and in Cantos 1-7," Paideuma, 7 (Spring-Fall, 1978), 73-111.

808 Monroe, Harriet. "Ezra Pound," Poets and Their Art. Freeport, NY: Bks. for Libraries Pr., 1967, pp. 12-20.

809 Moody, A. D. "Cantos I-III: Craft and Vision," Agenda, 17, #3-4, and 18, #1 (Aut-Wntr-Spr., 1979-80), 103-117.

810 _____. "The Democracy of the Cantos," TLS, #4038 (August 15, 1980), 917.

811 Moore, Marianne. "A Draft of XXX Cantos," Poetry, 39 (October, 1931), 37-50.

812 _____. "A Draft of Cantos," Criterion, 13 (April, 1934), 482-485.

813 _____. "Ezra Pound: The Cantos," A Marianne Moore Reader. New York: Viking Pr., 1961, pp. 149-166.

814 _____. "Ezra Pound: The Cantos," Predilections. New York: Viking Pr., 1955, pp. 62-75.

815 _____. "A Note," Agenda, 4 (October-November, 1965), 22.

816 _____. "A Tribute," Cf., #125, p. 21.

817 Moramarco, Fred. "Concluding an Epic: The Drafts and Fragments of the Cantos," AL, 49 (November, 1977), 309-326.

818 _____. "Italian Imagery in The Cantos," Contributi dell' Istituto di filologia moderna. Sergio Rossi, ed. Milano: Vita e Pensiero, Univ. Cattolica. [1974?]

819 _____. "The Malatesta Cantos," Mosaic, 12, #1 (1978), 107-118.

820 _____. "Schiavoni: 'That Chap on the Wood Barge,'" Paideuma, 4, #1 (Spring, 1975), 101-104.

821 Morrow, Bradford. "De Lollis' Sordello and Sordello: Canto 36," Paideuma, 4, #1 (Spring, 1975), 93-98.

822 _____. "A Source for 'Palace in smoky light': Pound and Dryden's Virgil," Paideuma, 3, #2 (Fall, 1974), 245-246.

823 Morse, Jonathan. "What's His Name," Paideuma, 10, #3 (Winter, 1981), 595-597.

824 Muir, Edwin. "Experimental Poetry," LonM, 31 (April, 1935), 594-595.

825 _____. "Recent Poetry," Purpose, 12 (July-December, 1940), 149-150.

826 _____. "Review: Fifth Decade of Cantos," Criterion, 17 (October, 1937), 148-149.

827 Mullins, Eustace Clarence. Cf., #92, pp. 176-179, passim.

828 Murphy, Richard. "Books and Writers," Spectator, 185 (November 17, 1950), 516.

829 Myers, Peter. "The Metre of Canto 47," Paideuma, 11, #1 (Spring-Summer, 1982), 91-92.

830 Namjoshi, Suniti Manohar. "Ezra Pound and Reality: A Study of the Metaphysics of the Cantos," DAI, 34, #2 (McGill (Canada): 1972), 785A.

831 Nanny, Max. Ezra Pound: Poetics for an Electric Age. Bern: Francke, 1973.

832 _____. "Ezra Pound's Cantos: The Tale of the Tribe," NZZ, (November, 1972), 51-52.

833 _____. "Oral Dimensions in Ezra Pound," Paideuma, 6 (Spring, 1977), 13-26.

834 Nassar, Eugene Paul. The Cantos of Ezra Pound: The Lyric Mode. Baltimore and London: Johns Hopkins U. Pr., 1975.

835 _____. "'This Stone Giveth Sleep': 'Io son la lune,'" Paideuma, 1, #2 (Winter, 1972), 207-211.

836 Neidhardt, Frances E. "From Apelles to Pound's 'Usury' Canto: Botticelli's 'La Calumnia' Goes Modern," Paideuma, 12, #2-3 (Fall-Winter, 1983), 427-445.

837 Nicholls, P. Ezra Pound: Politics, Economics, and Writing: A Study of the Cantos. England: Macmillan Pr., 1984.

838 Nicolescu, Vasile. "Ezra Pound: tragism si iluminare," Cantos, si alte poeme. Bucharest: Univers, 1975, pp. 5-10.

839 Niikura, Toshikazu. "Berryman's Significance," JBeSt, 1, #2
     (April, 1975), 14-18.

840 Nolde, John J. "The Sources for Canto 54: Part One,"
     Paideuma, 5, #3 (Winter, 1976), 419-453; "Part Two," Paideuma,
     6, #1 (Spring, 1977), 45-98.

841 _____. "The Sources for Canto 55," Paideuma, 7 (Spring-
     Fall, 1978), 189-247.

842 _____. "The Sources for the Chinese Dynastic Canto 56,"
     Paideuma, 8 (1979), 263-292, 485-511.

843 Norman, Charles. "Pound's Cantos and His Economic," Cf.,
     #93, pp. 335-354.

844 Oakes, Lois Ann. "An Explication of 'Canto 75' by Ezra
     Pound," WSCL, 5 (Summer, 1964), 105-109.

845 O'Connor, William Van. Ezra Pound. Minneapolis: U. of
     Minnesota Pr., 1963; also: #26 Pamphlets of American Writers.

846 Odlin, Reno. "Dinklage," Paideuma, 11, #2 (Fall, 1982), 283.

847 Olson, Charles. "First Canto," Paideuma, 3, #3 (Winter,
     1974), 295-300.

848 Olson, Paul A. "Pound and the Poetry of Perception,"
     Thought, 35, #138 (Autumn, 1960), 331-348; repr., #535,
     pp. 72-73.

849 Olsson, Theodore C. A. "Usura: Economics and Ethics in the
     Cantos of Ezra Pound," DAI, 35, #6 (Calif., Santa Barbara:
     1974), 3758A.

850 Overland, Orm. "Ezra Pound and Wilfrid Scawen Blunt: A
     Footnote to Canto 81," N&Q, 14 (July, 1967), 250-252.

851 Owen, Earl Ben. "Social Credit and The Cantos," Pound
     Newsletter, 2 (April, 1954), 6-10.

852 Paige, D. D. "Aspects of the Cantos: Three New Cantos,"
     Pound Newsletter, 6 (April, 1955), 2-4.

853 Paz, Octavio. The Bow and the Lyre. Trans. Ruth L. C.
     Simms. New York: McGraw-Hill, 1973, pp. 66-68.

854 _____. Children of the Mire: Modern Poetry from Romanti-
     cism to the Avant-Garde. Tr. by Rachel Phillips. Cambridge,
     Mass.: Harvard U. Pr., 1974, pp. 123-130, 132-138, passim.

855 Peachy, Frederic. "Aspects of the Cantos: The Greek Ele-
ment in the Cantos," Pound Newsletter, 8 (October, 1955),
8-10.

856 Peacock, Alan J. "Pound, Horace and Canto IV," ELN, 17
(June, 1980), 288-292.

857 Pearce, Roy Harvey. "'The Cantos,'" The Continuity of
American Poetry. Princeton, N.J.: Princeton U. Pr., 1961,
pp. 83-101, 286-289.

858 _____. "Toward an American Epic," HudR, 12, #3 (Autumn,
1959), 362-377.

859 Pearlman, Daniel. "Alexander Del Mar in The Cantos: A
Printout of the Sources," Paideuma, 1, #2 (Winter, 1972),
161-180.

860 _____. The Barb of Time: On the Unity of Pound's Cantos.
New York: Oxford U. Pr., 1969.

861 _____. "The Blue-Eyed Eel: Dame Fortune in Pound's
Later Cantos," Agenda, 9, #4-10 (Fall-Wntr, 1971-72), 60-77.

862 _____. "Canto 52: The Vivante Passage," Paideuma, 10,
#2 (1981), 311-314.

863 _____. "Canto 74: 'Lucifer' Elucidated," Paideuma, 9
(1980), 313-317.

864 _____. Review: [Cf., #834], MLQ, 37, #3 (1976), 298-300.

865 _____. "The Inner Metronome: A Genetic Study of Time
in Pound," Agenda, 8, #3-4 (Autumn-Wntr., 1970), 51-58.

866 _____. "Time and Major Form in the Cantos of Ezra
Pound," DAI, 31, #9 (Columbia U: 1968), 4789A.

867 Peck, John. "'Get a Dictionary': The Festus Behind Pound's
Festus," Paideuma, 2, #2 (Fall, 1973), 211-213.

868 _____. "Landscape as Ceremony in the Later Cantos:
From The Roads of France to Rock's World," Agenda, 9, #2-3
(Spr.-Summer, 1971), 26-69.

869 _____. "Pound's Lexical Mythography," Paideuma, 1, #1
(Spring-Summer, 1972), 3-36.

870 Perlès, Alfred. "From an Ancient Diary," Nimbus, 3, #1
(Summer, 1955), 6-11.

871 Peterson, Leland D. "Ezra Pound: The Use and Abuse of
     History," AQ, 17 (Spring, 1965), 33-47.

872 Pevear, Richard. "Notes on the Cantos of Ezra Pound,"
     HudR, 25, #1 (Spring, 1972), 51-70.

873 Powell, James A. "The Light of Vers Libre," Paideuma, 8, #1
     (Spring, 1979), 3-34.

874 Pritchard, William. "Two-tone Epic," TLS (July 23, 1976),
     926-927.

875 Quinn, Bernetta, O. S. F. "'All That Sandro Knew': The
     Boticellian Vision in The Cantos," Greyfriar, 20 (Fall, 1979),
     29-55.

876 _____. "The Cantos: From Erebus to Pisa," and "The
     Cantos: The Perilous Ascent," Ezra Pound: An Introduction
     to the Poetry. London; New York: Columbia U. Pr., 1972,
     pp. 101-128, 129-167.

877 _____. "Light from the East: The Cantos and Chinese
     Art," Greyfriar, 18 (1977), 49-63.

878 _____. "The Metamorphoses of Ezra Pound," WR, 15
     (Spring, 1951), 169-181; repr., EIE (1953), pp. 60-100; Cf.,
     #771.

879 _____. "A Note on Richard of St. Victor and the Moon
     Goddess," Paideuma, 5, #1 (Spring-Summer, 1976), 59-61.

880 Raaberg, Gloria Gwen. "Toward a Theory of Literary Collage:
     Literary Experimentalism and Its Relation to Modern Art in the
     Works of Pound, Stein, and Williams," DAI, 39, #5 (U. of
     Calif., Irvine: 1978), 2932A.

881 Rabaté, Jean-Michel. "Pound anathème," Degrés, (Spring-
     Summer, 1981), 26-27.

882 _____. "'Sounds Pound': History and Ideology in the
     China Cantos," Myth and Ideology in American Culture. Regis
     Durand, ed. (Cahiers Amer. 1.) Villeneuve d'Ascq: U. de
     Lille, III, pp. 21-41.

883 Raboni, Giovanni. "Appunti per una lettura dei Cantos," Let,
     Nos. 39-41 (maggio-agosto, 1959), 52-61.

884 Racey, Edgar Francis, Jr. "Pound's Cantos: The Structure
     of a Modern Epic," DA, 24, #6 (Claremont: 1963), 2484.

885 Read, Forrest, Jr. "A Man of No Fortunes," EIE, (1953),
     pp. 101-123; repr., #771, pp. 101-123.

886 _____. "The Mathematical Symbolism of Ezra Pound's Revolutionary Mind," Paideuma, 7 (Spring-Fall, 1978), 7-72.

887 _____. "Pound, Coke, or Gordon? Venus, Aeneas, or Tmesis? That's What's Wrong with Paideuma," Paideuma, 5, #1 (Spring, 1976), 199-208.

888 _____. "'76: The Cantos of Ezra Pound," StAR, 1, #1 (Fall-Winter, 1970), 11-16.

889 _____. '76: One World and the Cantos of Ezra Pound. Chapel Hill: U. of North Carolina Pr., 1981.

890 Read, Herbert E. "Ezra Pound," Cf., #125, pp. 7-20.

891 _____. "Ezra Pound," The Tenth Muse: Essays in Criticism. London: Routledge & Kegan Paul, c1957; Freeport, NY: Books for Libraries Pr., 1969, pp. 260-275.

892 _____. "Ideas in Action: Ezra Pound," True Voice of Feeling: Studies in English Romantic Poetry. New York: Pantheon Pr., 1953, pp. 116-138.

893 _____. "The Limits of Permissiveness," MalR, 9 (January, 1969), 37-50.

894 Reboni, Giovanni. "Appunti per una lettura dei Cantos," Let, 7 (1959), xxxix-xl, 52-61.

895 Reche, Denis. "Pour Ezra Pound," Tel Quel, #11 (Fall, 1962), 17-24.

896 Reck, Michael. "Reading the Cantos: Pound's Fugal Music," Cw, 83 (October 22, 1965), 93-95.

897 Reed, Victor B. "Toward The Cantos of Ezra Pound," DA, 28 (Columbia: 1965), 1445A-46A.

898 Regier, W. G. "Ezra Pound, Adam Smith, Karl Marx," MinnR, n.s., 12 (1979), 72-76.

899 Revell, Peter. "'Toward the Great Healing': The Cantos of Ezra Pound," Quest in Modern American Poetry. London: Vision Pr.; NJ: Barnes & Noble, 1981, pp. 98-136.

900 Rice, Philip Blair. "The Education of Ezra Pound," Nation, 139 (November 21, 1934), 599-600.

901 Riddel, Joseph N. "Pound and the Decentered Image," GaR, 29, #3 (Fall, 1975), 565-591.

902   Roberts, Michael. "A Draft of XXX Cantos," Adelphi, 7
      (December, 1933), 226-228.

903   _____. "Mr. Pound's Cantos," Spectator, 151 (October 13,
      1933), 492.

904   Rosenthal, M[acha] L[ouis]. "Canto XVI," Poetry and the
      Common Life. New York: Oxford U. Pr., 1974, p. 87.

905   _____. "The Cantos," A Primer of Ezra Pound. New York:
      Macmillan, 1960, pp. 42-51; repr., in Ezra Pound: A Collec-
      tion of Critical Essays. Walter Sutton, ed. Englewood Cliffs,
      NJ: Prentice-Hall, Inc., 1963, pp. 57-63; and in Ezra Pound:
      A Collection of Criticism. Grace Schulman, ed. NY: McGraw-
      Hill, 1974, pp. 125-131.

906   _____. "Dimensions of Pound: The Structuring of The
      Cantos," and "Voyage of Sensibility: Pound's Canto 47,"
      Sailing Into the Unknown: Yeats, Pound, and Eliot. New
      York: Oxford U. Pr., 1978, pp. 69-115, pp. 12-25.

907   _____. "The New Poets," American and British Poetry
      Since World War II. New York: Oxford U. Pr., 1967, passim.

908   _____. "The Pleasures of Pound," Nation, 190 (1960),
      368-371.

909   _____. "Poetic Means and Meanings," Nation, 182 (May 5,
      1956), 385.

910   _____. "Pound at His Best: Canto 47 as a Model of
      Poetic Thought," Paideuma, 6 (Winter, 1977), 309-321.

911   _____. "Some Notes on The Cantos," The Modern Poets:
      A Critical Introduction. New York: Oxford U. Pr., 1960,
      pp. 66-74.

912   _____. "The Structuring of Pound's Cantos," Paideuma, 6,
      #1 (Spring, 1977), 3-11.

913   Rosenthal, Marilyn. "The Impact of Confucius on Ezra
      Pound's Canto XIII: An Explication de Texte," ChC, 18
      (1977), 41-48.

914   Roskolenko, Harry. "The Cant in Pound's Cantos," Congress
      Weekly (April 11, 1949), 5-7.

915   Rubin, Louis D., Jr. "The Search for Lost Innocence,"
      Hollins Critic, I, #5 (December, 1964), 1-16.

916   Russell, Francis. "The Cantos of Ezra Pound," ContempI. 10
      (May-June, 1960), 117-142.

917 Sanders, Frederick K. "The 'French Theme' of Canto 70: An
     Examination of Ezra Pound's Use of Historical Sources," Paideu-
     ma, 2, #3 (Winter, 1973), 379-390.

918 Sawyer, Richard James. "The Great Periplus: A Study of the
     Structure of Ezra Pound's Cantos," DAI, 45, #2 (Toronto:
     1983), 517A.

919 Schafer, Murray. "Ezra Pound and Music," Canadian Music
     Journal, 5, #4 (Summer, 1961), 15-43.

920 Schimmel, Harold. "Historical Grit Gestation," Sagetrieb, 1,
     (1982), 220-254.

921 Schmidt, Gerd. "A Note on Canto CX," Paideuma, 8 (1979),
     55-56.

922 Schneidau, Herbert N. Ezra Pound: The Image and the Real.
     Baton Rouge: Louisiana St. U. Pr., 1969, pp. 126-127, 136-
     145.

923 Schneideman, Robert. "A Guide to Ezra Pound's Cantos (VII),"
     Analyst, No. 4 (June, 1954), 1-14.

924 Schwartz, Delmore. "Ezra Pound and History," NR, 142, #6
     (February 8, 1960), 17-19; Cf., #926, pp. 113-119.

925 _____. "Ezra Pound's Very Useful Labors," Poetry, 51, #6
     (March, 1938), 324-339; Cf., #926, pp. 102-112.

926 _____. Selected Essays of Delmore Schwartz. Donald A.
     Dike and David H. Zucker, eds., with an appreciation by
     Dwight MacDonald. Chicago: U. of Chicago Pr., 1970.

927 _____. "Notes on the Verification of the Cantos," Notes on
     Ezra Pound's Cantos: Structure and Metric. Norfolk, Conn.:
     New Directions, 1940, pp. 90-91.

928 Scott, Tom. "Two Plus Two Would Equal Four but for the
     Shadow," Agenda, 8, #3-4 (Autumn-Winter, 1970), 35-37.

929 Seferis, George. "A Note Appended to His Translation of
     Three Cantos," Cf., #239, pp. 77-83.

930 Shaheen, Mohammed Y. "A Note on the Spelling 'Habdimalich'
     for 'Abd-al-Malik' in The Cantos," Paideuma, 11, #2 (Fall,
     1982), 287-288.

931 _____. "The Story of Abd-el-Melik's Money in Canto XCVI
     and XCVII," Paideuma, 11, #3 (Winter, 1982), 420-428.

932 Shaw, Peter. "Ezra Pound on American History," PR, 44
     (1977), 112-124.

933 Shere, Charles. "Eastbay Artists Score Record Triumph,"
     Oakland Tribune (September 17, 1972), 7-9; Paideuma, 2
     (Spr., 1973), 7-9.

934 Sieburth, Richard. "Canto 119: Francois Bernouard,"
     Paideuma, 4, #2-3 (Fall-Winter, 1975), 329-332.

935 _____. "Ideas into Action: Pound and Voltaire,"
     Paideuma, 6, #3 (Winter, 1977), 365-390.

936 Singh, G. "The 'Cantos' of Ezra Pound," TLS, No. 3,497
     (March 6, 1969), p. 241; No. 3498 (March 13, 1969), p. 271;
     No. 3,500 (March 27, 1969), p. 327; No. 3,501 (April 3,
     1969), p. 368; No. 3,502 (April 10, 1969), p. 390.

937 _____. "Dante and Pound," CritQ, 17, #4 (Winter, 1975),
     311-328.

938 _____. "Ezra Pound Symposium," Paideuma, 3, (Fall,
     1974), 151-168.

939 _____. "Four Views of Ezra Pound," BA, 46 (Winter,
     1972), 61-63.

940 _____. "Meeting Ezra Pound," BA, 46 (Summer, 1972),
     403-409.

941 _____. "Pound and Cavalcanti," Essays in Honour of John
     Humphreys Whitfield Presented to Him on His Retirement from
     the Serena Chair of Italian at the University of Birmingham.
     Davis, H. C., D. G. Rees, J. M. Hatwell, and G. W. Slowey,
     eds. London: St. George's, 1975, 268-284.

942 Sitwell, Edith. "Ezra Pound," Aspects of Modern Poetry.
     London. Duckworth, 1934; repr., Freeport, NY: Bks. for
     Libraries Pr., 1970, pp. 178-214.

943 _____. "Ezra Pound," English and American Book of Eng-
     lish and American Poetry. Edith Sitwell, ed. Boston: Little,
     Brown & Co., 1958, pp. 993-1003.

944 _____. "Preface to Ezra Pound," YLM, 126, #5 (December,
     1958), 42-44.

945 Slatin, Myles. "A History of Pound's Cantos, I-XVI, 1915-
     1925," AL, 35, #2 (May, 1963), 183-195.

946 Smith, P. H., and A. E. Durant. "Pound's Metonymy: Re-
     visiting Canto 47," Paideuma, 8 (1979), 327-333.

947 Snodgrass, W. D. "Four Gentlemen; Two Ladies," HudR, 13,
     #1 (Spring, 1960), 120-125.

948 Spann, Marcella. "Beauty in Fragments," Agenda, 8, #3-4
     (Autumn-Winter, 1970), 40-43; repr., under title "Ezra Pound:
     Drafts and Fragments of Cantos CX-CXVII," Sou'wester (So.
     Ill. U.), Special Ezra Pound, Birthday Issue (October 30,
     1970), 55-58.

949 Spender, Stephen. "The Fifth Decad of Cantos," Left Review,
     3 (July, 1937), 361.

950 Splitter, Randolph. "Pound's Dream of the Gods: A Baker's
     Half-Dozen of the Cantos," Sou'wester, Special Ezra Pound,
     Birthday Issue, (October 30, 1970), 81-99.

951 Stauffer, Donald A. "Poetry as Symbolic Thinking," SatRL,
     30 (March 22, 1947), 9-10.

952 Steven, James C. "Modernist Form: Pound's Style in a Draft
     of XXX Cantos," DAI, 44, #6 (U. of Arkansas: 1983), 1787A.

953 Stock, Noel. "Balancing the Books," PoetA, 30 (October,
     1969), 42-52.

954 _____. Reading the Cantos: A Study of Meaning in Ezra
     Pound. London: Routledge & Kegan Paul; NY: Random
     House, 1966.

955 Stoicheff, Richard Peter. "Ezra Pound's 'Drafts & Fragments':
     A Study in Composition," DAI, 44, #9 (U. of Toronto: 1983),
     2768A.

956 _____. "CX/778 Revisited," Paideuma, 12, #1 (Spring,
     1983), 47-50.

957 Stone, Douglas. "Pound's 'Mr. Corles': Canto XXXV,"
     Paideuma, 2, #3 (Winter, 1973), 411-414.

958 Surette, Philip Leon. "The City in the Cantos of Ezra Pound:
     A Study of a Modern Epic," DAI, 32 (Toronto: 1969), 458A-
     459A.

959 _____. "The City of Dioce, U.S.A.: Pound and America,"
     BuR, 20, #2 (Fall, 1972), 14-34.

960 _____. "Ezra Pound's John Adams: An American Odyssey,"
     Prospects: Annual of American Cultural Studies, 2 (1976),
     483-495.

961 _____. "'Having His Own Mind to Stand by Him,'" HudR,
     27 (Winter, 1974-75), 491-510.

962   _____. "Helen of Tyre," Paideuma, 2, #3 (Winter, 1973),
419-421.

963   _____. "The Historical Pattern in Ezra Pound's Cantos,"
HAB, 22, #3 (1971), 11-21.

964   _____. "A Light from Eleusis," Paideuma, 3, #2 (Fall,
1974), 191-216.

965   _____. A Light from Eleusis: A Study of Ezra Pound's
Cantos. Oxford: Clarendon Pr.; NY: New York U. Pr.,
1979.

966   Sutton, Walter E. "Criticism as a Social Act," Modern American Criticism. Englewood Cliffs, NJ: Prentice-Hall, 1963,
pp. 281-283.

967   _____. "Ezra Pound: The Cantos," American Free Verse:
The Modern Revolution in Poetry. New York: New Directions,
1973, pp. 65-80.

968   Swabey, Henry. "Towards an A.B.C. of History," Cf., #239,
pp. 186-202.

969   Tate, Allen. "Ezra Pound," Collected Essays, Cf., #238,
pp. 350-357.

970   _____. "Ezra Pound," Essays of Four Decades. Chicago:
Swallow Pr., 1968, pp. 364-371.

971   _____. "Ezra Pound, 1931," On the Limits of Poetry: Selected Essays: 1928-1948. New York: Swallow Pr., and
Wm. Morrow Co., pp. 350-357.

972   _____. "Ezra Pound," Reactionary Essays on Poetry and
Ideas. New York: Charles Scribner's Sons, 1936.

973   _____. "Ezra Pound," Literary Opinion in America: Essays
Illustrating the Status, Methods, and Problems of Criticism in
the United States in the Twentieth Century. M. D. Zabel, ed.,
3rd ed. revised, Harper, 1951, pp. 237-242.

974   _____. "Ezra Pound's Golden Ass," Nation, 132 (June 10,
1931), 632-634; An Examination of Ezra Pound. New York:
New Directions, 1950, pp. 66-72.

975   _____. "Il vero cuore dei Cantos," FLe, 8, #43 (October
25, 1953), 3-4.

976   _____. "On Ezra Pound's Cantos," Essays of Four Decades,
Cf., #970, pp. 364-371.

977 _____. "Poetry and Politics," NR, 75 (August 2, 1933), 308-311.

978 Tay, William Shu-san. "The Sun on the Silk: Ezra Pound and Confucianism," DAI, 38 (U. of Calif., San Diego: 1977), 5450A.

979 Terrell, Carroll F. "Cabranez, the Mystery Man," Paideuma, 11, #3 (Winter, 1982), 451-453.

980 _____. "Canto XXXIV: The Technique of Montage," Paideuma, 6 (Fall, 1977), 186-232.

981 _____. "The Chinese Dynastic Cantos Generale de la Chine, 100-121," Paideuma, 5 (Spring-Summer, 1976), 95-99.

982 _____. A Companion to the Cantos of Ezra Pound. Published in cooperation with the National Poetry Foundation of California Pr., Berkeley: U. of Calif. Pr., 1980; Vol. 2, 1984.

983 _____. "A Commentary on Grosseteste with an English Version of De Luce," Paideuma, 2, #3 (Winter, 1973), 449-470.

984 _____. "A Couple of Glosses," Paideuma, 12, #1 (Spring, 1983), 51-52.

985 _____. "The Eparch's Book," Paideuma, 2, #2 (Fall, 1973), 223-311.

986 _____. "History, de Mailla, and the Dynastic Cantos," Paideuma, 5, #1 (Spring-Summer, 1976), 95-99.

987 _____. "John Adams Speaking: Some Reflections on Technique," Paideuma, 4, #2&3 (Fall-Winter, 1975), 533-538.

988 _____. "Magna Carta, Talbots, The Lady Anne, and Pound's Associative Technique in Canto 80," Paideuma, 5, #1 (Spring, 1976), 69-76.

989 _____. "The Na-Khi Documents, I: The Landscape of Paradise," Paideuma, 3, #1 (Spring, 1974), 91-122.

990 _____. "The Periplus of Hanno: Edited with a Commentary," Paideuma, 1, #2 (Winter, 1972), 223-232.

991 _____. "The Sacred Edict of K'ang-hsi," Paideuma, 2, #1 (Spring, 1973), 69-112.

992 _____, and David M. Gordon. "The Sources of Canto 53," Paideuma, 5, #1 (Spring, 1976), 95-152.

993 Thaniel, George. "George Seferis' Thrush and the Poetry of
     Ezra Pound," CLS, 11, #4 (December, 1974), 326-336.

994 Theroux, Paul. "Christopher Okigbo," Transition, 5, #22
     (1965), 18-20.

995 Thompson, J. S. "The Political Theme of Pound's Cantos,"
     L&I, 8 (1971), 43-56.

996 Trevisan, Lucio. "Il Canto 74 e el metodo poundiano," SA,
     17 (1971), 167-193.

997 Tritschler, D. M. "A Guide to Ezra Pound's Cantos (V),"
     Analyst, 2 (July, 1953), 1-7.

998 Tseng, Yueh-nung. "On Ezra Pound's Canto XIII," Chinese
     Cult (Taiwan), 2 (1959), 1-3.

999 Ullyatt, A. G. "Judging the Cantos: Paradox as Unity,"
     UES, 15, #2 (1977), 52-61.

1000 Untermeyer, Louis, "Poet in Extremis," SatRL, 17 (January
     29, 1938), 10.

1001 _____. "Yeats and Others," YR, 30 (Winter, 1941), 380-
     382.

1002 Vasse, William W. "Aspects of the Cantos: II: American
     History and the Cantos," PoundN, 5 (January, 1955), 13-19.

1003 _____. "A Note on the Text of the China Cantos," PoundN,
     6 (April, 1955), 15-19.

1004 _____. "Traveler in a Landscape: The Structure of His-
     tory in Ezra Pound's Cantos," DAI, 31 (Calif., Berkeley:
     1969), 772A.

1005 _____, and William W. Edwards. The Annotated Index to
     the Cantos of Ezra Pound. Berkeley and Los Angeles, Calif.,
     1957.

1006 Vettori, Vittorio. "Premessa" [for "Dai Cantos di Ezra
     Pound"], Dial, 6 (1958), 3-9.

1007 _____. "Pound in Italia," Il fiore dei Cantos: 18 Inter-
     pretazioni con un saggio introduttivo de Vittorio Vettori.
     Pisa: Giardini Editore, 1962.

1008 Véza, Laurette. "Les Cantos de Pound: Un Voyage au bout
     de la nuit," Le Voyage dans la littérature anglo-saxonne.
     Actes du Congres de Nice (1971): Soc. des Anglicistes de
     l'Enseignement Supérieur. Paris: Didier, 1972.

1009 Vidan, Ivo. "Znanje Pounda i glas 'Pjevanja,'" [Pound's knowledge and the voice of the Cantos.] Kritika (Zagreb), (12), (1970), 417-423.

1010 Von Hendy, Andrew John. "The Form and Principal Themes of Pound's Cantos," DA, 24 (Cornell: 1962), 306.

1011 Wagstaff, A. Christopher. "Make It New: A Study of the American Aspects of Ezra Pound's Cantos," DAI, 34 (Calif., Davis: 1973), 6668A.

1012 Wain, John. "The Reputation of Ezra Pound," LonM, II, #10 (October, 1955), 55-64.

1013 _____. "The Shadow of an Epic," Spectator, #6872 (March 11, 1960), 360.

1014 Walkiewicz, E. P. "A Reading of Pound's Canto CXX," NMAL, 4 (1980), Item 28.

1015 Walton, Eda Lou. "Eleven New Cantos by Ezra Pound," NYTBR, 5 (November 18, 1934), 4.

1016 _____. "Obscurity in Modern Poetry," NYTBR, 5 (April 2, 1933), 2.

1017 Wand, David Hsin-Fu. "To the Summit of the Tai Shan: Ezra Pound's Use of Chinese Mythology," Paideuma, 3, #1 (Spring, 1974), 3-12.

1018 Wanning, Andrews. "Current Letters: III: Ezra Pound, Poetry in an Ivory Tower," The Harkness Hoot, 3 (April, 1933), 33-39.

1019 Warren, Eugene. "The Temple Is Not for Sale,"--Canto 97, Sou'wester (So. Ill. U.), (October 30, 1970), 125-126.

1020 Watts, Harold H. "The Devices of Pound's Cantos," QRL, V, #2 (1949), 147-173.

1021 _____. Ezra Pound and the Cantos. Chicago: Henry Regnery, 1952; London: Routledge & Kegan Paul, 1951.

1022 _____. "Pound's Cantos: Means to an End," YPR, #6 (1947), 9-20.

1023 Wees, William C. "Ezra Pound as a Vorticist," WSCL, 6 (Winter-Spring, 1965), 56-72.

1024 Westcott, Glenway. "A Draft of Cantos," Dial, 79 (December, 1925), 501-503.

1025 Weston, K. Noel. "Cantos LII-LXXI," The Townsman, 3, #11
      (July, 1940), 27-29.

1026 Whigham, Peter. "Il Suo Paradiso Terrestre," Agenda, 8
      (Spring, 1970), 31-34.

1027 Wilhelm, James J. "The Dragon and the Duel: A Defense of
      Pound's Canto 88," TCL, 20 (April, 1974), 114-125.

1028 _____. "Guido Cavalcanti as a Mask for Ezra Pound,"
      PMLA, 89, #2 (March, 1974), 332-340.

1029 _____. "In Praise of Anselm: An Approach to Canto 105,"
      Paideuma, 2, #3 (Winter, 1973), 399-407.

1030 _____. The Later Cantos of Ezra Pound. New York:
      Walker, 1977.

1031 _____. "Notes and Queries," Paideuma, 2, #2 (Fall,
      1973), 333-339.

1032 _____. "Pound's Middle Cantos as an Analogue to Dante's
      Purgatorio: Purgatories Fictive and Real," IQ, 16, #64
      (1973), 49-66.

1033 _____. "Two Heavens of Light: Paradise to Dante and to
      Pound," Paideuma, 2, #2 (Fall, 1973), 175-191.

1034 Williams, John K., Jr. "The Hell-Cantos as Source of Satiric
      Imagery," IE, 4 (1975), 1-7.

1035 Williams, William Carlos. "Excerpts from a Critical Sketch:
      A Draft of XXX Cantos of Ezra Pound," Symposium, 2 (April,
      1931), 257-263; repr., in Ezra Pound: A Collection of Criti-
      cal Essays. Walter Sutton, ed. Englewood Cliffs, N.J.:
      Prentice-Hall, 1963, pp. 11-16; also repr., in Ezra Pound:
      A Critical Anthology. J. P. Sullivan, ed. Baltimore: Pen-
      guin Bks., 1970, pp. 116-122.

1036 _____. "The Later Pound," MassR, 14, #1 (Winter, 1973),
      124.

1037 _____. "Pound's Eleven New Cantos," New Democracy, 3
      #10-11 (January 15-February 1, 1935), 191-192.

1038 _____. "A Study of Ezra Pound's Present Position,"
      MassR, 14, #1 (Winter, 1973), 118-123.

1039 Wilson, T. C. "Rhythm and Phrase," SatRL, 9 (July 1,
      1933), 677.

1040 Winters, Yvor. "Ezra Pound's Techniques," Cf., #535,
      pp. 31-33.

1041 _____. "Primitivism and Decadence," The Anatomy of
      Nonsense. Norfolk, Conn.: New Directions, 1943; repr., in
      In Defense of Reason: Primitivism and Decadence. New
      York: Wm. Morrow & Co., 1947, pp. 95, 101-102.

1042 _____. "Problems of the Modern Critic of Literature,"
      The Function of Criticism: Problems and Exercises. Denver:
      Allen Swallow, 1967, pp. 12, 46-47.

1043 Witemeyer, Hugh. "The Flame-style King," Paideuma, 4,
      #2-3 (Fall-Winter, 1975), 333-335.

1044 _____. "Pound and the Cantos: 'Ply over Ply,'" Occident,
      7, #1 (1973), 229-235; Paideuma, 8 (1979?), 229-235.

1045 _____. Review, Paideuma, 5, #1 (1976), 191-193, [Cf.,
      #724]

1046 _____. "Ruskin and the Signed Capital in Canto 45,"
      Paideuma, 4, #1 (Spring, 1975), 85-88.

1047 Wolfe, Humbert. "Yes or No," EngRev, 57 (December, 1933),
      664-666.

1048 Yueh-nung, Tseng. "On Ezra Pound's Canto XIII," Chinese
      Culture, II (Taiwan), (March, 1959), 1-3.

1049 Zapatka, Francis E. "Crommelyn and del Valle: A Note on
      Canto 105," Paideuma, 2, #3 (Winter, 1973), 423.

1050 Zolla, Elémire. "I 'Cantos' di Ezra Pound," SPe, 8 (November,
      1955), 465-467.

1051 Zukovsky, Louis. "American Poetry, 1920-1930," Symposium,
      2, #1 (January, 1930), 71-73, 74.

1052 _____. "Cantos d'Ezra Pound," Echanges, 3 (June, 1930),
      145-172.

1053 _____. "The Cantos of Ezra Pound," Criterion, 10 (April,
      1931), 424-440.

1054 _____. "Ezra Pound," Prepositions: The Collected Critical
      Essays of Louis Zukovsky. Expanded Ed. Berkeley & Los
      Angeles: 1981, pp. 67-83.

1055 _____. "Ezra Pound: His Cantos," Observer (Memphis,
      Tenn.), 2 (January-February, 1934), 3-4, 8.

1056 _____. "Ezra Pound's XXX Cantos," Front, 4 (Amsterdam),
(June, 1931), 364-369.

1057 _____. "Cantos di Ezra Pound," L'Indice, (Genoa: 10,
April 25, May 10, 1931).

The Adams Cantos

1058 Davis, Kay. "Eleusis and the Structure of the Adams Cantos," ConP, 5, #1 (1982), 45-55.

1059 Gordon, David M. "Coke in the Adams and Pisan Cantos,"
Paideuma, 4, #2&3 (Fall-Winter, 1975), 223-299.

1060 McDonald, James R. "The 'Adams Cantos': Fact or Fiction,"
AntigR, 21 (1975), 97-107.

1061 _____. "'Norm of Spirit': The Adams Cantos of Ezra
Pound," DAI, 34, #10 (Toledo: 1973), 6650A.

1062 Sanders, Frederick Kirkland. John Adams Speaking:
Pound's Sources for the Adams Cantos. Orono: U. of
Maine Pr., 1975.

1063 _____. "A Source Book for the 'Adams Cantos' of Ezra
Pound," DAI, 32 (Georgia: 1971), 5805A-06A.

1064 Terrell, C. F. "John Adams Speaking: Some Reflections on
Technique," Paideuma, 4, #2&3 (Fall-Winter, 1975), 533-538.

The Pisan Cantos

1065 Amaral, José Vázquez. Introduction. Los Cantares de Pisa.
Mexico: Universidad Nacional de Mexico, 1956, p. 14.

1066 _____. "Words from Ezra Pound," RutgersRev, 3 (Winter,
1968), 40.

1067 Astaldi, Maria Luisa. "I Canti Pisani," Il Giornale d'Italia.
Rome: January 21, 1954.

1068 Bacigalupo, Massimo. "The Pisan Poem and Its Genesis,"
Cf., #437, pp. 1-4.

1069 Barton, David. "Difficult Methods: The Pisan Cantos,"
NConL, 8, iv (1978), 8-9.

1070   Benet, William Rose. "Phoenix Nest," Cf., #269.

1071   Berryman, John. Cf., #5.

1072   Bertacchini, Renato. "I Canti Pisani," Gazzetta dell-Emilia,
       Modena: (January 2, 1954).

1073   Bogan, Louise. Cf., #464.

1074   Bowra, C. M. "More Cantos from Ezra Pound," NS&N, 38
       (September 3, 1949), 250.

1075   Cantrell, Carol Helmstetter. Cf., #490.

1076   Caparelli, Giuseppe. "I Canti Pisani di Ezra Pound," La
       Giustizia. Rome: December, 1953.

1077   Chace, William M. "The Pisan Cantos: 'Paradise,'" The
       Political Identities of Ezra Pound and T. S. Eliot. Stanford,
       Calif.: Stanford U. Pr., 1973, pp. 86-105.

1078   Contino, Vittorugo. Ezra Pound in Italy: From the Pisan
       Cantos. Venice: G. Ivancich, 1970.

1079   Corrigan, Robert A. Cf., #172.

1080   Corsare, Antonio. "I Pisan Cantos," Il Giornale di Sicilia.
       Cantania: (April 12, 1954).

1081   Cousins, Norman, and Harrison Smith. Cf., #177.

1082   Cowley, Malcolm. Cf., #178.

1083   Crino, Anna Maria. "Observations on the Italian Translation
       of the Cantos by Alfredo Rizzardi," Idea, 5 (December 27,
       1953), 4.

1084   Davie, Donald. "The Pisan Cantos," Ezra Pound: A Collec-
       tion of Criticism. Grace Schulman, ed. New York: McGraw-
       Hill, 1974, pp. 114-124.

1085   _____. "The Pisan Cantos," TLS (January 11, 1957), 23.

1086   Decavalles, Anthony M. "Elysium in Fragments," IJAS, 2,
       #2 (December, 1972), 17-29.

1087   Dennis, Helen M. "The Elusinian Mysteries as an Organising
       Principle in The Pisan Cantos," Paideuma, 10, #2 (Fall,
       1981), 273-282.

1088   Deutsch, Babette. Cf., #562, p. 4.

1089 _____. Cf., #563, pp. 668-670.

1090 _____. Cf., #564, p. 7.

1091 Diggory, Terrence. "A Live Tradition: Ezra Pound," Yeats
and American Poetry: The Tradition of the Self. Princeton:
Princeton U. Pr., 1983, pp. 31-58.

1092 DuPlessis, Rachel Blau. "The Endless Poem: Paterson of
William Carlos Williams and The Pisan Cantos of Ezra Pound,"
DAI, 31 (Columbia: 1970), 5396A.

1093 Eberhart, Richard. "An Approach to the Cantos," See #535,
pp. 34-35.

1094 _____. Of Poetry and Poets. Urbana: U. of Illinois Pr.,
1979, pp. 126-140.

1095 _____. "Pound's New Cantos," QRL, 5, #2 (1949), 174-191.

1096 Emery, Clark. [Pisan Cantos]. Ideas Into Action. Coral
Gables, Fla.: U. of Miami Pr., 1958, pp. 79ff.

1097 Fang, Achilles. "Materials for the Study of Pound's Cantos,"
Diss., Harvard U., 1958. [Pisan Cantos]

1098 Ferril, Thomas Harnsby. "The New Poetry," San Francisco
Chronicle, (November 7, 1948), 11.

1099 Fitzgerald, Robert. "Addendum on Pound," NR, 119, #8
(August 23, 1948), 26.

1100 _____. "What Thou Lovest Well Remains," NR, 119
(August 16, 1948), 21-23.

1101 Fleming, William. Cf., #318, pp. 325-328.

1102 Flory, Wendy Stallard. "The 'Tre Donne' of the Pisan Cantos," Paideuma, 5, #1 (Spring, 1975-76), 45-52.

1103 Frankenberg, Lloyd. Cf., #624, Sec. 7, p. 14.

1104 Gerhardt, Rainer M. "Die Pisaner Gesange," Hossischer
Rundfunk, (March, 1952). [A radio program]

1105 Giovacchini, Graziella. "I Canti Pisani de Ezra Pound,"
Posta Letteraria (Lodi: April 3, 1954).

1106 Golffing, Francis. Pisan Cantos: Review. Furioso, 4
(Winter, 1949), 64.

1107 Gordon, David M. "Edward Coke: The Azalia Is Grown,"
      Cf., #651.

1108 Greenspan, Cory Robert. "Charles Olson and Ezra Pound:
      Modes of Language and Thought in Modern Poetry," DAI, 34
      (Buffalo: 1973), 5172A.

1109 Gregory, Horace. "Ezra Pound in Progress," NR, 94 (March
      23, 1938), 200-201.

1110 _____. "The Search for a Frontier," Cf., #657.

1111 _____, and Marya Zaturenska. A History of American
      Poetry, 1900-1940. New York: Harcourt, Brace & Co., 1946.

1112 Guidacci, Margherita. "Canti Pisani," Il Ponte, 10, #4
      (Florence: 1954).

1113 Guidi, Augusto. "I Pisan Cantos e la corrispondenza di
      Pound," Occasioni americane. Rome: 1958, pp. 92-99.

1114 _____. "Pound nei 'Pisan Cantos' e nella corrispondenza,"
      Letteratura, I (December, 1953), 153-159.

1115 Guidotti, Mario Colombi. "Canti Pisani," Gazzetta de Parma,
      (December 29, 1953).

1116 Hamburger, Michael. Pisan Cantos. [Review], World Review,
      8 (October, 1949), 78.

1117 Healy, J. V. "Pound and Tate," WR, 13, #2 (Winter, 1949),
      115-118.

1118 Hesse, Eva, tr. Die Pisaner Gesange. With Concluding Es-
      say. Zurich: Die Arche, 1956.

1119 _____. "New Light on Old Problems," Paideuma, 7 (Spring-
      Fall, 1978), 179-183.

1120 Humphries, Rolfe. "Jeffers and Pound," Nation, 167 (Septem-
      ber 25, 1948), 349.

1121 Hutchins, Patricia. "Ezra Pound's Pisa," SoR, 2, #1, n.s.
      (Winter, 1966), 77-93.

1122 Kennedy, Leo. "Poet Who Was 'Mad as a Fascist,'" Chicago
      Sun, (August 9, 1948).

1123 Kenner, Hugh. "In the Caged Panther's Eyes," HudR, 1, #4
      (Winter, 1949), 580-586.

1124 _____. Cf., #738, pp. 185ff.

1125 _____. "Pound's Cantos I," Expl, 11, #3 (December, 1952), Item 20.

1126 _____. "The Rose in the Steel Dust," Cf., #742, pp. 66-124.

1127 Kimpel, Ben D., and T. C. Duncan Eaves. "Pound's Canto LXXX," Explicator, 41, #3 (Spring, 1983), 43-44.

1128 _____ and _____. "Pound's Pisan Cantos," Expl, 40 (Fall, 1981), #43.

1129 King, Michael. "Ezra Pound at Pisa: An Interview with John L. Steel," TQ, 21, #4 (Winter, 1978), 48-61.

1130 Kurumisawa, Atsuo. "The 'Center of the World' as Implied in The Pisan Cantos," SELL, 31 (January, 1981), 19-37.

1131 Larkin, Greg. "From Noman to Everyman: Chinese Characters in the Pisan Cantos," TkR, 11, #3 (Spring, 1981), 307-315.

1132 Lenberg, Lore Marianne. The Coherence of the Pisan Cantos and Their Significance in the Context of Ezra Pound's "Poem of Some Length." Diss. Freiburg, 1958.

1133 _____. Rosen aus Feilstaub: Studien zu den Cantos von Ezra Pound. Wiesbaden: Limes, 1966.

1134 MacLeish, Archibald. Letter. The Case Against The Saturday Review of Literature. Cf., #215, pp. 59-62.

1135 _____. Poetry and Opinion: The Pisan Cantos of Ezra Pound: A Dialog on the Role of Poetry. Urbana: U. of Illinois Pr., 1950.

1136 Madge, Charles. "The Ellipse in the Pisan Cantos," An Examination of Ezra Pound: A Collection of Essays. Rev. & Enl. Peter Russell, ed. New York: Gordian Pr., 1973, pp. 119-133.

1137 Martz, Louis L. "Recent Poetry," YR, 38, #1 (Autumn, 1948), 144-151.

1138 Monk, Donald. "Intelligibility in The Pisan Cantos," JAmS, 9 (1975), 213-227.

1139 Montale, Eugenio. "Ezra Pound," Corriere della sera (Milan),

(November 19, 1953), p. 3; repr., in Nuova corrente, Nos.
5-6 (Genn.-giugno, 1956), pp. 21-27.

1140 _____. "Lo zio Ez," Studi e Opinioni su Ezra Pound. Alfredo Rizzardi, ed., NC, Nos. 5-6 (January-June, 1956),
21-27.

1141 _____. "Uncle Ez," NER, 4, #2 (Spring, 1982), 358-362.

1142 Moody, A. D. "The Pisan Cantos: Making Cosmos in the
Wreckage of Europe," Paideuma, 11, #1 (Spring-Summer,
1982), 135-146.

1143 Moramarco, Fred. "Thirty Years with The Pisan Cantos: A
Reading," MPS, 9 (Spring, 1978), 1-17.

1144 Mowrer, Deane. "Some Current Poetry," NMQ, 18 (Winter,
1948), 463-464.

1145 Nassar, Eugene Paul. "The Pisan Cantos," Cf., #834, pp.
71-98.

1146 Neame, Alan. "The Pisan Cantos: An Approach," The
European, #4 (June, 1953), 37-46. (Annotations to Canto
LXXIV, 11, 1-43.)

1147 _____. "The Pisan Cantos. II. Considerations in Criticism," European, #10 (December, 1953), 13-26.

1148 _____. "The Pisan Cantos: III," European (September,
1954), 17-29.

1149 _____. "The Pisan Cantos, IV: Construction Part I,"
European (January, 1955), 23-34.

1150 _____. "The Pisan Cantos, VI: Speech and Penalty,"
European, 10 (February, 1958), 351-360.

1151 Niikura, Shunichi. "Pound wo Motomete: Pisa Shihen no
Sekai," EigoS, 121 (1975), 407-408. ["In Search of Pound:
World of Cantos.]

1152 Niikura, Toshikazu. "The Pisan Cantos and Noh Drama,"
American Literature in the 1940's. Annual Report, 1975.
Tokyo: Tokyo and Chapter, Amer. Lit. Soc. of Japan, 1976,
pp. 132-140.

1153 Norman, Charles. The Case of Ezra Pound, Cf., #219.

1154 Nyren, Dorothy, ed. "Ezra Pound," A Library of Literary
Criticism: Modern American Literature. New York: Ungar
Pub. Co., 1960, pp. 380-385.

1155 O'Connor, William Van, and Edward Stone. A Casebook on
      Ezra Pound. Cf., #29.

1156 Olson, Paul A. Cf., #221.

1157 Patmore, Brigit. "Ezra Pound in England," Cf., #98.

1158 Pecorino, Jessica Prinz. "Resurgent Icons: Pound's First
      Pisan Canto and the Visual Arts," JML, 9, #2 (May, 1982),
      159-174.

1159 Petrocchi, Giorgio. "I Canti Pisani," Il Giornale d'Italia,
      Rome: (December 2, 1953).

1160 Pritchard, William H. "Pisan Cantos," Lives of the Modern
      Poets. New York: Oxford U. Pr., 1980, pp. 144, passim.

1161 Raine, Kathleen. "There Is No Trifling," NR, 126 (March 24,
      1952), 17, 22.

1162 Ratte, Eva. "Ezra Pound: I Canti Pisani," Umana (Trieste:
      January, 1954).

1163 Read, Forrest. "The Pattern of the Pisan Cantos," SR, 65
      (Summer, 1957), 400-419. Cf., E. San Juan, Jr., ed., #535,
      pp. 49-52.

1164 Rebora, Piero. "Ezra Pound: Canti Pisani," Italia Che Scrive.
      Rome (January, 1954).

1165 Reck, Michael. "The Pisan Cantos," Cf., Michael Reck, #109,
      pp. 11-12, 64-65.

1166 Rizzardi, Alfredo. "La maschera e la poesia di Ezra Pound,"
      Canti pisani di Ezra Pound. Bologna: Guanda, 1953, pp.
      vii-xlv. Cf., #518, Jung, Angela, and Guido Palandri, eds.,
      pp. 55-76.

1167 _____. "The Mask of Experience: A Chapter upon Ezra
      Pound's Pisan Cantos," SUS, 35 (1960), 135-159.

1168 Rosenthal, Macha Louis. "The Pisan Cantos," A Primer of
      Ezra Pound. Cf., #905, p. 49.

1169 Roskolenko, Harry. "The Cant in Pound's Cantos," Cf.,
      #914, pp. 5-7.

1170 Rossi, Alberto. "I Canti Pisani," La Stampa (Turin: March
      31, 1954).

1171 Sanesi, Roberto. "I Canti Pisani," Aut-Aut, 18 (November,
      1953).

1172 Sanguineti, Edoardo. "I 'Canti Pisani,'" Aut-Aut, #22 (luglio, 1954), 329-334.

1173 Scalero, Liliano. "I 'Canti Pisani' di Ezra Pound," La Giustizia, (Juno 1, 1954), 3.

1174 Schlauch, Margaret. "The Anti-Humanism of Ezra Pound," Science and Society, 13 (Summer, 1949), 258-269; repr., in Critics on Ezra Pound. E. San Juan, ed., Cf., #535, pp. 44-46.

1175 Schuldiner, Michael. "Pound's Progress: The Pisan Cantos," Paideuma, 4, #1 (Spring, 1975), 71-81.

1176 Shapiro, Karl. "Letter to the Editor," Cf., #227, p. 16.

1177 Sieburth, Richard. "He Do the Enemy in Different Voices," Poetry, 134 (August, 1979), 292-302.

1178 Sillen, Samuel. "A Prize for Ezra Pound," Cf., #231.

1179 Smith, Harrison. "Lock, Stock, and Barrel," Cf., #233.

1180 Spagnoletti, Giacinto. "Canti Pisani di Ezra Pound," Epoca, Milan (May 2, 1954).

1181 Squires, Radcliffe. "Ambassador of Culture," Cf., #235.

1182 Stevens, Peter. "Climbing the Poundian Alps," CRevAS, 12, #3 (Winter, 1981), 355-360.

1183 Stock, Noel. "The Pisan Cantos, 1948," Cf., #954, pp. 72-90.

1184 Surette, Philip Leon. "Also Sprach Ezra: Pound Exposed," Mosaic, 15 #2 (June, 1982), 57-62.

1185 _____. "'Having His Own Mind to Stand by Him.'" Cf., #961.

1186 Sutton, Walter. "Ezra Pound: The Pisan Cantos," American Free Verse. Cf., #967, pp. 77-86.

1187 _____. "The Pisan Cantos: The Form of Survival," Sense and Sensibility in Twentieth Century Writing: A Gathering in Memory of William Van O'Connor. Brom Weber, ed. Carbondale and Edwardsville: So. Ill. U. Pr., 1970, pp. 118-129.

1188 Tay, William. "Confucianism as Leitmotif: The Four Books in the Pisan Cantos," TkR, 9 (1978), 235-267.

1189 Viereck, Peter. "My Kind of Poetry," Cf., #249.

1190 _____. "Parnassus Divided," AtlM, 184 (October, 1949),
      69-70.

1191 Watts, Harold H. "Points on the Circle," SR, 57, #2 (Spring,
      1949), 303-306.

1192 Weissman, David L. ["The Pisan Cantos"], Cf., #252.

1193 Whittemore, Reed. "Pound on Pound," Poetry, 73 (Novem-
      ber, 1948), 108-110.

1194 Williams, David Park. "The Background of The Pisan Can-
      tos," Poetry, 73, #4 (January, 1949), 216-221.

1195 Williams, William Carlos. "The Fistual of the Law," Imagi, 4,
      #4 (Spring, 1949), 10-11.

1196 Woods, John. "Brief: In William Duffy's Hammock," NWR, 15,
      #1 (Summer, 1975), 15-20.

1197 Woodward, Anthony. Ezra Pound and The Pisan Cantos.
      Boston: Routledge & Kegan Paul, 1980.

1198 Woodward, Kathleen M. "Ezra Pound and the Pisan Cantos:
      The Teachings of Confucius, the Teachings of Ezra Pound,"
      At Last, the Real Distinguished Thing: The Late Poems of
      Eliot, Pound, Stevens, and Williams. Ohio State U. Pr.,
      1980, pp. 69-98.

The Rock-Drill Cantos

1199 Alvarez, Alfred. "Rock-Drill Cantos," Observer (March 3,
      1957), 3.

1200 Bacigalupo, Massimo. "Rock-Drill--'In the Sibyl's Cave'"
      The Forméd Trace: The Later Poetry of Ezra Pound. New
      York: Columbia U. Pr., 1980, pp. 219ff.

1201 Baumann, Walter. "Secretary of Nature, J. Heydon," New
      Approaches to Ezra Pound: A Co-ordinated Investigation of
      Pound's Poetry and Ideas. Eva Hesse, ed. Berkeley; Los
      Angeles: U. of Calif., 1969, pp. 303-319.

1202 Cambon, Glauco. "Ezra Pound: Section: Rock-Drill 85-95
      de los cantares," Il Verri (Autunno 1956), 98-102.

1203 Ciardi, John. "For Ezra Pound: Section: Rock-Drill," The

Yale Literary Magazine, 127, #5 (December, 1958), 17; The Poetry Circus. New York: Hawthorn Bks., 1967, p. 139.

1204 Cookson, William. "Some Notes on Rock-Drill and Thrones," Agenda (London), 4, (October-November, 1965), 30-37.

1205 Davie, Donald. "Bed-Rock," NS&N, 53 (March 9, 1957), 316-317.

1206 _____. "The Rock-Drill Cantos," Modern Poetry: Essays in Criticism. John Hollander, ed. London; New York: Oxford U. Pr., 1968, pp. 447-472.

1207 _____. "Res and Verba in Rock-Drill and After," Paideuma, 11, #3 (Winter, 1982), 382-394.

1208 Fitts, Dudley. "Prelude to Conclusion," SatRL, 39 (May 12, 1956), 18-19.

1209 Gordon, David. "Ezra Among the Old Bones," Paideuma, 4, #2-3 (Fall-Winter, 1975), 355-359.

1210 Grieve, Thomas. "Annotations to the Chinese in Section: Rock-Drill," Paideuma, 4, #2-3 (Fall-Winter, 1975), 362-508.

1211 Kenner, Hugh. "Homage to Musonius," Poetry, 90, #4 (July, 1957), 237-243. Reply: J. R. Hendrickson, Poetry, 91 (December, 1957), 209-211.

1212 _____. "Rock-Drill by Ezra Pound," HudR, 9 (1957), 457.

1213 _____. "Rock-Drill: A Review of Cantos 88-89," Pound Newsletter, 8 (October, 1955), 15-17.

1214 _____. "Rock Drill, Cantos 88-89," Studi e Opinioni su Ezra Pound. Alfredo Rizzardi, ed. Nuova Corrente, Nos. 5-6 (January-June, 1957), 197-204.

1215 _____. "Rock-Drill," The Pound Era. Berkeley and Los Angeles, Calif.: U. of Calif. Pr., 1971, pp. 528-532, passim.

1216 _____. "Under the larches of Paradise," Gnomon: Essays on Contemporary Literature. New York: McDowell-Obolensky, 1958, pp. 280-296.

1217 Kimpel, Ben, and T. C. Duncan Eaves. "American History in Rock-Drill and Thrones," Cf., #745, pp. 417-439.

1218 Korg, Jacob. "Jacob Epstein's Rock-Drill and the Cantos," Paideuma, 4, #2&3 (Fall-Winter, 1975), 310-313.

1219 _____. "The Music of Lost Dynasties: Browning, Pound and History," ELH, 39 (1972), 420-440.

1220 Lewis, Wyndham. "The Rock-Drill," Ezra Pound: Perspectives. Noel Stock, ed. Cf., #125, pp. 198-203.

1221 Lucas, John. "Our Foreign Agents: Rock Drill Dinner-Date," Carleton Miscellany, I, #3 (Summer, 1960), 91-94.

1222 Neault, D. James. "Apollonius of Tyana: The Odyssean Hero of Rock-Drill as a Doer of Holiness," Paideuma, 4, #1 (Spring, 1975), 3-36.

1223 _____. "Richard of St. Victor and Rock-Drill," Paideuma, 3, #2 (Fall, 1974), 219-227.

1224 _____. "Spring Ice and Tiger's Tail: A Study of Major Sources in Ezra Pound's Rock-Drill," DAI, 35 (Ohio: 1974), 7916A.

1225 Rosen, Aaron. "The Enormous Dream--Its Rhetoric," Pound Newsletter, 10 (April, 1956), 6-9.

1226 Rosenthal, M. L. "Poetic Means and Meanings," Nation, 182, #18 (May 5, 1956), 384-386.

1227 Stock, Noel. "Rock-Drill," Meanjin, 15 (March, 1956), 112-114.

1228 _____. "Rock-Drill, 1955," Reading the Cantos: A Study of Meaning in Ezra Pound. London: Routledge & Kegan Paul, 1967, pp. 91-103.

1229 Tay, William. "History as Poetry: The Chinese Past in Ezra Pound's Rock-Drill Cantos," TkR, 10 (1979), 97-125.

Seven Lakes Canto

1230 Kenner, Hugh. "More on the 'Seven Lakes Canto,'" Paideuma, 2 (Spring, 1973), 43-46.

1231 Palandri, Angela J. "The 'Seven Lakes Canto' Revisited," Paideuma, 3, #1 (Spring, 1974), 51-54.

CATHAY

1232   Ford, Ford Madox. "On Ezra Pound's Cathay," Agenda, 20,
       #3-4 (Autumn-Winter, 1982-83), 65-66.

1233   Lee, Pen-Ti, and Donald Murray. "The Quality of Cathay:
       Ezra Pound's Early Translations of Chinese Poems," LE&W, 10
       (September, 1961), 264-277.

1234   Orage, A[lfred] R[ichard]. "Mr. Pound's 'Cathay,'" The
       Art of Reading. New York: Farrar & Rinehart, 1930, pp.
       143-146.

1235   Sanehide, Kodama. "Cathay and Fenollosa's Notebooks,"
       Paideuma, 11, #2 (Fall, 1982), 207-240.

1236   Toki, Tsuneji. "Technique of Ezra Pound--on Cathay,"
       Metropolitan, 7 (March, 1962), 17-22.

1237   Wells, Tanya. "Ezra Pound's Cathay and the American Idea
       of China," DAI, 44, #11 (Arizona State: 1983), 3381A.

1238   Yip, Wai-Lim. "Ezra Pound's 'Cathay,'" DA, 29 (Princeton:
       1967), 280A.

1239   _____. Ezra Pound's Cathay. Princeton: University of
       Princeton Pr., 1969.

CLASSIC ANTHOLOGY

1240   Blissett, William. Classic Anthology. Review: Canadian
       Forum, 34 (October, 1954), 166-167.

1241   "Classic Anthology," Review: NY, 30, #38 (November 6,
       1954), 195-196.

1242   Cookson, William. "A Note on The Classic Anthology,"
       Agenda, 17 #3-4, (Autumn-Winter-Spring, 1979-80), 218-219.

1243   Fitts, Dudley. "From Some Three Millennia," NYT (Septem-
       ber 12, 1954), 42.

1244   Ford, Ford Madox. "'From China to Peru,'" Outlook, 35
       (June 19, 1915), 800-801.

1245   Fussell, Paul. "The Book of Odes Made New," Pound News-
       letter, 5 (January, 1955), 10-13.

1246   Garcia Terres, Jaime. Classic Anthology. Universidad de
       Mexico, 9, #5-6 (January-February, 1955), 31-32.

1247   Jung, Angela. "Classic Anthology," Review: Comparative
       Literature, 7, #1 (Winter, 1955), 91-93.

1248   _____. "Pound's Translation of 'Book of Poetry' Is a Re-
       creation," Asian Student, 3, #2 (San Francisco: September
       21, 1954), 4.

1249   Liu, Wu-Chi. Classic Anthology. LE&W, 2 (Summer, 1955),
       36-37.

1250   Muir, Edwin. "Odes from the East," Observer (March 6,
       1955).

1251   Smith, G. D. Gilling. [Under initials H. B.] Review:
       Classic Anthology, European (June, 1955).

                          EXULTATIONS

1252   Bennett, John. "Ezra Pound's Exultations: A Study in
       Structure," AmerS (Taiwan), 7, #3 (September, 1977), 27-39.

1253   Brenner, Milton. "A Panel of Poets," Bookman, 35 (April,
       1912), 156-161.

1254   "Current Poetry," LitD, 50, #9 (February 26, 1910), 402-404.

1255   Flint, F. S. "Publications Received," EngRev, 4 (December,
       1909), 160-161.

1256   _____. "Verse," New Age, 6 (January 6, 1910), 233-234.

                      GAUDIER-BRZESKA

1257   Ede, H. S. A Life of Gaudier-Brzeska. London: William
       Heinemann, 1930.

1258   "Gaudier-Brzeska." Review: American Review of Reviews,
       54 (August, 1916), 238.

1259   "Gaudier-Brzeska," Review: Dial, 61 (August 15, 1916), 112

1260 "Gaudier-Brzeska," Review: Nation, 103 (August 31, 1916), 207.

1261 "Gaudier-Brzeska," Review: NYTBR (August 13, 1916), 314.

1262 "Gaudier-Brzeska," Review: TLS (August 27, 1916), 199.

1263 "Gaudier-Brzeska," Review: Pittsburg, 21 (November, 1916), 485.

1264 Materer, Timothy. "Ezra Pound and Gaudier-Brzeska: Sophie's Diary," JML, 6 (April, 1977), 315-321.

1265 _____. "Gaudier's 'Three Ninas,'" Cf., #795, pp. 323-324.

1266 Matthias, John E. "Statement," Sou'wester (October 30, 1970), 135-136.

1267 Perloff, Marjorie. "The Portrait of the Artist as Collage-Text: Pound's Gaudier-Brzeska and the 'Italic' Texts of John Cage," APR, 11, #3 (May-June, 1982), 19-29.

GUIDE TO CULTURE (American, 1938)
GUIDE TO CULTURE (England, 1938)

1268 Bogan, Louise. "Make It New," Nation, 148 (April 29, 1939), 504-505.

1269 _____. "Make It New," Cf., #465, pp. 138-141.

1270 "Briefly Noted: Fiction," NY, 28, #33 (October 4, 1952), 137.

1271 Deutsch, Babette. "A Baedeker in Code," NY Herald Tribune (Book Rev.), (February 26, 1939), 18.

1272 Fitts, Dudley. "Right Thinking," SatRL, 20 (Mary 13, 1939), 16.

1273 Friedrich, Otto. "Ezra Pound: The Guide to Kulchur," New World Writing, 17 (1960), 161-202.

1274 Healy, J. V. "The Pound Problem," Poetry, 57, #3 (December, 1940), 200-214.

1275 Jack, Peter Monroe. "Ezra Pound's Culture," NYT (February 26, 1939), 14.

1276 Kenner, Hugh. "Pound and the Provision of Measures,"
      Poetry, 83, #1 (October, 1953), 29–35.

1277 Queneau, Raymond. "Guide to Kulchur," Nouvelle Revue
      Francaise (October, 1939).

1278 Williams, William Carlos. "Penny Wise, Pound Foolish," NR,
      99 (June 28, 1939), 229–230.

GUIDO CAVALCANTI

1279 Anderson, David. "Cavalcanti: Canzone to Fortune,"
      Paideuma, 12, #1 (Spring, 1983), 41–46.

1280 _____. "The Techniques of Critical Translation: Ezra
      Pound's Guide Cavalcanti, 1912," Paideuma, 8 (Fall, 1979),
      215–226.

1281 Gilson, Etienne. "Books of the Quarter," Criterion, 12
      (October, 1932), 106–112.

1282 Henderson, Archie. "Ezra Pound: Composer," Paideuma, 12,
      #2-3 (Fall-Winter, 1983), 499–509.

1283 Mangan, Sherry. "Poetry for Scholars, Scholarship for
      Poets," Poetry, 41 (March, 1933), 336–339.

1284 Mayor, A. Hyatt. "Cavalcanti and Pound," H&H, 5 (April-
      June, 1932), 468–471.

1285 Oderman, Kevin. "'Cavalcanti': That the Body Is Not
      Evil," Paideuma, 11, #2 (Fall, 1982), 257–279.

HOMAGE TO SEXTUS PROPERTIUS

1286 Blackmur, R. P. "Masks of Ezra Pound," H&H, 7 (January-
      March, 1934), 184–191; repr., in The Double Agent. Glou-
      cester, Mass., 1962; also in Language as Gesture. New
      York: Harcourt, Brace, 1952.

1287 Bush, Ronald. "Gathering the Limbs of Orpheus: The Sub-
      ject of Pound's Homage to Sextus Propertius," Ezra Pound
      and William Carlos Williams: The University of Pennsylvania

Conference Papers. Daniel Hoffman, ed. Philadelphia: U. of Pennsylvania Pr., 1983, pp. 61-78.

1288 Chauvet, Paul. Review: Homage to Sextus Propertius and Make It New," RAA (June, 1934), 445-446.

1289 Drew-Bear, Thomas. "Ezra Pound's 'Homage to Sextus Propertius,'" AL, 37, #2 (May, 1965), 204-210.

1290 Espey, John. "Towards Propertius," Paideuma, 1, #1 (Spring-Summer, 1972), 63-74.

1291 _____. "Vers Propertius," Les Cahiers de l'Herne. D. de Roux, ed. Paris: 1965, Vol. 2, pp. 502-507.

1292 Fletcher, John Gould. "Some Contemporary Poets," Chapbook: A Monthly Miscellany. No. 11 (May, 1920), 23-25.

1293 Forbes, Clarence A. "Ezra Pound and Sextus Propertius," CJ, 42, #3 (December, 1946), 177-179.

1294 Friar, Kimon. "On Translation," CLS, 8, #3 (September, 1971), 197-213.

1295 Hale, William G. "Pegasus Impounded," Poetry, 14, #1 (April, 1919), 52-55.

1296 Heppenstall, Rayner. "Homage to Sextus Propertius," Adelphi, 9 (January, 1935), 253-254.

1297 Hesse, Eva. "Pound oder der Verlängerie Konflikt [Pound: or, the Protracted Battle]," Diagonale, 5 (1967), 26-29.

1298 Highet, Gilbert. "Beer-bottle on the Pediment," Cf., #700.

1299 Holder, Alan. "Anne Bradstreet Resurrected," CP, 2, #1 (Spring, 1969), 11-18.

1300 Iwasaki, Ryozo. "Ezura Paundo no 'Puroperuchiusu' Santan," [Pound's Homage to Propertius], Shiho (Poetical Methods), 2, #2 (February 1, 1935), 74-76.

1301 Joseph, Terry Brint. "Ezra Pound's Approaches to the Long Poem in 'Near Propertius' and 'Hugh Selwyn Mauberly,'" DAI, 42, #9 (U. of Calif., Irvine: 1981), 4000A.

1302 Kenner, Hugh. The Poetry of Ezra Pound, Cf., #738, pp. 146-163.

1303 _____. "Scatter," StAR, 1, #1 (Fall-Winter, 1970), 51-55.

1304 Laughlin, James. "Ezra Pound's Propertius," SR, 46
      (October-December, 1938), 480-491. Cf., #1545, pp. 320-329.

1305 Levi, Peter. "Pound and the Classics," Cf., #777, pp. 42-45.

1306 Lewis, Wyndham. "Mr. Ezra Pound," Observer (October 18,
      1920), 5. See also #778, pp. 169ff.

1307 MacDiarmid, Hugh. "The Esemplastic Power," Cf., #782, pp.
      27-30.

1308 _____. "The Master Voyager of Our Age," Agenda, 10
      (1972-73), 139-145.

1309 _____. "The Return of the Long Poem," Cf., #125, pp.
      90-108.

1310 _____. "Tribute to Ezra Pound," CamR, 94 (June 8,
      1973), 168-170.

1311 Messing, Gordon M. "Pound's Propertius: The Homage and
      the Damage," Poetry and Poetics from Ancient Greece to the
      Renaissance: Studies in Honor of James Hutton. G. M. Krik-
      wood, ed. Cornell Studies in Classical Philology, 38. Ithaca:
      Cornell U. Pr., 1975, pp. 105-133.

1312 Miller, Vincent E. "The Serious Wit of Pound's Homage to
      Sextus Propertius," ConL, 16 (Autumn, 1975), 452-462.

1313 Nichols, Robert. "Poetry and Mr. Pound," Observer (Janu-
      ary 11, 1920), 6.

1314 Orage, A[lfred], R[ichard]. "Mr. Ezra Pound as Metricist,"
      The New Age. New Age Press, 1918; repr., in Readers and
      Writers (1917-1921). London: Allen & Unwin, 1922, pp. 57-
      60.

1315 _____. "Readers and Writers," New Age, 16, #3 (Novem-
      ber 19, 1914), 69.

1316 Porteus, Hugh Gordon. "Propertius Transmuted," New Eng-
      lish Weekly, 6 (March 7, 1935), 432-433.

1317 Richardson, Lawrence. "Ezra Pound's Homage to Propertius,"
      YPR, 6 (1947), 21-29.

1318 Rosenthal, M. L. The Modern Poets: A Critical Introduction.
      New York: Oxford U. Pr., 1960, pp. 55-56.

1319 Ruthven, K. K. "Propertius, Wordsworth, Yeats, Pound and
      Hale," N&Q, 15, #2 (February, 1968), 47-48.

1320 Sinclair, May. "The Reputation of Ezra Pound," NAR, 211
      (May, 1920), 658-668.

1321 Speirs, John. "Mr. Pound's Propertius," Scrutiny, 3 (Sep-
      tember, 1934), 409-418.

1322 Spender, Stephen. "Homage to Sextus Propertius," Review.
      Spectator, 153 (December 14, 1934), 938.

1323 Sullivan, John Patrick. Ezra Pound and Sextus Propertius:
      A Study in Creative Translation. London: Faber & Faber;
      Austin, Texas: U. of Texas Pr., 1964.

1324 _____. "Ezra Pound's Classical Translations," TQ, 10, #4
      (Winter, 1967), 57-62.

1325 _____. "The Poet as Translator: Ezra Pound and Sextus
      Propertius," KR, 23 (Summer, 1961), 462-481.

1326 _____. "Pound and Propertius: Some Techniques of
      Translation," Hereditas: Seven Essays on the Modern Ex-
      perience of the Classical. Will, Frederic, ed. Austin, Texas:
      U. of Texas Pr., 1964, pp. 95-129.

1327 _____. "Pound's Homage to Propertius: The Structure of
      a Mask," EIC, 10 (July, 1960), 239-249; Agenda (London), 4,
      #2 (October-November, 1965), 57-61.

1328 Turner, Mark. "Propertius through the Looking Glass: A
      Fragmentary Glance at the Construction of Pound's Homage,"
      Paideuma, 5, #2 (Fall, 1976), 241-265.

                              HOW TO READ

1329 Brulé, A. "Active Anthology," RA&A (October, 1934), 76-77.

1330 _____. "Revue of How to Read," RA&A (August, 1932),
      559-560.

1331 Ford, Ford Madox. "Pound and 'How to Read,'" New Review,
      11 (April, 1932), 39-45.

1332 Leavis, Frank Raymond. How to Teach Reading: A Primer
      for Ezra Pound. Cambridge, England: Heffer, (Minority
      Press Pamphlet), 1932.

1333 _____. How to Teach Reading: Education and the Univer-
      sity. London: Chatto & Windus, 1943.

1334 _____. New Bearings on English Poetry, Cf., #774, pp.
133-157.

1335 McGreevy, Thomas. "Pound and How to Read," New Review,
2 (April, 1932), 45-48.

1336 Stafford, Clayton. "Reading and Writing," H&H, 7 (July-
September, 1934), 731-736.

1337 Tate, Allen. "How Is Writing Taught," Poetry, 44 (April,
1934), 53-55.

1338 _____. "Laundry Bills," Poetry, 41 (November, 1932),
107-112.

HUGH SELWYN MAUBERLEY

1339 Bacigalupo, Massimo. "Lineaments of Space: From Hugh
Selwyn Mauberley to the Early Cantos," Cf., #437, pp. 5-51.

1340 Bell, Ian F. A. "In the Real Tradition: Edgar Lee Masters
and Hugh Selwyn Mauberley," Criticism, 23, #2 (Spring,
1981), 141-154.

1341 _____. "Instruments for Design: Mauberley's Sieve,"
ELN, 17 (June, 1980), 294-297.

1342 _____. "Mauberley's Barrier of Style," Ezra Pound: The
London Years: 1908-1920. Philip Grover, ed., Cf., #52,
pp. 89-115.

1343 _____. "The Phantasmagoria of Hugh Selwyn Mauberley,"
Paideuma, 5, #3 (Winter, 1976), 361-385.

1344 Berryman, Jo Brantley. "The Art of the Image: Allusions
in Pound's 'Medallion,'" Paideuma, 6 (Winter, 1977), 295-308.

1345 _____. Circe's Craft: Ezra Pound's 'Hugh Selwyn Mauberley.' UMI Research Press, Ann Arbor, Michigan, 1983.

1346 _____. "Ezra Pound Versus Hugh Selwyn Mauberley: A
Distinction," DAI, 34, #10 (So. Calif.: 1973), 6624A.

1347 _____. "Mauberley, Logopoeia, and the Language of
Modernism,: SAQ, 83, #1 (Winter, 1984), 18-43.

1348 _____. "'Medallion': Pound's Poem," Paideuma, 2, #3
(Winter, 1973), 391-398.

1349   _____ and Donald Davie. "'Medallion': Some Questions,"
        Paideuma, 8 (1979), 151-157.

1350   Bornstein, George. "The Forest of His Mind: Mauberley
        and The Cantos," Cf., #467, pp. 60-72.

1351   Brumm, Anne-Marie. "Mouths Biting Empty Air: Ezra Pound's
        'Hugh Selwyn Mauberley' and Henry James's 'Lambert
        Strether,'" RLC, 54 (January-March, 1980), 47-70.

1352   Bueltmann, Faith. "Mauberley's 'Medallion,'" N&Q, 7, #4
        (n.s.), (April, 1960), 148.

1353   Campos, Augusto de. "Nota Sobre 'Hugh Selwyn Mauberley,'"
        ESPSL, (October 30, 1965), 3.

1354   Connolly, Thomas E. "Further Notes on Mauberley," Accent,
        16 (Winter, 1956), 59-67.

1355   D'Agostino, Nemi. "La Sequenza di Hugh Selwyn Mauberley,"
        La Fiera Letteraria, 8, #43 (October 25, 1953), 3-4.

1356   Davie, Donald. Ezra Pound. Frank Kermode, ed. New York:
        Viking Pr., 1975.

1357   _____. "Ezra Pound's Hugh Selwyn Mauberley," The Mod-
        ern Age. Boris Ford, ed. Pelican Guide to English Litera-
        ture. New York: Penguin Books, 1961, VII, pp. 315-329.

1358   DeCampos, Augusto. "Nota sobre 'Hugh Selwyn Mauberley,'"
        ESPSL, (October, 1965), 3.

1359   Demirovic, Hamdija. "Tekst i kaos: Slika umjetnika u svijetu
        rasapa vrijednosti u poemi 'Hugh Selwyn Mauberley' Ezre
        Pounda," Izraz, 22 (1978), 1557-1602.

1360   Deutsch, Babette. This Modern Poetry. New York: W. W.
        Norton, Inc., 1935, pp. 115-118, passim.

1361   Donoghue, Denis. "James's The Awkward Age and Pound's
        Mauberley," N&Q, 17 (February, 1970), 49-50.

1362   Duffey, Bernard. "Ezra Pound's Mauberley," AL, 27
        (January, 1956), 601-602.

1363   Duncan, Ronald. "A Supervision with Dr. Leavis on Mauber-
        ley," All Men Are Islands: An Autobiography. London:
        Rupert Hart-Davis, 1964, pp. 84-87.

1364   Egudu, R. N. "'The Idyll Sham: Ezra Pound and Nigerian
        Wole Soyinka on War,'" Paideuma, 5, #1 (Spring, 1976), 31-41.

1365   Emery, Clark M. "Pound as Mauberley," HINL, 4 (January, 1958), 6-8.

1366   Emslie, Macdonald. "Pound's 'Hugh Selwyn Mauberley,' I, iii, 13-16," Expl, 14, #4 (January, 1956), Item 26.

1367   Espey, John. Ezra Pound's Mauberley: A Study in Composition. London: Faber & Faber, 1955; Berkeley and Los Angeles: U. of Calif. Pr., 1955.

1368   Faas, Egbert. "Formen der Bewusstseinsdarstellung in der dramatischen Lyrik Pounds und Eliots," GRM, 18, #2, n.s. (April, 1968), 172-191.

1369   Feder, Lillian. Ancient Myth in Modern Poetry. Princeton, N.J.: Princeton U. Pr., 1971, pp. 99-105.

1370   Findley, Timothy. Famous Last Words. New York: Delacorte Pub. Co., 1982.

1371   Fraser, G. S. "Pound: Masks, Myth and Man," Cf., #114, pp. 172-185.

1372   French, A. L. "'Olympian Apathein': Pound's Hugh Selwyn Mauberley and Modern Poetry," EIC, 15, #4 (October, 1965), 428-445.

1373   _____. "Mauberley: A Rejoinder," EIC, 16 (July, 1966), 356-359. Cf., #1407.

1374   Friar, Kimon, and John Malcolm Brinnin. "Hugh Selwyn Mauberley," Cf., #626, pp. 525-531.

1375   Giovannini, G. "'Pound's Hugh Selwyn Mauberley,' I, iii, 22," Expl, 16 (March, 1958), Item 35.

1376   Gregory, Horace. "This Side of Poetry," Poetry, 44 (August, 1934), 291-294.

1377   Grover, Philip, ed. "Mauberley's Barrier of Style," Ezra Pound: The London Years, 1908-1920. Philip Grover, ed. Cf., #52, pp. 89-115, 155-164.

1378   Hoffman, Frederick J. "The Text: Ezra Pound's Hugh Selwyn Mauberley," The Twenties: American Writing in the Postwar Decade. New York: Viking, 1955, pp. 36-46.

1379   Holbrook, David. "The Lack of a Creative Theme: Ezra Pound's Stone Mouths Biting Empty Air and Eliot's Hollow Men," Lost Bearings in English Poetry. London: Vision Pr., 1977, pp. 64-91; New York: Barnes & Noble, 1977, pp. 58-100.

1380   Holder, Alan. "The Lesson of the Master: Ezra Pound and
       Henry James," Cf., #706, pp. 71-79.

1381   Homberger, Eric. "Towards 'Mauberley,'" AntigR, 13 (Spring,
       1973), 35-44.

1382   Hombitzer, Eleonore. "Ezra Pound: 'Medallion,'" NS, 16,
       #10 (October, 1967), 499-503.

1383   Houston, John Porter. "Hugh Selwyn Mauberley," French
       Symbolism and the Modernist Movement, Cf., #711, pp. 46-48.

1384   Jenner, E. A. B. "'Medallion':   Some Questions," Paideuma,
       8 (1979), 153-157.

1385   Joseph, Terri Brint. "The Decentered Center of Ezra Pound's
       Hugh Selwyn Mauberley," REALB, 1 (1982), 121-151.

1386   _____. "Ezra Pound's Approaches to the Long Poem in
       'Near Perigord,' Homage to Sextus Propertius, and Hugh
       Selwyn Mauberley," Cf., #1301, p. 4000A.

1387   Kenner, Hugh. "Broken Mirrors and the Mirror of Memory,"
       Cf., #731, p. 26, and #771.

1388   _____. "Critic of the Month: III--Ghosts and Benedic-
       tions," Poetry, 113, #2 (November, 1968), 109-125.

1389   _____. "Mauberley," The Poetry of Ezra Pound, Cf.,
       #738, pp. 164-182.

1390   _____. "Mauberley," Ezra Pound: A Collection of Critical
       Essays. Walter Sutton, ed. Englewood Cliffs, NJ, Prentice-
       Hall, Inc., 1951, pp. 41-56.

1391   Knox, George. "Glaucus in Hugh Selwyn Mauberley," ES,
       45, #3 (June, 1964), 236-237.

1392   _____. "Pound's Hugh Selwyn Mauberley':   A Vortex
       Name," Spirit, 36, #2 (1969), 23-28.

1393   Leavis, F. R. "Ezra Pound--Mauberley," New Bearings in
       English Poetry. Cf., #774, pp. 133-157.

1394   Libby, Gary R. "Image or Image: An Unnoticed Allusion in
       'Hugh Selwyn Mauberley,'" Paideuma, 1, #2 (Winter, 1972),
       205-206.

1395   Link, Franz H. "A Note on Samothrace in Pound's Hugh
       Selwyn Mauberley," Paideuma, 6 (Winter, 1977), 329.

1396 Long, Richard A. "Pound's Hugh Selwyn Mauberley," Expl,
      10 (June, 1952), Item 56; repr., in The Explicator Cyclopedia,
      Vol. I, p. 231.

1397 McCuaig, Ronald. "Mauberley Again," The Bulletin, (Syd-
      ney), (May 4, 1955), p. 2.

1398 Madge, Charles. "The Ellysse in the Pisan Cantos," An Ex-
      amination of Ezra Pound. Peter Russell, ed., Cf., #1136,
      pp. 121-123.

1399 Malkoff, Karl. "Allusion as Irony: Pound's Use of Dante in
      Hugh Selwyn Mauberley," MinnR, 7, #1 (1967), 81-88.

1400 _____. Escape from the Self: A Study in Contemporary
      American Poetry and Poetics. New York: Columbia U. Pr.,
      1977, pp. 31-32, 106-107, passim.

1401 Mazzeno, Laurence W. "A Note on Hugh Selwyn Mauberley,"
      Paideuma, 4, #1 (Spring, 1975), 89-91.

1402 Mills, Lloyd L. "English Origin of 'Still-born' and 'Dumb-
      born' in Mauberley," AN&Q, 10, #5 (January, 1972), 67-68.

1403 Muir, Edwin. "Hugh Selwyn Mauberley," [Review], New
      Age, 21 (October, 1922), 288.

1404 Pratt, William C. "Ezra Pound and the Image," Ezra Pound:
      The London Years: 1908-1920, Cf., #52, pp. 15-30.

1405 Quartermain, Peter. "'Blocked. Make a Song out of That':
      Pound's 'E.P. Ode pour l'élection de son sépulchre,'" KRev,
      1, i (1980), 32-48.

1406 Quinn, Sr. M. Bernetta. "A Poem Too Interesting for
      Burial," Pound Newsletter, 7 (July, 1955), 1-3. [Review:
      John J. Espey's Ezra Pound's Mauberley, #1367.]

1407 Reiss, Christopher. "In Defence of Mauberley," EIC, 16
      (July, 1966), 351-355; Rejoinder by A. L. French, Cf.,
      #1373, pp. 356-359.

1408 Rosenthal, M. L. "Ezra Pound: The Poet as Hero, ...
      Mauberley: Alienation of the Citizen-Artist," The Modern
      Poets: A Critical Introduction. New York: Oxford U. Pr.,
      1960, pp. 49-74.

1409 _____. "The Mauberley Sequence," A Primer for Ezra
      Pound, Cf., #905, pp. 29-41.

1410 San Juan, E[pifanio], Jr., ed. "Ezra Pound's Craftsmanship:

An Interpretation of Hugh Selwyn Mauberley," Critics on
Ezra Pound, Cf., 535, pp. 106-124.

1411   Sanavio, Piero. "'Hugh Selwyn Mauberley,'" Nuova corrente,
       Nos. 5-6 (genn.-giugno, 1956), 165-183.

1412   Schmidt, A. V. C. "Crumpets in Coriolan, Muffins in Pick-
       wick," N&Q, 23 (July, 1976), 298-299.

1413   Sergeant, Howard. Review: John J. Espey's Ezra Pound's
       Mauberley English, 10, #59 (Summer, 1955), 192-193. [John
       J. Espey: #1367].

1414   Sitwell, Edith. "Ezra Pound," An Examination of Ezra Pound.
       Peter Russell, ed. Cf., #114, pp. 44-50.

1415   Spanos, William V. "The Modulating Voice of Hugh Selwyn
       Mauberley," WSCL, 6 (Winter-Spring, 1965), 73-96.

1416   Sparrow, John. "Doubts about Pound and 'Mauberley,'"
       Sense and Poetry: Essays on the Place of Meaning in Con-
       temporary Poetry. London: Constable, 1934, pp. 122-132.

1417   Sutton, Walter E. "Ezra Pound: Early Poems and Mauber-
       ley," American Free Verse: The Modern Revolution in Poetry.
       New York: New Directions, 1973, pp. 47-64.

1418   _____. "Mauberley, The Waste Land, and the Problem of
       Unified Form," WSCL, 9, #1 (Winter, 1968), 15-35.

1419   Tillyard, E. M. W. Poetry, Direct, and Oblique. London:
       Chatto and Windus, 1934, pp. 34-35.

1420   Wallace-Crabbe, Chris. "Auden's New Year Letter and the
       Fate of Long Poems," Melbourne Critical Rev, 5 (1962), 129-
       136.

1421   Widmer, Kingsley. "The Waste Land and the American
       Breakdown," The Twenties: Fiction, Poetry, Drama. War-
       ren French, ed. Cf., #671, pp. 479-480.

1422   Witemeyer, Hugh. "Hugh Selwyn Mauberley as Bhlooming
       Ulysses," The Poetry of Ezra Pound: Forms and Renewal,
       1908-1920. Berkeley and Los Angeles: U. of Calif. Pr.,
       1969, pp. 161-195.

IMPACT: ESSAYS ON IGNORANCE AND THE
DECLINE OF AMERICAN CIVILIZATION

1423   Fitts, Dudley. "Impact," New York Times Book Review (July
       3, 1960), Review.

1424   _____. The Caged Panther: Ezra Pound at St. Elizabeth's
       by Harry M. Meacham. Cf., #361, p. 88.

1425   Heymann, C. David. "Impact," Ezra Pound: The Last
       Rower, Cf., #57, pp. 268, 348.

1426   Kenner, Hugh. "Apples, Planets, Dollars," National Review,
       10 (March 25, 1961), 183-185.

1427   Stock, Noel, Ed., with Introduction. Impact: Essays on
       Ignorance and the Decline of American Civilization. Chicago:
       H. Regnery Co., 1960.

1428   _____. "Impact," Poet in Exile: Ezra Pound. Cf., #402,
       pp. 12, 175.

IN A STATION OF THE METRO

1429   Beck, Warren. "Boundaries of Poetry," CE, 4 (March,
       1943), 346-347.

1430   Bell, Ian F. A. "'In a Station of the Metro' and Carpenterian
       Transformations," N&Q, 29, #4 (August, 1982), 345-346.

1431   Bevilaqua, Ralph. "Pound's 'In a Station of the Metro': A
       Textual Note," ELN, 8 (June, 1971), 293-296.

1432   Brooks, Cleanth, and Robert Penn Warren. Understanding
       Poetry. New York: 1938, pp. 175-176; Revised Ed., New
       York: Holt, 1951, pp. 78-80.

1433   Bryer, Jackson R., ed. Fifteen Modern American Authors:
       A Survey of Research and Criticism. Durham, N.C.: Duke
       U. Pr., 1969, pp. 335ff.

1434   _____. Sixteen Modern American Authors: A Survey of
       Research and Criticism. Durham, N.C.: Duke U. Pr., 1974,
       pp. 457ff.

1435   Espey, John J. "Pound's 'In a Station of the Metro,'" Expl,
       11 (June, 1953), #59.

1436 Friend, Joseph H. "Teaching the 'Grammar of Poetry,'" CE,
      27 (February, 1966), 362-363.

1437 Haefner, Gerhard. "Zur Wandlung des Imagismus Ezra
      Pounds," Poetica, 4, #3 (1971), 325-332.

1438 Hanzo, Thomas A. "Pound's 'In a Station of the Metro,'"
      Expl, 11 (February, 1953), No. 26.

1439 Kann, Hans-Joachim. "Translation Problems in Pound's 'In a
      Station of the Metro,'" LWU, 6 (1973), 234-240.

1440 Lasser, Michael L., and Yoshiyuki Iwamoto. "Pound's 'In a
      Station of the Metro,'" Expl, 19 (February, 1961), No. 30.

1441 Link, Franz H. "A Note on the Apparition of These Faces
      ... in 'In a Station of the Metro,'" Paideuma, 10, #2 (Fall,
      1981), 327.

1442 Nicolaisen, Peter. "Ezra Pounds 'In a Station of the Metro,'"
      LWU, 1, #3 (1968), 198-204.

1443 Rosenthal, Machia Louis, and A. J. M. Smith. Exploring
      Poetry. New York: Macmillan, 1955, pp. 157-158.

1444 Smith, Richard Eugene. "Ezra Pound and the Haiku," CE,
      26, #7 (April, 1965), 522-527.

1445 Wilson, Donald D. "Penny-Wise Pound," Paideuma, 1, #2
      (Winter, 1972), 203-204.

1446 Wimsat, W. K. ["In a Station of the Metro"], Day of the
      Leopards: Essays in Defense of Poems. New Haven and
      London: Yale U. Pr., 1976, p. 217.

INSTIGATIONS

1447 Blum, W. C. "Super Schoolmaster," Dial, 69 (October,
      1920), 422-423.

1448 Brooks, Van Wyck. "Reviewer's Notebook," Freeman, 1
      (June 16, 1920), 334-335; repr., in Van Wyck Brooks: The
      Early Years, A Selection from His Works, 1908-1921. Claire
      Sprague, ed. New York: Harper & Row, 1968.

1449 Colum, Padriac. "Studies in the Sophisticated," NR, 25
      (December 8, 1920), 52-54.

1450 Dale, Peter. "Pound and De Gourmont," Agenda, 17, #3-4
      (1979-80), 284.

1451 Kay, Bernard. "The Singing Sinologue," NS&N, 44 (June 4,
      1955), 788.

1452 Sieburth, Richard. Instigations: Ezra Pound and Remy de
      Gourmont. Diss., Cambridge: Harvard UP., 1978.

JEFFERSON AND/OR MUSSOLINI

1453 A. M. "For Mussolini, God, Moscow and Major Douglas,"
      New Verse, #16 (August-September, 1935), 18-20.

1454 Falbo, Ernest S. "Ezra Pound's 'Lombard Writer, Friend,'"
      Paideuma, 3, #2 (Fall, 1974), 247-249.

1455 Hawkins, A. Desmond. "Prejudices," NS&N, 10 (August 31,
      1935), 284-285.

1456 Kenner, Hugh. "Jefferson and/or Mussolini," The Poetry of
      Ezra Pound. Cf., #738, pp. 320-323.

1457 Olson, Charles. "This Is Yeats Speaking," Cf., #374.

LITERARY ESSAYS

1458 Bloom, E. A. "Literary Essays," Review. SatRL, 37
      (April 3, 1945), 30.

1459 Brown, Ashley. "The Translations and Literary Essays,"
      Review. Shenandoah, 5, #3 (Summer, 1954), 61-65.

1460 Carter, Thomas H. "Ezra Pound the Critic," KR, 16, #3
      (Summer, 1954), 490-496.

1461 Cole, Thomas. "Literary Essays," Review. Imagi, 6, #4
      (1955).

1462 Davie, Donald. "Instigations to Procedures," NS&N, 47
      (March 27, 1954), 410, 412.

1463 Deutsch, Babette. "Pound's Enduring Criticism," NY Herald
      Tribune Book Review (June 6, 1954), 14.

1464   Duclos, Jacques. "Personae, Literary Essays, Translations,"
        Revue Des Langues Vivantes, 21, #1 (1955), 70-72.

1465   Eliot, T. S., ed. Introduction by T. S. Eliot. The Literary
        Essays of Ezra Pound. Norfolk, Conn.: New Directions,
        1954.

1466   Freedman, Ralph. "The Serious Artist and the Verbal Icon,"
        WR, 19, #3 (Spring, 1955), 221-229.

1467   Fuller, Roy. "Literary Essays." Review. London Magazine,
        1 (May, 1954), 94, 96, 99, 100.

1468   "The Greatness of Critics," TLS (May 28, 1954), 345.

1469   "Literary Essays," Review. The Listener, 51 (April 29,
        1954), 749.

1470   "Literary Essays of Ezra Pound," Review, NY, 30, #6
        (March, 1954), 118-119.

1471   "Literary Essays." Review. St. Louis Post-Dispatch
        (March 15, 1954).

1472   McLuhan, Marshall. "The Criticism of Ezra Pound," Cw, 60,
        #20 (August 20, 1954), 492-493.

1473   "Pound as Critic," Nation, 178, #18 (May 1, 1954), 388-389.

1474   Robson, W. W. "Literary Essays." Review. Blackfriars, 35
        (April, 1954), 184-185.

1475   Stanford, Derek. "Sun-Spots and Blind-Spots," Month, 197
        (April, 1954), 239-241.

1476   Stock, Noel. "Literary Essays," Review. Meanjin, 2 (Mel-
        bourne, 1955), 273-277.

1477   Tomlinson, Charles. "Literary Essays." Review. Spectator,
        192 (February 19, 1954), 212.

                                LUSTRA

1478   Bodenheim, Maxwell. "A Poet's Opinion," Little Review, 4
        (June, 1917), 28.

1479   Buss, Kate. "Ezra Pound: Some Evidence of His Rare

Chinese Quality," Boston Evening Transcript (December 6, 1916), Sec. 3, p. 5.

1480 Cronin, G. W. "Classic Free Verse," New York Call (December 20, 1917), 18.

1481 "Current Poetry," LitD, 55 (December 29, 1917), 51-52.

1482 Deutsch, Babette. "Ezra Pound: Vorticist," Ready's Mirror (St. Louis), 26 (December 21, 1917), 860-861.

1483 Grover, Philip. "Manuscript Corrections in Lustra," Paideuma 9, (1980), 357-358.

1484 Hasegawa, Mitsuaki. "Sexual Mockery in Lustra," HSELL, 19, #2 (1973), 33-44.

1485 "Lustra," LitD, 55, #24 (December 15, 1917), 38.

1486 M. T. "Ezra Pound and Others," NR, 13, #168 (January 19, 1918), 352-353.

1487 Michelson, Max. "A Glass-Blower of Time," Poetry, 11 (March, 1918), 330-333.

1488 Orage, A. R. "Readers and Writers," New Age, 23 (July 25, 1918), 201.

1489 Reid, B. L. The Man from New York: John Quinn and His Friends. New York: Oxford U. Pr., 1968, p. 340.

1490 Rittenhouse, J. B. "Contemporary Poetry," Bookman, 46 (January, 1918), 577-578.

1491 Thomas, Ronald E. "Catullus, Flaminius, and Pound in 'Blandula, Tenella, Vagula,'" Paideuma, 5, (Winter, 1976), 407-412.

1492 Untermeyer, Louis. "China, Provence, and Points Adjacent," Dial, 63 (December 20, 1917), 633-635.

1493 Witemeyer, Hugh. "Aspects of Lustra," The Poetry of Ezra Pound: Forms and Renewal, 1908-1920. Berkeley: U. of Calif. Pr., 1969, pp. 122-160.

MAKE IT NEW

1494 C. R. A. "Make It New," Review. AL, 9, #3 (November, 1937), 393.

1495 Chauvet, Paul. "Make It New," Review, RAA (June, 1934), 445-446.

1496 Chesterton, G. K. "Make It New," Review, Listener, 12 (November 28, 1934), 921.

1497 Deutsch, Babette. "Indomitable Ezra Pound," NYHBR (June 2, 1935), 18.

1498 Dobree, Bonamy. "Make It New," Criterion, 14 (April, 1935), 523-526.

1499 DuBois, Arthur E. "Make It New," Review, SR, 44, #2 (April-June, 1936), 254-256.

1500 Gregory, Horace. "Pound as Essayist," YR, 24 (March, 1935), 608-610.

1501 John, K. "The Eternal Schoolboy," NS&N, 8 (November 3, 1934), 630-632.

1502 King, William. "Essays," EngRev, 59 (December, 1934), 745-746.

1503 McCole, Camille. "Make It New," CathW, 141 (May, 1935). 244.

1504 Powell, Dilys. "The Jackdaw of Paris," LonMer, 31 (November, 1934), 81-82.

1505 Roberts, Michael. "Off with the Motley," Spect, 153 (November 2, 1934), 684-686.

1506 S. C. C. "Make It New," Review, CSMM (April 3, 1935), 10.

1507 Walton, Eda Lou. "Mr. Pound as a Critic Is Not Bound by Any Group," NYT, 6 (June 30, 1935), 3.

1508 Wilson, T. C. "Pound as Critic," NR, 85 (November 27, 1935), 80-81.

1509 Young, G. M. "Make It New," Review, Observer (October 7, 1934), 7.

1510 _____. "Ezra Pound Again," Springfield Republican (October, 1934), 7e.

NEAR PERIGORD

1511 Connolly, Thomas E. "Ezra Pound's 'Near Perigord': The Background of a Poem," CL, 8 (Spring, 1956), 110-121.

1512 Joseph, Terry Brint. "'Near Perigord': A Perplexity of Voice," Paideuma, 11, #1 (Spring-Summer, 1982), 93-98.

1513 Kenner, Hugh. "The Broken Mirrors and the Mirror of Memory," Cf., #731, #771.

1514 Schmidt, Gerd. "Ezra Pound: 'Near Perigord,'" NS, 18 (October, 1969), 502-512.

THE NOH PLAYS

1515 Eliot, T. S. "The Noh and the Image," Egoist, 4 (August, 1917), 102-103.

1516 Keith, Nobuko T. "Ezra Pound and Japanese Noh Plays: An Examination of Sotoba Komachi and Nishikigi," LE&W, 15-16 (1971-72), 662-679.

1517 _____. "Ezra Pound's Relationship with Fenollosa and the Japanese Noh Plays," Cf., #728.

1518 Lewin, Bruno. "Literarische Begegnungen zwischen Amerika und Japan," JA, 14 (1969), 25-39.

1519 Miller, Felicia. "Pound, Fenollosa, and the Noh," Occident, 7, #1 (1973), 63-65.

1520 Packard, William. "An American Experiment in Noh," First Stage 4, #2 (Summer, 1965), 60-61.

1521 Saitoh, Kuniharu. "Some Critical Comments on 'Fenollosa-Pound' Translations of Noh Plays," Meiji Gakuin Review (1966), referred to in Sixteen Modern American Authors, Jackson R. Bryer, ed., Cf., #1434, p. 459.

1522 Sato, Toshihiko. "A Study of Noh, The Robe of Feathers," CLAJ, 16 (September, 1972), 72-80.

1523 Taylor, Richard. "Ezra Pound: Editor of Nō," Paideuma, 4, #2-3 (Fall-Winter, 1975), 345-353.

1524 Teele, Roy E. "A Balance Sheet on Pound's Translation of
      Noh Plays," BA, 39 (Spring, 1965), 168-170.

1525 _____. "Translations of Noh Plays," CL, 9, #4 (Fall,
      1957), 345-368.

1526 Tsukui, Nobuko. "Ezra Pound and the Japanese Noh Plays,"
      DAI, 28 (Nebraska: 1967), 2267A-68A; United Pr. of Amer-
      ica, Inc., Washington, D.C., 1983.

                           A PACT

1527 D'Avanzo, Mario L. "Pound's 'A Pact,'" Expl, 24 (February,
      1966), Item 51.

1528 Kahn, Sholom J. "Whitman's 'New Wood,'" WWR, 15, #4
      (December, 1969), 201-214.

                          PAPYRUS

1529 Byrnos, Robert S. "Modern Poetry," The Courier Mail
      (Brisbane), (March 31, 1954). (An attack on Pound's
      "Papyrus" and a reply by Roger Covell.)

1530 Collinge, N. E. "Gongyla and Mr. Pound," N&Q, n.s., 5,
      #6 (June, 1958), 265-266.

1531 Daniels, Earl. "Papyrus," The Art of Reading Poetry. New
      York: Farrar & Rinehart, Inc., 1941; Bks. for Libraries
      Pr., 1969, p. 9.

1532 Dawson, Christopher M. "Pound's Papyrus," Expl, 9 (Febru-
      ary, 1951), Item 30.

1533 Fang, Achilles. "A Note on Pound's Papyrus," MLN, 67, #3
      (March, 1952), 188-190.

1534 _____. "Metaphysics and Money-Making," NMQ, 23, #1
      (Spring, 1953), 91-94.

1535 Highet, Gilbert. "The Symbolist Poets ...," The Classical
      Tradition: Greek and Roman Influences on Western Litera-
      ture. New York: Oxford U. Pr., 1957, p. 517, passim.

1536 Murray, Robert Duff, Jr. "A Note on Sappho and Ezra
      Pound," Classical Journal, 46 (March, 1951), 304-305.

PATRIA MIA

1537 Deutsch, Babette. "Ezra Pound's Early Credo," NY Herald
      Tribune Bk. Review (September 17, 1950), 19.

1538 Kenner, Hugh. "Prophets of Renaissance," HudR, 3 (Fall,
      1950), 474-478.

1539 MacFall, Russell. "Patria Mia," Review. Chicago Sunday
      Tribune, (July 2, 1950), 5.

1540 Richie, Donald. "Belles-Lettres Notes," SatRL, 33 (Octo-
      ber 14, 1950), 42.

1541 Runnquist, Åke. "Notiser från vöster," Dagens-Nyheter
      (Stockholm), (August 21, 1950).

1542 Wilson, Edmund. "Patria Mia," NY, 26 (August 5, 1950),
      64-67.

PAVANNES AND DIVISIONS

1543 Aiken, Conrad. "A Pointless Pointillist," Dail, 65 (October
      19, 1918), 306-307.

1544 Carnevali, Emanuel. "Irritation," Poetry, 15 (January,
      1920), 211-221.

1545 Hale, W. G. "Pegasus Impounded," Poetry, 14 (April, 1919),
      52-55; repr., in Ezra Pound: The Critical Heritage. Eric
      Homberger, ed. London; Boston: Routledge & Kegan Paul,
      1972, pp. 155-157.

1546 "Mr. Pound as Critic," TLS (September 19, 1918), 437; repr.,
      in American Writing Today: Its Independence and Vigor.
      Allan Angoff, ed. New York U. Pr., 1957, pp. 332-335.

1547 Untermeyer, Louis. "Ezra Pound, Proseur," NR, 16 (August
      17, 1918), 83-84.

PERSONAE

1548 Aiken, Conrad. "Personae," Review. Indep, 118 (February 26, 1927), 246.

1549 _____. "Personae," Poetry, 44, #5 (August, 1934), 276-279.

1550 _____. "Vagabondia," NR, 51, #655 (June 22, 1927), 131-132.

1551 Benet, William Rose. "Personae," The Collected Poems of Ezra Pound, Review. YR, 17 (January, 1928), 366-374.

1552 Blackmur, R. P. "A Variety of Masks," SatRL, 3, #40 (April 30, 1927), 784.

1553 Braybrooke, Neville. "Personae," Review. English, 9, #51 (Autumn, 1952), 108-109.

1554 Bronner, Milton. "A Panel of Poets," Bookman, 35 (April, 1912), 156-158.

1555 Brooke, Rupert. "Personae," Review. CamR, 31 (December 2, 1909), 166-167.

1556 _____. The Letters of Rupert Brooke. Chosen and edited by Geoffrey Keynes. New York: Harcourt, Brace & World, 1968, pp. 332, 470.

1557 Courtney, W. L. "Personae," Review. Daily Telegraph (April 23, 1909), 6.

1558 "Current Poetry," LitD, 60 (February 26, 1910), 402-404.

1559 Deutsch, Babette. "Personae," Review. Bookman, 65 (April, 1927), 220.

1560 Eliot, T. S. Ezra Pound: His Metric and Poetry. New York: Alfred A. Knopf, 1917; repr., in To Criticize the Critic. New York: Farrar, Straus & Giroux, 1965, pp. 162-182.

1561 _____. "Isolated Superiority," Dial, 84 (January, 1928), 4-7.

1562 Flint, F. S. "Verse," The New Age, 5 (May 27, 1909), 101-102.

1563 Ford, Ford Madox. "Personae," NY Herald Tribune BR (January 9, 1927), 1, 6.

1564 Gorman, H. S. "Personae," Review. NYTBR (January 23,
      1927), 2.

1565 Harris, Frank. "L'Homme Moyen Sensuel," The Little Review,
      4 (October, 1914), 40.

1566 Hassall, Christopher. Rupert Brooke: A Biography. New
      York: Harcourt, Brace & World, 1964, p. 210.

1567 Hollander, John. "The Poem in the Eye," Shenandoah, 23
      (Spring, 1972), 24.

1568 McFarland, Ronald E. "A Note on Monsieur Verog,"
      Paideuma, 11, #3 (Winter, 1982), 446-448.

1569 Mathews, Elkin. Personae: Die Masken Ezra Pounds.
      Verlag der Arche, Zürich, 1959, pp. 12-15.

1570 Nanny, Max. "Context, Contiguity and Contact in Ezra
      Pound's Personae," ELH, 47 (Summer, 1980), 386-398.

1571 Petter, C. G. "Pound's Personae: From Manuscript to
      Print," Studies in Biblio. Vol. 35, pp. 111-132. Fredson
      Bowers, ed. Published for the Biblio Soc. of University of
      Virginia by University Pr. of Virginia, 1982, pp. 111-132.

1572 Ruthven, K. K. A Guide to Ezra Pound's Personae.
      Berkeley; Los Angeles: U. of Calif. Pr., 1969.

1573 Sitwell, Edith. "Ezra Pound," An Examination of Ezra
      Pound. Peter Russell, ed. Rev. and Enlarged. New
      York: Gordian Pr., 1973, pp. 39-40.

1574 Thomas, Edward. "Two Poets," English Review, 2 (June,
      1909), 627-632.

1575 Van Doren, Mark. "First Glance," Nation, 124 (February 2,
      1927), 120.

1576 Williams, W. C. "Personae," Review. LiteraryRev (February,
      1927), 1.

1577 Wright, George T. "Modern Poetry and the Personae: The
      Device and Its Aesthetic Context, as Exhibited in the Work
      of Eliot, Yeats and Pound," Diss. U. of Calif., at Berkeley,
      1956.

1578 _____. The Poet in the Poem: The Personae of Eliot,
      Yeats, and Pound. Berkeley. U. of Calif. Pr., 1960.

PHANOPOEIA

1579 Hombitzer, Eleonore. "Ezra Pound: 'Phanopoeia': Hinweise
      zu einer Interpretation," NS, 14, #7 (July, 1965), 568-578.

POEMS: 1918-1921

1580 Bishop, John Peale. "The Intelligence of Poets," Vanity
      Fair, 17 (January, 1922), 13-14.

1581 Bodenheim, Maxwell. "Isolation of Carved Metal," Cf., #462.

1582 Geddes, Virgil. "Ezra Pound Today," Poetry, 21 (November,
      1922), 95-100.

1583 Howard, Brian. Brian Howard: Portrait of a Failure.
      Marie-Jacqueline Lancaster, ed. London: Anthony Blond,
      1968, p. 56.

1584 LeGallienne, Richard. "Poems: 1918-1921," Review. NYT
      (February 5, 1922), 2.

1585 McClure, John. "New Poems of Ezra Pound," Double Dealer,
      2 (May, 1922), 269-271.

1586 Monroe, Harriet. "Ezra Pound," Cf., #85.

1587 Wilson, Edmund. "Mr. Pound's Patchwork," NR, 30, #385
      (April 19, 1922), 232-233; repr., in The Shores of Light: A
      Literary Chronicle of the Twenties and Thirties. New York:
      Farrar, Straus & Young, Inc., 1952, pp. 44-48.

POLITE ESSAYS

1588 Brown, E. K. "Mr. Pound's Conservatism," Canadian Forum,
      20 (April, 1940), 24.

1589 Evans, B. I. "Polite Essays." Review. Manchester Guardian
      (March 25, 1937), 7.

1590 Healy, J. V. "The Pound Problem," Cf., #1274, p. 75.

1591   Mortimer, Raymond. "Polite Essays," Review. NS&N, 13
       (May 15, 1937), 813-814.

1592   Mowrer, Deane. "Pound Wise," NR, 102 (February 12, 1940),
       220.

1593   "Polite Essays," Review. CSMM (March 16, 1940), 10.

1594   "Polite Essays," Review. Nation, 150 (March 23, 1940), 401.

1595   "Polite Essays," Review. New Yorker, 15 (January 20, 1940),
       64.

1596   "Polite Essays," Review. Time, 35 (January 1, 1940), 47.

1597   Roberts, Michael. "Mr. Pound's Criticism," Spectator, 158
       (February 19, 1937), 324.

1598   Wright, Cuthbert. "Criticism," Cw, 31 (February 23, 1940),
       390.

PORTRAIT D'UNE FEMME

1599   Barry, Elaine. "'Portrait d'une Femme,' Frost's Comments
       on Pound," Robert Frost on Writing. New Brunswick, New
       Jersey: Rutgers U. Pr., 1973, pp. 170-172.

1600   Giannone, Richard J. "Eliot's 'Portrait of a Lady' and
       Pound's 'Portrait d'une Femme,'" TCL, 5 (October, 1959),
       131-134.

1601   Grieder, Josephine. "Robert Frost on Ezra Pound, 1913:
       Manuscript Corrections of 'Portrait d'une Femme,'" NEQ, 44
       (June, 1971), 301-305.

1602   Hagelstango, Rudolf. "Ezra Pound und die fallstricke der
       Politik," Suddeutsche Zeitung (July 24/25, 1954).

PROFILE

1603   Arns, K. "How to Read," Deutsche Schulzeitung. Hannover:
       1931, pp. 307-308.

1604 _____. "Profile," Englische Studien, 69 (1934), 281-282.

1605 Parkes, H. B. "Two Pounds of Poetry," New English Weekly,
      2 (December 22, 1932), 227-228.

PROVENÇA

1606 Dell, Floyd. "Provença," Ezra Pound: The Critical Heritage.
      Eric Homberger, ed. Cf., #1545, pp. 70-72.

1607 _____. "Friday Literary Review," Chicago Evening Post,
      (January 6, 1911), p. 5.

1608 Mencken, H. L. "Provença," Review in Smart Set (April,
      1911), Repr., in Ezra Pound: The Critical Heritage. Eric
      Homberger, ed., Cf., #1545, pp. 73-74.

1609 Nolte, William H., ed. H. L. Mencken's Smart Set Criticism.
      Cornell U. Pr., 1969, pp. 76-78.

1610 Stock, Noel. "Provença," The Life of Ezra Pound. Cf.,
      #127, pp. 80, 90, 92-93.

1611 Tanselle, G. Thomas. "Two Early Letters of Ezra Pound,"
      AL, 34, #1 (March, 1962), 114-119.

THE RETURN

1612 Deutsch, Babette. "The Return," Poetry in Our Time. New
      York: Henry Holt & Co., 1952, pp. 124-125.

1613 "Experiment in Verse--'The Return,'" TLS (August 17,
      1956), Special Number, #3.

1614 Friar, Kimon, and John Malcolm Brinnin, eds. "The Re-
      turn," Modern Poetry. New York: Appleton-Century-
      Crofts, 1951, pp. 138, 531.

1615 Israel, Calvin. "Imitation and Meaning in Ezra Pound's 'The
      Return,'" LHR, 8 (1966), 31-36.

1616 Kenner, Hugh. "The Return," Cf., #738, p. 122.

1617   M. M.   "Pound's 'Return,'" Expl, 12, #3 (December, 1953),
       Q. 1.

1618   Rosenthal, M. L.   "The Return," The Modern Poets, Cf.,
       #911, pp. 51-53.

1619   Taupin, René.   L'Influence de Symbolisme Français sur la
       Poèsie Américaine, (de 1910 à 1920).   Paris: 1929, pp. 114,
       133-158.

RIPOSTES

1620   Alden, Raymond Macdonald.   "The New Poetry," Nation, 96
       (April 17, 1913), 386-387.

1621   Bell, Ian F. A.   "Pound's 'Silet,'" Expl, 38, #4 (Summer,
       1980), 14-16.

1622   Child, Harold.   Ripostes.   Review.   TLS (December 12,
       1912).

1623   Flint, F. S.   "The 'Ripostes' of Ezra Pound with 'The Com-
       plete Poetical Works' of T. E. Hulme," Poetry and Drama, I,
       #1 (March, 1913), 60-62.

1624   Ingber, Richard Geoffrey.   "Ezra Pound and the Classical
       Tradition Backgrounds and Formative Influences," DAI, 44,
       #9 (U. of Toronto: Canada, 1983), 2759A.

1625   Kenner, Hugh.   "Ripostes," The Pound Era, Cf., #732,
       passim.

1626   Monroe, Harriet.   "In Defense of Poetry," Dial, 54 (May 16,
       1913), 106-107, 409.

1627   _____.   A Poet's Life, Cf., #86, passim.

1628   Rice, Wallace.   "Pound and Poetry," Dial, 54 (May 1, 1913),
       370-371.

1629   Witemeyer, Hugh.   "Ripostes: Recapitulations and Innova-
       tions," Cf., #1422, pp. 140-121.

SEAFARER

1630 Adams, S. J. "A Case for Pound's Seafarer," Mosaic, 9, #2
      (Winter, 1976), 127-146.

1631 Alexander, Michael. "Ezra Pound's 'Seafarer,'" Agenda, 13,
      iv-14; i (Winter, 1975; Spring, 1976), 110-126.

1632 Bessinger, J. B. "The Oral Text of Ezra Pound's 'The Sea-
      farer,'" QJS, 47 (April, 1961), 173-177.

1633 Chaplin, Sherry. "Pound's Seafarer: An Assessment of
      Value," UES, 15, #2 (1977), 42-45.

1634 Herzbrun, Philip. "Mr. Pound and The Seafarer," TLS
      (August 20, 1954), 529. [Letter concerning "The Greatness
      of Criticism," TLS (May 28, 1954).]

1635 Hesse, Eva, ed., with Introduction. New Approaches to
      Ezra Pound, Cf., #41, pp. 35, 332-334, passim.

1636 Kenner, Hugh. The Poetry of Ezra Pound, Cf., #738, pp.
      134, 140, 316.

1637 _____. The Pound Era, Cf., #732, pp. 349-354, passim.

1638 _____. "Song's Sooth Reckoned," Poetry, 111, #6 (March,
      1968), 395-399.

1639 Lucas, F. L. Criticism and Poetry. (The Wharton Lecture,
      British Academy) Oxford U. Pr., 1933.

1640 _____. "Translation," TLS (September 10, 1954), 573.
      [Letter has mention of Pound's Seafarer]

1641 Robinson, Fred C. "'Might of the North': Pound's Anglo-
      Saxon Studies and The Seafarer," YR, 71, #2 (Winter, 1982),
      199-224.

1642 Sarang, Vilas. "Pound's Seafarer," CP, 6, #2 (Fall, 1973),
      5-11.

1643 Savoia, Dianella. "Traduzione e poesia nel Seafarer di Ezra
      Pound," Contributi dell'Instituto di filologia moderna. Sergio
      Rossi, ed. Milano: Vita e Pensiero. U. of Cattolica, 1974,
      pp. 210-238.

1644 Sisam, Kenneth. "Mr. Pound and the Seafarer," TLS (June
      25, 1954), 409.

1645 Sutherland, James R. "Mr. Pound and 'The Seafarer,'"
      TLS, (July 9, 1954), 447. [Reply to Kenneth Sisam, TLS
      (June 25, 1954).]

                    SELECTED POEMS (1928; 1949)

1646 Bowra, C. M. "More Cantos from Ezra Pound," NS&N, 38
      (September 3, 1949), 250.

1647 Burford, William. "On Louis Coxe's Review of Ezra Pound,"
      Poetry, 92, #3 (June, 1958), 195-196.

1648 Cole, Thomas. "Ends and Means," Imagi, 5 (1949), 11.

1649 Coxe, Louis O. "Temperament and Subject," Poetry, 91, #6
      (March, 1958), 389-393; repr., Discussion, 92 (June, 1958),
      195-197.

1650 Duncan, Robert. "On Louis Coxe's Review of Ezra Pound,"
      Poetry, 92, #3 (June, 1958), 196-197.

1651 Eliot, T. S. "Introduction," Selected Poems (by Ezra
      Pound). London: Faber & Gwyer, 1928, pp. vii-xxv.

1652 Espey, John. "Ezra Pound: 'Selected Poems,'" Fifteen
      Modern American Authors. Jackson R. Bryer, ed. Cf.,
      #1433, p. 324.

1653 _____. "Ezra Pound: 'Selected Poems,'" Sixteen Modern
      American Authors. Jackson R. Bryer, ed., Cf., 1434,
      p. 446.

1654 Ferril, Thomas Harnsby. Review: Selected Poems. San
      Francisco Chronicle (January 8, 1950), 25.

1655 Fletcher, John Gould. Review: "Selected Poems," Cf., #618.

1656 Froula, Christine. A Guide to Ezra Pound's "Selected Poems."
      New York: New Directions, 1983.

1657 Lucas, F. L. "The Criticism of Poetry," (Warton Lecture on
      English Poetry). Proceedings of the British Academy. Lon-
      don: Oxford U. Pr., 1933, pp. 171-172.

1658 McDonald, Gerald. Review: Selected Poems. Library Jour-
      nal, 74 (December 15, 1949), 1909.

1659   Meyer, G. P. "A Sampling of Pound and Modern Man,"
       SatRL, 32 (December 24, 1949). 14.

1660   Roberts, Michael. "Ezra Pound's Unpopularity," NEW, 1
       (May 5, 1932), 67-69.

1661   Roskolenko, Harry. "What Manner of Man Is This?" Voices,
       141 (1950), 41-43.

1662   Russell, Peter. Review: Selected Poems. WorldRev, 7
       (September, 1949), 76.

SELECTED PROSE, 1909-1965

1663   Cookson, William, ed. Introduction. Selected Prose, 1909-
       1965. New York: New Directions, 1973.

1664   Read, Forrest. Review: Ezra Pound: Selected Prose, 1909-
       1965. Paideuma, 3, #1 (Spring, 1974), 125-128.

SEPARATION ON THE RIVER KIANG

1665   Graham, D. B. "From Chinese to English: Ezra Pound's
       'Separation on the River Kiang,'" LE&W, 13 (June, 1969),
       182-195.

1666   Meyer, William J. "The Imagist and the Translator: Ezra
       Pound's 'Separation on the River Kiang,'" Sou'wester (So.
       Ill. U), (October 30, 1970), 72-80.

THE SPIRIT OF ROMANCE

1667   Coffman, Stanley K., Jr. Review: Spirit of Romance. BA,
       27, #4 (Autumn, 1953), 385.

1668   Espey, "Ezra Pound: 'Spirit of Romance,'" Fifteen Modern
       American Authors, Cf., #1433, p. 324; Cf., #1434, p. 446.

1669   Halsband, Robert. "Pound Revisited," SatRL, 36, #19 (May
       9, 1953), 47-48.

1670 Kenner, Hugh. "Pound and the Provision of Measures,"
      Poetry, 83, #1 (October, 1953), 29-35.

1671 Littlefield, Walter. Review: The Spirit of Romance, NYT
      (November 17, 1910), 714.

1672 "Pound Revisited," Review: The Spirit of Romance, SatRL,
      36 (May 9, 1953), 47-48.

1673 "The Spirit of Romance," Review: NY, 29 (May 23, 1953),
      138.

1674 Stern, Richard G. "Pound as Translator," Accent, 13, #4
      (Autumn, 1953), 265-268.

1675 Thomas, Edward. Review: "The Spirit of Romance," Morning
      Post (August 1, 1910); repr., Ezra Pound: The Critical
      Heritage. Eric Homberger, ed. Cf., #1545, pp. 68-69.

                    LE TESTAMENT DE VILLON

1676 Antheil, George. "Salons de Paris," Bad Boy of Music.
      Garden City, New York: Doubleday, Dorn & Co., 1945,
      pp. 117-123.

1677 _____. "Why a Poet Quit the Muses," Paideuma, 2, #1
      (Spring, 1973), 3-6.

1678 Hughes, Robert. "Ezra Pound's Opera: Le Testament de
      Villon," Paideuma, 2, #1 (Spring, 1973), 11-16.

1679 Lucas, John. "'Villon'--Made New and Well," CaM, 13
      (1973), 78-84.

1680 Lyall, Larry. "Pound/Villon: Le Testament de François
      Villon," Paideuma, 2, #1 (1973), 17-22.

1681 Rodker, John. "Pound's 'Villon' on the Radio," Transatlantic-
      Rev, I, #4 (Winter, 1931), 389.

1682 Straus, H. "American Music via Europe," Nation, 119 (Sep-
      tember 10, 1924), 268.

THE TRANSLATIONS

1683 Alvarez, A[lfred]. "Ezra Pound: The Qualities and Limitations of Translation-Poetry," EIC, 6 (1956), 171-189.

1684 Davie, Donald. "Translation Absolute," NS&N, 46 (September 5, 1953), 262.

1685 De Schloezer, Boris. "Stravinsky: His Technique," (Trans. by Ezra Pound), Dial, 86 (1929), 9-26, passim.

1686 Dudek, Louis. Review: The Translations, CIV/n, No. 4 (Montreal: 1953), 17-18.

1687 Edwards, John. "Pound's Translations," Poetry, 83, #4 (January, 1954), 233-238.

1688 Ferlinghetti, Lawrence. "Among the New Books," San Francisco Chronicle, (October 4, 1953), 26.

1689 Fiedler, Leslie. "Sufficient Unto the Day," PR, 22 (Winter, 1955), 118-122; repr., in Partisan Review Anthology. William Phillips and Philip Rahv, eds. New York: Holt, Rinehart & Winston, 1962, pp. 457-459.

1690 Fitts, Dudley. "The Tea-Shop Aura," NR, 130 (January 4, 1954), 18-19.

1691 Graham, Stephen. "Pound Sterling," Poetry Review, 44, #4 (October-December, 1953), 472-473.

1692 Guenther, Charles. "Eloquent Scholarship," St. Louis Post-Dispatch, (November 30, 1953), 2E.

1693 Haley, Martin. Review: Translations, TC (Australia), (Autumn, 1954).

1694 Keith, Nobuko Tsukui. "Aoi no Ue and Kinuta: An Examination of Ezra Pound's Translations," Paideuma, 8 (1979), 199-214.

1695 Kenner, Hugh. "Introduction." The Translations of Ezra Pound. London: Faber; New York: New Directions, 1953.

1696 McNaughton, William. "Pound's Translations and Chinese Melopoeia," TQ, 10, #4 (Winter, 1967), 52-56.

1697 Muir, Edwin. "New Poems for Old," Observer (August 2, 1953).

1698 Murphy, Richard. "The Art of a Translator," Spectator, 190
      (September 18, 1953), 303-304.

1699 Sontag, Susan. "Translation as Art," New Leader (June 28,
      1954), 26-27.

1700 Stern, Richard G. "Pound as Translator," Cf., #1674.

1701 Stevenson, Anne. Review: "The Translations." Michigan
      Daily, (March 4, 1954).

1702 "Translations." Review: New Yorker, 30 (May 1, 1954), 112.

1703 Ward, Charlotte, ed. "Translations," IowaR, 12, #1 (Winter,
      1981), 37-49.

1704 Whicher, George F. Review: "Translations," AL, 26, #1
      (March, 1954), 119-121.

1705 _____. "Translations and Poetry," NY Herald Tribune
      Book Review (October 25, 1953). 25.

      THE UNWOBBLING PIVOT and THE GREAT DIGEST

1706 Breit, Harvey. "Repeat Performances Approved," NYT Bk.
      Rev., (February 3, 1952), 29.

1707 Chan, Wing-tsit. "The Unwobbling Pivot and The Great
      Digest," Philosophy, East & West, 3, #4 (January, 1954),
      371-373.

1708 Fang, Achilles. "Metaphysics and Money-Making," Cf.,
      #1534.

1709 Ferlinghetti, Lawrence. "Poetry Shelf," San Francisco
      Chronicle (February 3, 1952), 27.

1710 Raine, Kathleen. "There Is No Trifling," Cf., #1161.

1711 Tay, William. "Between Kung and Eleusis: Li Chi, The
      Eleusinian Rites, Erigena and Ezra Pound," Paideuma, 4, #1
      (Spring, 1975), 37-54.

1712 _____. "Cheng Ming: The New Paideuma of Ezra Pound,"
      Asian Cult, 7 (1979), 29-46.

1713 "The Unwobbling Pivot." NY, 28 (May 31, 1952), 98.

1714   "The Unwobbling Pivot," San Francisco Chinese World (January 21, 1954), (English Section), p. 2.

WOMEN OF TRACHIS

1715   Bowra, C. M. "The Women of Trachis: A Symposium," Pound Newsletter, 2 (January, 1955), 3-8.

1716   Dick, Bernard F. "Sophocles Com-Pounded," Classical World, 54 (1961), 236-237.

1717   Donoghue, Denis. "Ezra Pound and Women of Trachis," The Third Voice: Modern British and American Verse Drama. Princeton, N.J.: Princeton U. Pr., 1959, pp. 213-222.

1718   Earp, F. R. "The Women of Trachis: A Symposium," Pound Newsletter, 5 (January, 1955), 3-8.

1719   Eliot, T. S. "The Women of Trachis," Cf., #1718.

1720   Espey, John. "Ezra Pound--'Women of Trachis,'" Cf., #1433, pp. 340-341.

1721   _____. "Ezra Pound: Women of Trachis," Cf., #1434, pp. 462-463.

1722   Goacher, Denis. "The Critics and the Master," European, 15 (May, 1954), 24-37.

1723   _____. "Notes from Abroad: London," Shenandoah, 6, #1 (Winter, 1954), 84-87.

1724   Ingber, Richard. "Ezra Pound's Women of Trachis: A Song for the Muses' Garden," AmS, 23 (1978), 131-146.

1725   Kenner, Hugh. "Some Elders," Poetry, 83, #6 (March, 1954), 357-366.

1726   _____. "Homage to Musonius," Cf., #1211.

1727   Lattimore, Richmond. "The Women of Trachis: A Symposium," Cf., #1718.

1728   Levi, Peter. "Ezra Pound's Translation of Sophokles' Women of Trachis," Agenda, 7, #1 (1969), 17-22.

1729   _____. "Pound and the Classics," Cf., #777.

1730   Mason, H. A.   "The Women of Trachis," Arion, 2 (1963),
        59-81, 105-121; revised version, Cambridge Qt, 4 (1969),
        244-272.

1731   "Melpomene in the West," TLS (August 27, 1954), 537-538.

1732   Pasquier, Marie-Claire, tr.   "Les Femmes de Trachis," CRB,
        103 (1982), 67-150.

1733   Peachy, Frederic.   "The Women of Trachis: A Symposium,"
        Pound Newsletter, 5 (January, 1955), 3-8.

1734   "Pound Takes on Sophocles: Women of Trachis Staged,"
        The Times, (November 23, 1962), p. 16, col. 7.

1735   Slavitt, David.   "Eliot, Pound Played in Three Quarter
        Round," Yale Daily News (March 24, 1955), 8. (Review of
        the Yale performance of the Women of Trachis, March 23-25,
        1955.)

1736   Sutherland, Donald.   "Ezra Pound or Sophocles," ColQ, 8,
        #2 (Autumn, 1959), 182-191.

1737   Trewin, J. C.   "Women of Trachis," Review of Performance.
        Listener, 51 (April 29, 1954), 755.

III. SUPPLEMENTAL WORKS

ABC OF ECONOMICS

1738 Coulter, John W. "Reviews," Adelphi (May 6, 1933), 142-144.

1739 Gregory, Horace. "The ABC of Ezra Pound," Poetry, 46 (August, 1935), 279-285.

1740 Hazlitt, Henry. "Studies in Money and Power," New York Times (April 7, 1940), 22.

1741 Healy, J. V. "The Pound Problem," Cf., #1274.

ABC OF READING

1742 Arvin, Newton. "Primer for Pedants," NR, 82 (February 20, 1935), 54.

1743 B[regy], K[atherine]. Review of ABC of Reading, Catholic World, 140 (December, 1934), 371.

1744 Bridson, D. G. "ABC OF READING," Criterion, 14 (October, 1934), 123-125.

1745 Brown, Ivor. "Ezra Pound Speaks," Springfield Republican, 22 (July, 1934), 7e.

1746 Burke, Kenneth. "Gastronomy of Letters," Nation, 139 (October, 1934), 458-459.

1747 Deutsch, Babette. "With Seven League Boots," New York Herald Tribune (November 25, 1934), 18.

1748 Gregory, Horace. "The ABC of Ezra Pound," Cf., #1739.

1749 _____. "Pound as Essayist," Yale Review, 24 (March, 1935), 608-610.

1750 Haley, Martin. "Ezra Pound as Literary Teacher Writes Sensibly," Advocate (Melbourne), (August 26, 1954), 9.

1751 Halsband, Robert. "Belles-Lettres Notes," SatRL, 34 (July 14, 1951), 48.

1752 John, K. "Mr. Pound's Exhibits," NSt&N, 7 (June 23, 1934), 952.

1753 Mairet, Philip. Review: ABC of Reading. New English Weekly (June 14, 1934).

1754 Palmer, Leslie H. "Matthew Arnold and Ezra Pound's ABC of Reading," Paideuma, 2, #2 (Fall, 1973), 193-198.

1755 Peel, Robert. Review: ABC of Reading, CSMM (October 31, 1934), 12.

1756 Peschman, Herman. "ABC of Reading," Poetry Review, 42, #5 (September-October, 1951), pp. 273-275.

1757 Rainer, Dachine. "ABC of Reading," Retort, 5 (1951), 48.

1758 Ransom, John Crowe. "ABC of Reading," SatRL, 11 (January 19, 1935), 434-435.

1759 Sjostrand, Osten. "Konsten all lasa," Morgon-Tindningen (Stockholm) (August 1, 1951).

THE ALCHEMIST

1760 Materer, Timothy. "Ezra Pound and the Alchemy of the Word," JML, 11, #1 (March, 1984), 109-124.

1761 Rosenthal, M[achia], L[ouis]. "The Alchemist--Ezra Pound: The Poet as Hero," The Modern Poets: A Critical Introduction. Cf., #911, p. 53.

A LUME SPENTO

1762 Accrocca, E. F. "'A Lume Spento' di Ezra Pound, nel cinquantenario del primo libro," FLe, 13 (November 16, 1958), 1-2.

1763   Diesendorf, Margaret.   Cf., #31.

1764   Falck, Colin.   "A Lume Spento," Encounter, 27 (August,
       1966), 82.

1765   Levi, Peter, S. J.   "Ezra Pound Assessed," Jubilee, 13, #10
       (February, 1966), 56-57.

1766   Schmidt, Gerd.   "Pound's 'In Epitaphium Eius,'" Expl, 40,
       #3 (Spring, 1982), 44-45.

ANTHEIL AND THE TREATISE ON HARMONY

1767   Engel, Carl.   "Views and Reviews," Musical Quarterly, 12,
       #4 (October, 1926), 631-641.

1768   Frank, Mortimer H.   "Ezra Pound's Musical Excursions," UWR,
       15, i-ii (1979-80), 5-12.

1769   Haggin, Bernard H.   "Antheil and the Treatise on Harmony,
       with Supplementary Notes," Music in the Nation.   New York:
       Wm. Sloane Associates, Inc., 1949, pp. 325-327.

1770   Robinson, E.   "Antheil," NY Evening Post (November 5,
       1927), 12.

1771   Rorem, Ned.   "Introduction," Antheil and the Treatise on
       Harmony by Ezra Pound.   New York: Da Capo Pr., 1968,
       pp. 1-16.

1772   Schafer, Murray.   "Ezra Pound and Music," Cf., #919.

THE APPROACH TO PARIS

1773   Hutchins, Patricia.   "Ezra Pound's Approach to Paris," SoR,
       6, #2 (New Series), (April, 1970), 340-355.

THE BALLAD OF THE GOODLY FERE

1774   Abad, Gemino H.   "Ballad of the Goodly Fere," A Formal

Approach to Lyric Poetry. Quezon City, Philippines: U. of
Philippines Pr., 1978, pp. 168-169, 172-173, passim.

1775 Buxbaum, Katherine. "Ezra Pound's 'Ballad of the Goodly
Fere,'" Poet's Lore, 40 (Spring, 1929), 142-143.

1776 Hughes, Glenn. "Ezra Pound: 'Ballad of the Goodly Fere,'"
Imagism and the Imagists: A Study in Modern Poetry. New
York: Humanities Pr., 1960, pp. 230-231.

1777 Link, Franz H. "Two Notes on the Early Poetry," Paideuma,
7 (Fall, 1978), 185-186.

1778 Mencken, H. L. "Ezra Pound," H. L. Mencken's Smart Set
Criticism. Sel., and ed., by William H. Nolte. Ithaca, New
York: Cornell U. Pr., 1968, pp. 77-78.

1779 Riding, Laura, and Robert Graves. "Ballad of the Goodly
Fere," A Survey of Modernist Poetry. New York: Doubleday, Doran & Co., 1928, pp. 140-142.

1780 Schneidau, Herbert N. "Style and Sacrament in Modernist
Writing," GeorgiaRev, 31, #2 (Summer, 1977), 427-452.

1781 Tanselle, G. Thomas. ["Ballad of the Goodly Fere"], "Two
Early Letters of Ezra Pound," AL, 34, #1 (March, 1962),
114-119.

BLANDULA, TENELLA, VAGULA

1782 McDougal, Stuart. "The Presence of Pater in 'Blandula,
Tenella, Vagula," Paideuma, 4, 2&3 (Fall-Winter, 1975), 317-
321.

1783 Thomas, Ronald. "Catullus, Flaminius, and Pound in 'Blandula, Tenella, Vagula," Cf., #1491.

IV. GENERAL CRITICISM

1784 Aaron, Daniel. Writers on the Left: Episodes in American Literary Communism. New York: Harcourt, Brace & World, 1961, 114-116, 201-202, passim.

1785 Abbs, Peter, ed. The Black Rainbow: Essays on the Present Breakdown of a Culture. London: Heineman, 1975, passim.

1786 Abse, Dannie. "Ezra Pound," [Poem about Ezra Pound], Commentary, 26 (November, 1958), 410.

1787 _____. "Ezra Pound and My Father," TC, 176 (1st Qt., 1968), 42-44.

1788 Accrocca, Elio Filippo. "Pound e l'ideogramma," Stagione, 2, #7 (Rome: 1955), 4.

1789 Ackroyd, Peter. Ezra Pound and His World. Cf., #1.

1790 Adams, Robert M. "A Hawk and a Handsaw for Ezra Pound," Accent, 8 (Summer, 1948), 205-214.

1791 _____. "The Pound in Your Pocket," Review: Ezra Pound by Donald Davie. TLS (February 6, 1976), 128-129.

1792 Adams, Stephen J. "Ezra Pound and Music," DAI, Cf., #429.

1793 _____. "Ezra Pound and Provencal Melopoeia," FDP, 2 (1978), 27-48.

1794 _____. "More on Pound," CRevAS, 13, #2 (Fall, 1982), 245-251.

1795 _____. "Musical Neofism: Pound's Theory of Harmony in Context," Mosaic, 13, #2 (Winter, 1980), 49-69.

1796 _____. "Pound, Olga Rudge, and the 'Risveglio Vivaldiano,'" Paideuma, 4, #1 (Spring, 1975), 111-118.

1797 _____. "Pound's Quantities and 'Absolute Rhythm,'" ELWIU, 4 (1977), 95-109.

1798 _____. "T. S. Eliot's So-Called Sestina: A Note on 'The Dry Salvages,' II," ELN, 15, #3 (March, 1978), 203-208.

1799   Agresti, Olivia Rosetti. "The Ambassador," Pound Newsletter, #8 (October, 1955), 19-20.

1800   _____. "Ezra Pound: A Tribute," Civ/n (Canada), 6 (1954), 25-27.

1801   _____. "Ricordo di Ezra Pound," Il Secolo d'Italia (December 1, 1953), 3.

1802   Aiken, Conrad. "Ezra Pound: 1914," Ezra Pound: Perspectives. Cf., #125, pp. 2-6.

1803   _____. "The Place of Imagism," NR, 3, #29 (May 22, 1915), 75-76.   .

1804   _____. "A Pointless Pointillist: Ezra Pound," Cf., #1543, pp. 136-142.

1805   _____. "Ezra Pound," Reviewer's ABC, Cf., #260, pp. 323-327.

1806   _____. Selected Letters of Conrad Aiken. Joseph Killorin, ed. New Haven and London: Yale U. Pr., 1978, pp. 21-23, passim.

1807   Aldington, Richard. "The Art of Poetry," Dial, 69 (August, 1920), 168-180.

1808   _____. "Blast," Egoist, 1 (July 15, 1914), 272-273.

1809   _____. "A Book for Literary Philosophers," Poetry, 16 (July, 1920), 213-216.

1810   _____. "Des Imagistes," SatRL, 21 (March 16, 1940), 3-4.

1811   _____. "Des Imagistes," The Saturday Review Gallery. New York: Simon & Schuster, 1959, pp. 269-275.

1812   _____. Ezra Pound and T. S. Eliot: A Lecture. Hurst, Berkshire: The Peacocks Pr., 1954.

1813   _____. Ezra Pound: Perspectives. Noel Stock, ed., Cf., #125, pp. 122-124.

1814   _____. "Farewell to Europe," AtlM, 166 (October, 1940), 518-530.

1815   _____. Life for Life's Sake. New York: Viking Pr., Inc., 1941, pp. 134-135.

1816   _____. "Modern Poetry and the Imagists," Egoist, I, ii (June 1, 1914), 201-203.

1817 _____. "Penultimate Poetry: Xenophilometropolitania," Egoist, I, 2 (January 15, 1914), 36.

1818 _____. Literary Studies and Reviews. London; New York: Allen & Unwin, and Dial Press, 1924; repr., Books for Libraries Pr., 1968.

1819 _____. "The Poetry of Ezra Pound," Egoist, 2 (May 1, 1915), 71-72.

1820 Aleksic, Branko. "X-Ray Pound i poetika imazizma," Izraz, 42 (1977), 1202-1231.

1821 Alexander, Michael. The Poetic Achievement of Ezra Pound. Cf., #432.

1822 _____. "Two Reviews," Agenda, 17, #3-4, and 18, #1 (Autumn-Winter-Spring, 1979-80), 122-129.

1823 Alpert, Barry S. "Ezra Pound, John Price, and The Exile," Paideuma, 2, #3 (Winter, 1973), 427-448.

1824 _____. "Permanence and Violence: Ezra Pound, The English Review, and BLAST," Occident, 8 (Spring, 1974), 80-96.

1825 _____. "The Unexamined Art: Ezra Pound and the Aesthetic Mode of the Little Magazine," DAI, 32 (Stanford: 1971), 5771A.

1826 Alsterlund, B. "Ezra Pound," Wilson Library Bulletin, 20 (January, 1946), 326.

1827 _____. "Newsmen and Their Wares," Wilson Library Bulletin, 18 (September, 1943), 6.

1828 Altieri, Charles. "Objective Image and Act of Mind in Modern Poetry," PMLA, 91 (1976), 101-114.

1829 Alvarez, A[lfred]. "Ezra Pound: Craft and Morals," The Shaping Spirit: Studies in Modern English and American Poets. London: Chatto & Windus, 1958; American Edition, entitled Stewards of Excellence. New York: Scribner, 1971.

1830 _____. "Ezra Pound: The Qualities and Limitations of Translation-Poetry," Cf., #1683.

1831 _____. "Two Faces of Pound," Observer (March 6, 1960).

1832 Amaral, José Vazquez. "Ezra Pound: Poeta del mundo nuevo," Universidad de Mexico, 8, #11 (July, 1954), 9-11.

1833 _____. "Notes from Abroad," Shenandoah, 6, #2 (Spring, 1955), 88-89.

1834 _____. "Words from Ezra Pound," Cf., #1066.

1835 Amdur, Alice Steiner. The Poetry of Ezra Pound. Cambridge, Mass., 1936; New York: Russell & Russell, 1966.

1836 Anant, Victor. "'Pop' Fiction," London Spectator, 14 (February, 1958), 197-198.

1837 Anceschi, Luciano. "Ezra Insegna Ancora," Stagione, 2, #7 (Rome: 1955), 3.

1838 _____. "Ezra Pound y el humanismo Americano," Cuadernos Hispanoamericanos, 32 and 35 (Madrid: August-November, 1953).

1839 _____. "Palinsesti del Protoumanesimo americano," Litteratura Arte Contemporanea (August, 1950), 34-44; (December, 1950), 30-38.

1840 _____. "Palinsesti del protoumanesimo poetico Americano," Poetica americana e altri studi contemporanei de poetica. Pisa: Nistri-Lischi, 1953, pp. 13-50, 131-133.

1841 Anderson, David. "Breaking the Silence: The Interview of Vanni Ronsisvalle and Pier Paolo Pasolini with Ezra Pound in 1968," Paideuma, 10, #2 (Fall, 1981), 331-345.

1842 _____. "Rapallo, 1941," Paideuma, 8 (1979), 431-442.

1843 Anderson, Margaret. My Thirty Years' War. New York: Covici, Friede, 1930, pp. 158-172, 174-175.

1844 Angoff, Allan, ed. "The Poems of Ezra Pound," American Writing Today: Its Independence and Vigor. New York: New York U. Pr., 1957, pp. 305-360.

1845 Angoff, Charles. "The Mystique of The Smart Set," Literary Review, 11, #1 (Autumn, 1967), 49-60.

1846 Antheil, George. "Salons de Paris," Bad Boy of Music. New York: Doubleday, Doran & Co., Inc., 1945, pp. 117-123.

1847 _____. "Why a Poet Quit the Muses," Paideuma, 2 (Spring, 1973), 3-6.

1848 Antonini, A. "A Lume Spento," Book News Monthly, 27 (May, 1909), 719.

1849 Apter, Ronnie Susan. "Creative Translation: The Influence
      of Ezra Pound on the Translation of Poetry," DAI, 40, #12,
      Part 1 (Fordham: 1980), 6285A.

1850 Arce, Armando Uribe. "Pound," Santiago: Centro de In-
      vestigaciones de Literatura Comparada de la Universidad de
      Chile. [1963]. Rev. by Bernard F. Engel, AL, 37, #1
      (March, 1965), 89-90.

1851 Arendt, Hannah. Men in Dark Times. New York: Harcourt,
      Brace & World, 1968, pp. 211-212.

1852 Armanini, Ante. "Ezra Pound," Delo, 22, #10 (1976), 91-109.

1853 Ashleigh, Charles. "Des Imagistes," Little Review, 1 (July,
      1914), 15-17.

1854 Avedon, Richard, and Truman Capote. "Observations on
      Ezra Pound," Cf., #17, pp. 74, 76.

1855 Awiszus, Sabine. "Kurg in Venedig: Die Erscheinung Ezra
      Pounds," Vergleichen und Verändern. Festschrift für Helmut
      Motekat. Albrecht Goetze and Pflaum Gunther, eds. München:
      Hueber, 1970, pp. 385-393.

1856 _____. "The Poet Professorially Examined," Agenda, 17,
      #2 (1979), 64-67.

1857 _____. "Statements on Pound's Prose," Agenda, 17, #3-4;
      18, #1 (Autumn-Winter-Spring, 1979-80), 266-272.

1858 Axelrod, Steven Gould. Robert Lowell: Life and Art. Cf.,
      #434.

1859 Ayscough, Florence, and Amy Lowell. Correspondence of a
      Friendship. Harley F. MacNair, ed. Chicago: U. of Chicago
      Pr., 1945, pp. 253-256.

1860 Baar, Ron. "Ezra Pound: Poet as Historian," Cf., #435.

1861 Bab, Julius. [Essay on Pound]. Amerikas Dichter der
      Gegenwart. Berlin: Christian Verlag, 1951, pp. 128-134.

1862 Bacigalupo, Massimo. The Forméd Trace: The Later Poetry
      of Ezra Pound. Cf., #437.

1863 _____. "The Later Pound, [Ezra Pound's Poetry, 1945-
      1960]," DAI, 36, #5 (Columbia U.: 1975), 2817-2818A.

1864 Baconsky, A. E. "Ezra Pound," Panorama Poeziei universale
      contemporane. [The scene of the world contemporary poetry.]
      Burcuresti: Albatros, 1972, pp. 629-632.

1865 Bailey, Bruce. "T. S. Eliot's The Waste Land in Parody,
      Travesty, and Satire," Yeats-Eliot Review, 5, #1 (1978), 3.

1866 Baisch, Dorothy R. "Ezra Pound," London Literary Circles,
      1910-1920, with Special Reference to Ford Madox Ford, Ezra
      Pound, D. H. Lawrence, and Virginia Woolf. Diss. Cornell
      U., 1950.

1867 Baker, Carlos. "Pound in Venice, 1965," Cf., #3.

1868 Baldner, Ralph W. "Ezra Pound: Image of Theophile Gautier,"
      ArQ, 14, #3 (Autumn, 1958), 246-256.

1869 Banerjee, Ron D. K. "Dante Through the Looking Glass:
      Rossetti, Pound, and Eliot," CL, 24, #2 (Spring, 1972), 136-
      149.

1870 Barbour, Douglas. "Ezra Pound's Legacy: 'What Thou Lovest
      Well Remains,'" QQ, 80 (Autumn, 1973), 450-454.

1871 Barbour, Linda Lee. "Lyric Definition: Poetry as Definitive
      Play," DAI, 43, #9 (U. of Calif., Irvine: 1982), 2987A.

1872 Barfoot, Gabriels. "Dante in T. S. Eliot's Criticism," EM, 23
      (1972), 231-246.

1873 _____. "The Theme of Usury in Dante and Pound," RLMC,
      30 (1977), 254-283.

1874 Barilli, Renato. Poetica e Retorica. Milano: Mursia, 1969.

1875 Barnard, Harry. "The Lost Liberals," Cw, 56, #8 (May 30,
      1952), 198-199. (Cf., Peter Viereck, "Symbols: Hiss and
      Pound," Cf., #251.)

1876 Barnard, Mary. "A Communication on Greek Metric, Ezra
      Pound, and Sappho," Agenda, 16, #3-4 (1978-79), 62-68.

1877 Barricalli, Gian Piero. "A Poet of a Poet: Comments on
      Pound's Translation of Leopardi's 'Sopra il Ritratto di una
      Bella Donna,'" IQ, 16:64 (July, 1973), 68-75.

1878 Barry, Elaine. "Frost's Comments on Pound," Cf., #1599,
      pp. 170-172.

1879 Barry, Iris. "The Ezra Pound Period," Bookman, 74, #2
      (October, 1931), 159-171.

1880 Batavia, Ludovico von. "USA--Botschaft, Schwedische
      Akademie: zu Ezra Pound und dem nobel-Preis [American
      Ambassador, Swedish Academy: of Ezra Pound and the Nobel
      Prize], Diagnole, 8 (1969), 28-31.

1881   Bates, Eveline. "Ezra Pound and the Critics," ChR, 24, #4
       (Spring, 1973), 108-115.

1882   Bates, Margaret. "Ezra Pound: Maker of Connections,"
       Paideuma, 6 (1977), 114-115.

1883   Baumann, Walter, "Carleton, Paquin and Salzburg," Paideuma,
       11, #3 (Winter, 1982), 442-445.

1884   _____. "Ezra Pound and Magic: Old World Tricks in a
       New World Poem," Paideuma, 10, #2 (Fall, 1981), 209-224.

1885   _____. "Gerhart--with the Standebuch of Sachs in Yr/
       Luggage," Paideuma, 10, #3 (Winter, 1981), 589-594.

1886   _____. "Pound and Layamon's Brut," JEGP, 68, #2 (April,
       1969), 265-276.

1887   _____. "Secretary of Nature, J. Heydon," New Approaches
       to Ezra Pound. Eva Hesse, ed., Cf., #41, pp. 303-318.

1888   Beach, Joseph Warren. "Ezra Pound," Obsessive Images:
       Symbolism in Poetry of the 1930's and 1940's. Minneapolis,
       Minn.: Lund Pr., Inc., 1960, passim.

1889   _____. "Pound, the Imagists, Sandburg," Concept of
       Nature in Nineteenth-Century English Poetry. New York:
       Pageant Book Co., 1956, pp. 547-559.

1890   Beach, Sylvia. "Mr. and Mrs. Pound," Shakespeare and
       Company. London; New York: Harcourt, Brace & Co.,
       1959, pp. 26-27, passim.

1891   _____. "Une lettre sur Ezra Pound," Mercure, 306 (June,
       1949), 379-380.

1892   Beaujour, Michel. "Pound in France," Punto de Contacto/
       Point of Contact. (New York), 1, #2 (1976), 61-68.

1893   Bednár, Kamil. "Malé úvahy nad dilem Ezry Pounda,"
       Plamen, 10, #8 (1968), 66-70. [Considering Pound's work.]

1894   Beer, J. B. "Ezra Pound," TLS, #3, 710 (April 13, 1973),
       421.

1895   Bell, Ian F. A. Critic as Scientist: The Modernist Poetics
       of Ezra Pound. London; New York: Methuen, 1981.

1896   _____. "Divine Patterns: Louis Agassiz and American
       Men of Letters," JAmS, 10, #3 (December, 1976), 372-373.

1897 _____. "Pound, Emerson and 'Subject Rhyme,'" Paideuma, 8 (1979), 237-239.

1898 _____. "Pound's Vortex: Shapes Ancient and Modern," Paideuma, 10, #2 (Fall, 1981), 243-271.

1899 _____. "'Red Bloods': Pound's 'The Condolence' and William James," N&Q, 30 [228], #4 (August, 1983), 333-334.

1900 Benet, William Rose. "Poetry by the Pound," Dial, 54 (June 1, 1913), 450.

1901 _____. "Poets in Collected Editions," Cf., #1551.

1902 Bennett, Mitchell Bruce. "In Altera Persona: The Dramatic Monologue in the Poetry of Pound, Eliot and Frost," Diss. Harvard: 1967.

1903 Benton, Richard P. "A Gloss on Pound's 'Four Poems of Departure,'" LE&W, 10 (September, 1966), 292-301.

1904 Berezin, Charles. "The Quest for Disconnection in the Poetry of George Oppen," Research Studies, 48, (1980), 167-182.

1905 Berger, T. L. "Orwell as Essayist: Pound as Correspondent," Intro, I (1951), 98-100.

1906 Bergman, Herbert. "Ezra Pound and Walt Whitman," AL, 27 (March, 1955), 56-61.

1907 Bergonzi, Bernard. "From Imagism to Fascism," Cf., #451.

1908 Bernard, Mary. "A communication on Greek Metric, Ezra Pound, and Sappho," Agenda, 16 (1978), 62-68.

1909 Berri, Pietro. "Una tradizione che non si spengne," Il Mare (Rapallo, 7) (Novombor 7, 1915), 2-3.

1910 Berryman, John. "The Poetry of Ezra Pound," Critics on Ezra Pound. E. San Juan, Jr., ed. Cf., #535, pp. 38-43.

1911 _____. "The Poetry of Ezra Pound," The Freedom of the Poet. New York: Farrar, Straus and Giroux, 1976, pp. 253-269.

1912 Bertacchini, Renato. "Saggi letterari," Lettere Italiane (genn.-marzo, 1958), pp. 106-112.

1913 _____. "Saggismo di Ezra Pound," Idea, 15 (1959), 622-628.

1914 Berti, Luigi. "Ezra Pound," Storia della letteratura americana.
      Milano: 1964, Vol. IV, pp. 102-127.

1915 _____. "Poesia e memetismo con Ezra Pound," Boccaporto
      secondo, Florence: Parenti, 1940, pp. 117-164; also in
      Letteratura, 4 (1940), 140-145; 5 (1941), 123-134.

1916 Bertolucci, Attilio. "Riterno di Pound," Illustrazione italiana,
      (sett. 1958), pp. 33-39.

1917 Betocchi, Carlo. "Ragioni mie per Pound," Stagione, 2, #7
      (Rome), (1955), p. 5.

1918 Bewley, Marius. The Complex Fate. New York: Gordian
      Pr., 1952; 1967, pp. 166-167.

1919 _____. "Eliot, Pound, and History," Masks and Mirrors:
      Essays in Criticism. New York: London: Chatto & Windus,
      1970, pp. 302-323.

1920 Beyer, W. H. "Contemporary Literature in Review," Sch&Soc,
      74, (July 7, 1951), 8-10.

1921 Bhatnagar, I. "Rabindranath Tagore and Ezra Pound," AsSt,
      12 (October 5, 1974).

1922 Bianchi, Ruggero. "Aspetti dell'estetica del primo Pound,"
      RdE, 8 (1963), 88-108.

1923 _____. "Fenollosa, Hulme e gli Imagisti," EM, 12 (1961),
      123-145.

1924 Bigongiari, Piero. "Appunti," Paragone, 72 (December,
      1955), 126.

1925 _____. "Per Ezra Pound," Stagione, 2, #7 (Rome: 1955),
      5-6.

1926 Bilenchi, Romano. "Rapallo, 1941," Paideuma, 8 (1979),
      431-432.

1927 _____. Amici: Vittorini, Rosae, e altre incontre. Torino:
      Einaudi, 1976, p. 18.

1928 Bishop, John Peale. "Homage to Hemingway," NR, 89, #1145
      (November 11, 1936), 39-42.

1929 _____. "Intelligence of Poets," and "Talk of Ezra Pound,"
      Collected Essays of John Peale Bishop. Ed. with Introduction
      by Edmund Wilson. New York: Scribners, 1948, pp. 263-
      269, 327-330. See also #457.

1930 Blackburn, Paul. "Das Kennerbuch," NMQ, 23, #2 (Summer, 1953), 215-219.

1931 Blackburn, Thomas. "Ezra Pound," The Price of an Eye. London: Longmans, Green, 1961; New York: Wm. Morrow & Co., 1961, pp. 66-68.

1932 Blackmur, R. P. "An Adjunct to the Muses' Diadem: A Note on Ezra Pound," American Critical Essays: Twentieth Century. Harold L. Beaver, ed. Oxford, 1959, pp. 202-210. Cf., #459.

1933 _____. "A Critic's Job of Work," Form and Value in Modern Poetry. New York: Anchor Books, 1957, pp. 113-120.

1934 _____. "Lord Tennyson's Scissors: 1912-1950," KR, 14, #1 (Winter, 1952), 1-20.

1935 Bly, Robert. "On English and American Poetry," MFS, 5, #2 (Summer, 1959), 45-47.

1936 Bock, Layeh Aronson. "The Birth of Modernism: Des Imagistes and the Psychology of William James," DAI, 41, #2 (Stanford: 1980), 666A.

1937 Bode, Carl, ed. The New Mencken Letters. New York: Dial Pr., 1977, passim.

1938 Boensch, Maria R. "Colloqui con Ezra Pound," Borghese, (31 luglio, 1958), 181-183.

1939 Boer, Charles. Charles Olson in Connecticut. Chicago: Swallow Pr., 1975, pp. 84-87.

1940 Bogan, Louise. Achievement in American Poetry--1900-1950. Chicago: Henry Regnery Co., 1951, passim.

1941 _____. "Modernism in American Literature," Selected Criticism: Prose, Poetry. New York: Noonday, 1955, pp. 178-180.

1942 _____. "Poetry," America Now: An Inquiry into Civilization in the United States by Thirty-six Americans. Harold Edmund Stearns, ed. New York: Scribners, 1938, pp. 48-61.

1943 _____. A Poet's Alphabet: Reflections on the Literary Art and Vocation. Robert Phelps and Ruth Limmer, eds. New York: McGraw-Hill, 1970, passim.

1944 _____. "Verse," NY, 32, #28 (September 1, 1956), 32-92.

1945   Bonner, Paul Hyde. "Goodby to Good Manners," Esquire, 12
       (December, 1939), 271-272.

1946   Booth, Frederick Joseph. "Ovid and Pound: Myth and Meta-
       morphosis," DAI, 44, #12, Pt. 1 (New Jersey, New Brunswick:
       1983), 3676A-77A.

1947   Booth, Marcella, and Carroll F. Terrell. "An Interlude:
       Creating and Sweeping Up," Paideuma, 4, #1 (Spring, 1975),
       189-195.

1948   Bornstein, George. "The Last Romanticism of W. B. Yeats,"
       Transformations of Romanticism in Yeats, Eliot, and Stevens.
       Chicago: U. of Chicago Pr., 1976, pp. 79-80, passim.

1949   _____. "Pound and Eliot," AmLS (1977), pp. 119-134.

1950   _____. " 'What Porridge Had John Keats?' Pound's 'L'Art'
       and Browning's 'Popularity,' " Paideuma, 10, #2 (Fall, 1981),
       303-306.

1951   _____, and Stuart Y. McDougal. "Pound and Eliot,"
       AmLS (1978), pp. 111-126.

1952   _____, and _____. "Pound and Eliot," AmLS (1979),
       pp. 115-132.

1953   _____, and Hugh H. Witemeyer. "From 'Villain' to Vision-
       ary: Pound and Yeats on Villon," CL, 19, #4 (Fall, 1967),
       308-320.

1954   Boselli, Mario. "Alcune osservazioni sui saggi critici di Ezra
       Pound," NC, Nos. 5-6 (January-June, 1956), 70-80.

1955   _____. "Some Observations on the Critical Essays of Ezra
       Pound," Italian Images of Ezra Pound: Twelve Critical Essays.
       Angela Jung and Guido Palandri, eds., and trs., Cf., #518,
       pp. 77-86.

1956   Bosschère, Jean de. "Ezra Pound," Egoist, 4 (January-
       February, April, 1917), 7-8, 27-29, 44.

1957   Bottrall, Ronald. "Ezra Pound," Adelphi, 28 (2nd Qt.,
       1952), 16-24.

1958   Boussard, Leon. "Ezra Pound ou le poète déraciné," Nouvelle
       Revue des Deux Mondes (December, 1972), 735-737.

1959   Boveri, Margaret. "Klassizist und Revolutionar--Ezra Pound,"
       Der Verrat im 20. Jahrhundert, 1 (1956), 125-130.

1960 Bowen, Stella. Drawn from Life. London: Collins Pubs.,
      1941, pp. 142-143.

1961 Bowers, Frederick. "Arthur Hugh Clough: The Modern
      Mind," SELit, 6 (1967), 709-716.

1962 Bowra, Cecil Maurice. Poetry and Politics, 1900-1960. Cam-
      bridge: Cambridge U. Pr., 1966, p. 32.

1963 Boyers, Robert. R. P. Blackmur: Poet-Critic: Toward a
      View of Poetic Objects. A Literary Frontier Edition. Colum-
      bia; London: U. of Missouri Pr., 1980, pp. 82-84.

1964 Bradbrook, Muriel C. "The Roles of Pound and Quinn,"
      T. S. Eliot: The Making of "The Wasteland," Published for
      The British Council by Longman Group, Ltd., 1972, pp. 26-36.

1965 Bradbury, Malcolm. "The Scenario for Modernism," NSt, 78,
      #2010 (September 19, 1969), 378-379.

1966 _____. The Social Context of Modern English Literature.
      Oxford: Basil Blackwell; New York: Schocken Bks., 1971,
      passim.

1967 Bradley, Edward Sculley, Richard Croom Beatty, and Ed.
      Hudson Long, eds. The American Tradition in Literature.
      Vol. 2. New York: W. W. Norton Co., 1956, pp. 881-889.

1968 Braithwaite, Willian Stanley. "Imagism: Another View," NR,
      3 (June 12, 1915), 154-155.

1969 Brandabur, Edward. "Ezra Pound and Wassily Kandinsky: A
      Language in Form and Color," JAE, 7, #2 (1973), 91-107.

1970 Breslin, James E. "Whitman and the Early Development of
      William Carlos Williams," PMLA, 82 (December, 1967), 613-621.

1971 Brounig, Le Roy. "F. S. Flint, Imagism's 'Maitre d'Ecole,'"
      CL, 4 (Spring, 1952), 118-136.

1972 Bridgman. Richard. "Ernest Hemingway," Ernest Hemingway:
      Five Decades of Criticism. Linda Welshimer Wagner, ed.
      East Lansing: Michigan State U. Pr., 1974, pp. 162, 165-166.

1973 Bridson, D. G. "Ezra Pound," TLS, #3892 (October 15,
      1976), 1306.

1974 _____. "Ezra Pound: Translater of Sophocles," Radio
      Times (April 25, 1954), 4.

1975 _____. "The Genius of Ezra Pound," Radio Times (August
      13, 1954), 8.

1976   Brinnin, John Malcolm. The Third Rose: Gertrude Stein and Her World. Gloucester, Mass.: Peter Smith, 1968, passim.

1977   Brooker, Peter. "The Lesson of Ezra Pound: An Essay on Poetry, Literary Ideology and Politics," Ezra Pound: Tactics for Reading. Ian F. A. Bell, ed. Cf., #449, pp. 9-49.

1978   _____. A Student's Guide to the Selected Poems of Ezra Pound. Cf., #477.

1979   Brooke-Rose, Christine. "'Legt mich zu Aurelie, den Sonnenaufgang zu Stonehenge,'" Ezra Pound: 22 Versuche über einen Dichter. Eva Hesse, ed. and trans. Frankfurt: Athenaum, 1967, pp. 304-331.

1980   Brooks, Van Wyck. An Autobiography. New York: E. P. Dutton & Co., Inc., 1965, passim.

1981   _____. The Confident Years, 1885-1915. New York: E. P. Dutton & Co., 1952, pp. 513-538, passim.

1982   _____. The Opinions of Oliver Allston. New York: E. P. Dutton & Co., Inc., 1941, p. 240.

1983   _____. "Religion of Art," SatRL, 34 (December 1, 1951), 13-14, 48-52.

1984   Brown, C. "The Color Symphony before and after Gautier," CL, 5 (Fall, 1953), 289-309.

1985   Brown, John. "Larbaud et al jeune poésie amércaine," Valery Larbaud et la littérature de son temps. Actes du colloque de Vichy, 17-19, juin 1977, pp. 39-39. (Assn. Internat. des Amis de Valery Larbaud) Paris: Klincksieck, 1978.

1986   Brown, John L. "Ezra Pound, Comparatist," YCGL, 20 (1971), 37-47. Cf., Actes du VIe Congres de l'Association Internationale de Litterature Comparee/Proceedings of the 6th Congress of the International Comparative Literature Association. Michel Cadot, et al., eds. Stuttgart: Bieber, 1975, pp. 727-729.

1987   _____. "Ezra Pound and the Social Responsibility of the Artist," World Lit. Today, 51 (Spring, 1977), 233-234.

1988   Brown, Merle. "Criticism as the Animus of Poetry," Stand, 8 (1967), 45-52.

1989   Browne, Robert. "Convention in Productive Theories: Ezra Pound and T. S. Eliot," Theories of Convention in Contempo-

rary American Criticism. Diss. Catholic U. of America,
Washington, D.C., 1956, pp. 44-69.

1990 Broyard, A. [Pound and Eliot], New York Times Bk. Rev.,
87 (May 30, 1982), 27.

1991 Bruce, Elizabeth Esther. Pound and Vorticism. Diss., U.
of Alberta, Canada, 1968.

1992 Bruns, Gerald L. Modern Poetry and the Idea of Language.
New Haven: Yale U. Pr., 1974, p. 195.

1993 Bryer, Jackson R., ed. Fifteen Modern American Authors.
Cf., #1433, pp. 323-344.

1994 _____. "Joyce, 'Ulysses' and the 'Little Review,'" SAQ,
66 (Spring, 1967), 148-164.

1995 _____, ed. Sixteen Modern American Authors. Cf.,
#1434, pp. 445-472, passim.

1996 Bryher, [Annie Winifred Ellerman]. The Heart to Artemis:
A Writer's Memoirs. London: Collins, 1963, pp. 194, 195-
197, 210.

1997 Bullaro, John Joseph. "The Dantean Image of Ezra Pound,
T. S. Eliot and Hart Crane," DA, 22 (Wisconsin: 1962),
4012.

1998 Bullough, Geoffrey. "The Individual and the Racial Image in
Modern Poetry," Mirror of Minds: Changing Psychological
Beliefs in English Poetry. London; Toronto: U. of Toronto
Pr., 1962, pp. 212-213, 216.

1999 Burgess, Anthony. "The Milton Revolution," Spectator,
#7244 (April 28, 1967), 487-488.

2000 Burne, Glenn S. Remy de Gourmont: His Ideas and Influence in England and America. Carbondale: So. Ill. U. Pr.,
1963, passim.

2001 Bush, Douglas. "American Poets," Mythology and the Romantic Tradition in English Poetry. New York: Pageant Bk. Co.,
1957, pp. 481-525.

2002 _____. Pagan Myth and Christian Tradition in English
Poetry. American Philosophical Soc., Independence Square,
Philadelphia, 1968, pp. 89-92, passim.

2003 Bush, Ronald. "Pound and Spengler: Another Look,"
Paideuma, 5, #1 (Spring, 1976), 63-65.

2004 Butor, Michel. "La Tentative Poétique d'Ezra Pound," Cri-
      tique (Paris), 14 (March, 1956), 206-219; repr., in Butor's
      Répertoire: Etudes et Conferences 1948-1959 (1960).

2005 Butturff, Douglas R. "Ezra Pound and the Medieval Tradi-
      tion," Paideuma, 4, #2&3 (Fall-Winter, 1975), 539-545.

2006 Bynner, Witter. Journey with Genius: Recollections and
      Reflections Concerning the D. H. Lawrences. New York:
      John D. Co., 1951, pp. 144-145, 194-195.

2007 Byrd, Don. "The Poetry of Production," Sagetrieb, 2, #2
      (Summer-Fall, 1983), 7-43.

2008 Cady, Frank C. "The Unitary Phenomenon: The Phenome-
      nology of Martin Heidegger and the Poetry of Ezra Pound,
      William Carlos Williams, and Charles Olson," DAI, 33 (Stan-
      ford: 1973), 6903A.

2009 Caesar, Terry Paul. "'Violating the Shrine': Parody Inside
      and Outside Literature," DAI, 40 (Washington: 1979), 3311A.

2010 Călinescu, Matei. "Conceptual Modern de poezie--modernism şi
      tradiţie: Ezra Pound şi 'imagismul,'" SXX, 13, #5 (1970), 8-28.

2011 _____. "Dupǎ simbolism: modernism şi tradite in poetica
      lui Ezra Pound şi u liǔ T. S. Eliot," Conceptul Modern de
      Poezie. De la romantism la avangardǎ. Bucureşti: Editura
      Eminescu, 1972, pp. 141-177.

2012 Callaghan, Morley. That Summer in Paris: Memories of
      Tangled Friendships with Hemingway, Fitzgerald, and Some
      Others. New York: Coward-McCann, Inc., 1963, passim.

2013 Caloro, Bonaventura. "Chi ha paura di Ezra Pound?" FLe,
      48, #25 (1972), 8-11.

2014 Cambon, Glauco. "Dante's Presence in American Literature,"
      Dante's Craft: Studies in Language and Style. Minneapolis:
      U. of Minn. Pr., 1969, pp. 127-136, passim.

2015 _____. "Ezra Pound as Translator of Italian Poetry," SA,
      19-20 (1976), 201-236.

2016 _____. The Inclusive Flame: Studies in Modern American
      Poetry. Bloomington, Indiana: U. of Indiana Pr., 1963,
      passim.

2017 _____. "La poesia di Pound come experienza spaziale,"
      NC, Nos. 5-6 (genn.-giugno, 1956), 81-91; repr., in La
      Lotta con Proteo. Milan: 1963, pp. 245-255.

2018 _____. "Poesie di Pound scelte dal poeta, tradotte da Rizzardi, introdotte da Eliot," FLe, 15 (November 6, 1960), 5.

2019 _____. "Pound's Poetry as Spatial Experience," in Italian Images of Ezra Pound. Angela Jung and Guido Palandri, eds. & trs., Cf., #518, pp. 112-122.

2020 _____. "Sulla strada di Joyce," FLe (February 7, 1954).

2021 _____. "La Testimonianza epistolare di Pound," Aut-Aut, 33 (May, 1955), 221-230.

2022 _____. "The Waste Land as Work in Progress," Mosaic, 6, #1 (Fall, 1972), 191-200.

2023 _____. "William Carlos Williams and Ezra Pound: Two Examples of Open Poetry," CE, 22, #6 (March, 1961), 387-389.

2024 Campbell, Sue Ellen. "The Enemy Attacks: Wyndham Lewis Versus Ezra Pound," JML, 10, #2 (June, 1983), 247-256.

2025 Campos, Augusto de. "Ezra Pound aos oitenta anos," ESPSL, 30 (1965), 2.

2026 _____, and Haroldo de Campos. "Ezra Pound: a beleza e dificil," Diario de São Paulo (August 16, 1953), 8; (August 23, 1953), 8-10.

2027 Campos, Haroldo de. "Ezra Pound: La vida, texto," Plural, 50 (1975), 23-27.

2028 Capellán Gonzalo, Angel. "La obra poética de Ezra Pound," CHA (1974), 32-87.

2029 _____. "Sobre Ezra Pound," CdA, 10 (1974), 36-38.

2030 Caproni, Giorgio. "Due 'pesci d'oro': Ezra Pound e Luciano Erba," FLe, 14 (November 8, 1959), 1-2.

2031 _____. "Omaggio a Pound e a Guillén," FLe, 14 (January 11, 1959), 3.

2032 _____. "Ricordo di Pound," Stagione, 2, #7 (Rome: 1955), 6.

2033 Cargill, Oscar. "American Decadence--[Ezra Pound]," Intellectual America: Ideas on the March. New York: Macmillan, 1941, pp. 229-238, passim.

2034 Carleton, Samuel. "Trachiniae 1046-1063: Sophocles, Cicero,

and Ezra Pound," Proceedings: Pacific Northwest Conference
on Foreign Languages. Walter C. Kraft, ed. Twenty-third
Annual Meeting, April 28-29, 1972. Corvallis: Oregon State
U., 1972, pp. 19-23.

2035 Carmichael, Frank Charles, Jr. "Ezra Pound, Romanticism,
and Explanation," DAI, 36 (South Carolina: 1975), 7418A-19A.

2036 Carne-Ross, D. S. "New Metres for Old: A Note on Pound's
Metric," Arion, 6 (Summer, 1967), 216-232.

2037 Carruth, Hayden. "Ezra Pound and the Great Style," SatRL,
49 (April 9, 1966), 21-22, 56; excerpt: "Vision and Style,"
in Critics of Ezra Pound. E. San Juan, Jr., ed. Cf., 535,
pp. 100-101.

2038 _____. "Here Today: A Poetry Chronicle," HudR, 24
(1971), 320-336.

2039 _____. "La poesia di Ezra Pound," Prospetti, #16 (1956),
137-166; "The Poetry of Ezra Pound," PUSA, #16 (Summer,
1956), 129-159.

2040 Carruthers, Ian, tr. "A Translation of Fifteen Pages of Ito
Michio's Autobiography, Uksukushiku naru Kyoshito," CJIS,
2, #1 (1976), 32-43.

2041 Cary, Joseph. "Evangelism, Epic and Ethical," Pound Newsletter, 10 (April, 1956), 11-12.

2042 Casamayor, Enrique. "Ezra Pound, un poeta encadenado a la
política de los EE.UU," CHA, 49 (January, 1954), 104-107.

2043 Casillo, Robert. "Anti-Semitism, Castration, and Usury in
Ezra Pound," Criticism, 25, #3 (Summer, 1983), 239-265.

2044 Casillo, Robert Faulkner. "The Parallel Design in John
Ruskin and Ezra Pound," DAI, 38 (Johns Hopkins: 1978),
6712A.

2045 Casper, Leonard. "Apprenticed in Provence," Poetry, 81
(December, 1952), 203-211.

2046 Cassell, Richard A. Ford Madox Ford: A Study of His
Novels. Baltimore: Johns Hopkins Pr.; London: Oxford U.
Pr., 1961, passim.

2047 _____. "A Visit with Ezra Pound," Paideuma, 8 (1979),
64-67.

2048 Castellani, Leonardo. "Ezra Pound Recitante," Il Mondo
(Rome), (January 3, 1956), 12.

2049 Cenci, Lino. "Pound e la politica," FLe, 13, #3 (May 4, 1958), 3.

2050 Cerf, Bennett. "Ezra Pound and the American Poet," AmQ, 34 (March, 1972), 101-113.

2051 Chace, William M. "Ezra Pound and the Marxist Temptation," AQ, 22 (Fall, 1970), 714-725.

2052 _____. "'Make It Not So New,' The Waste Land Manuscript," SoR, 9, #1 (January, 1973), 476-480.

2053 _____. "Modern Poetry," ConL, 17 (1976), 570-590.

2054 _____. "The Political Affinities of T. S. Eliot and Ezra Pound," DA, 29, #12 (Berkeley, Calif.: 1968), 4479A-80A.

2055 _____. "Talking Back to Ezra Pound," SoR, 8 (1972), 225-233.

2056 Chakravarty, Amiya. "A Note on Pound," IJAS, 2, #2 (December, 1972), 12-14.

2057 Chapman, Robert T. Wyndham Lewis: Fictions and Satires. New York: Barnes & Noble, 1973, passim.

2058 Charlesworth, Barbara. "Pound und die Tradition des ungeteilten Lichtes," Ezra Pound: 22 Versuche über einen Dichter. Eva Hesse, ed. Cf., #1979, pp. 217-226.

2059 _____. The Tensile Light: A Study of Ezra Pound's Religion. MA Diss: Coral Gables Fla., U. of Miami, 1957.

2060 Charters, Jimmie. "The White Winers," Esquire, 2 (August, 1934), 42-43, 126.

2061 Chase, Richard. "Pound of Flesh," PR, 18, #5 (September-October, 1951), 586-590.

2062 Cherchi, Luciano. "Un appello per Ezra Pound," Conv, 24 (July-August, 1955), 503-504.

2063 Chiara, Piero. "Ezra Pound," L'Italia (Milan: March 11, 1954).

2064 Chiareno, Aldo. "Saggismo di Ezra Pound," Idea, 15 (1959), 622-631.

2065 Chiari, Joseph. T. S. Eliot: Poet and Dramatist. New York: Harper & Row, 1973, pp. 56-59, passim.

2066 Chilanti, Felice. Ezra Pound fra i sediziosi degli anni

quaranta. Milan: All'insegna del pesce d'oro, 1972. Cf.,
#286.

2067 Chisolm, Lawrence W. Fenollosa: The Far East and American
Culture. New Haven, Conn.: Yale U. Pr., 1963.

2068 Christensen, Paul. Charles Olson: Call Him Ishmael.
George F. Butterick, ed. Austin, Texas: U. of Texas Pr.,
1975, pp. 14-15, 75-79, passim.

2069 _____. "The New American Romances," TCL, 26 (Fall,
1980), 269-277.

2070 Chung, Ling. "Ezra Pound's Interpretation of 'cheng ming'
and His Literary Theories," Kushner, Eva, and Roman Struc,
eds. Actes du VIIᵉ congrès de l'Association Intérnationale de
Litterature Comparée/Proceedings of the 7th Congress of the
International Comparative Literature Association, II: La
Littérature comparée aujourd'hui: Théorie et pratique/
Comparative Literature Today: Theory and Practice. (Lib.
of CRCL 3.) Stuttgart: Bieber, 1979, pp. 689-692.

2071 Chute, Desmond. "Poets in Paradise," Listener, 55 (January
5, 1956), 14-15.

2072 _____. "Poet's Paradise," Pound Newsletter, 8 (October,
1955), 12-14.

2073 Cianci, Giovanni. "Futurism and the English Avant-Garde:
The Early Pound between Imagism and Vorticism," ArAA, 6,
#1 (1981), 3-39. [Sum., 3; tr. and revision of "Futurismo e
Avanguadia Inglese: il Primo Pound tra Imagismo e Vorticis-
mo," Quarderno 9, (1979), 9-66.]

2074 Ciardi, John. "For Ezra Pound," [poem], Sou'wester (October 30, 1970), 137-138.

2075 Cimatti, Pietro. "La patria di Pound," FLe, 13 (December 7,
1958), 5.

2076 Claes, Paul. "Ezra Pound: Apologia voor 'a poet's poet,'"
Streven, 26 (1973), 355-361.

2077 Clare, John. "Form in Vers Libre," English, 27 (1978), 450-
470.

2078 Clark, David R. "Stretching and Yawning with Yeats and
Pound," MalR, 29 (1974), 104-117.

2079 Clarkson, William Ellis. "A Rage for Order: The Development of Ezra Pound's Poetics and Politics, 1910-1945," DAI,
35, #8 (Virginia: 1974), 5391A.

2080 _____. "Ezra Pound LTD," SR, 85, #4 (Fall, 1977), 667-670.

2081 Clearfield, Andrew. "Pound, Paris, and Dada," Paideuma, 7 (Spring-Fall, 1978), 113-140.

2082 Clemons, Walter. "A Tough, Wrongheaded Genius," Newsweek, 85, #20 (November 13, 1972), 63.

2083 Coblentz, Stanton A. "Freedom Through Dictatorship," The Poetry Circus. New York: Hawthorn Bks, Inc., 1967, pp. 13-14, 45-46, 177-178, passim.

2084 Coffman, Stanley K., Jr. "Imagism: The Contribution of T. E. Hulme and Ezra Pound to English Poetry, 1908-1917," DA, 57 (Ohio State, 1948), 39-45.

2085 _____. "Imagism and Symbolism," and "Ezra Pound and Imagist Theory," Imagism: A Chapter for the History of Modern Poetry. Norman, Oklahoma: U. of Okla. pr., 1951, pp. 74-103, 120-162, passim.

2086 Cohen, J. M. "Virgin Soil," Poetry of This Age, 1908-1958. Philadelphia: Dufour Eds., 1962, pp. 210-216.

2087 Colaneri, John. "Reflection of a Man: Guido Cavalcanti," Paideuma, 1, #2 (Winter, 1972), 199-204.

2088 Cole, Thomas. "William Carlos Williams," SatRL, 32, #40 (October 1, 1949), 22.

2089 _____. "Williams and Pound Remembered," William Carlos Williams Rev, 7, #2 (Fall, 1981), 4-20.

2090 Coles, R. "Pound Speaking," NYTimes Bk. Rev, 84 (January 14, 1979), 9ff.

2091 Colinas, Antonio. "Ezra Pound: Una poética con rigor," NE, 1 (1979), 47-50.

2092 Colum, Mary M. From These Roots: The Ideas That Have Made Modern Literature. New York: Chas. Scribner's Sons, 1938, pp. 178, 338.

2093 _____. Life and the Dream. Garden City, New York: Doubleday & Co., 1947, pp. 306-308, passim.

2094 Conarroe, Joel. "'You Can't Steal Credit': The Economic Motif," William Carlos Williams' Paterson: Language and Landscape. Philadelphia: U. of Penn. Pr., 1970, pp. 117-118.

2095 Connolly, Cyril. "The Breakthrough in Modern Verse,"
      Previous Convictions. New York: Harper & Row, 1963, pp.
      235-251; Cf., #20.

2096 _____. "Ezra Pound: 1, 2, 3," The Evening Colonnade.
      New York: Harcourt, Brace & Jovanovich, 1975, pp. 217-
      221, 221-225, 226-228.

2097 _____. "Ezra Pound as Critic," Previous Convictions.
      Cf., #2095, pp. 255-257.

2098 Conquest, Robert. "Ezra Pound," London Magazine, 3, #1
      (new series), (April, 1963), 33-49.

2099 Contini, Gianfranco. "From Dante to the Duce," TLS, #3916
      (April 1, 1977), 395-396.

2100 Cook, Howard Willard. "Ezra Pound," Our Poets of Today.
      New York: Moffat, Yard & Co., 1919, pp. 139-142.

2101 Cook, Reginald L. "Robert Frost in Context," Frost: Cen-
      tennial Essays III. Jac Tharpe, ed. Jackson: Miss U. Pr.,
      1978, pp. 157-162.

2102 Cookson, William. "Notes on Pound's Confucian Odes,"
      Agenda, 20, #3-4 (Autumn-Winter, 1982-83), 61-64.

2103 Cork, Richard, ed. Vorticism and Abstract Art in the First
      Machine Age. Berkeley and Los Angeles: U. of Calif., 1976,
      2 vols., passim.

2104 Cornevali, Emanuel. "Irritation," Poetry, 15 (January, 1920),
      211-221.

2105 Coronel-Urtecho, Jose. "Ezra Pound's Case," Universidad de
      México (Mexico City), (February, 1957).

2106 Corrigan, Matthew. "The Poet's Intuition of Prose Fiction:
      Pound and Eliot on the Novel," UWR, 2, #1 (Fall, 1965), 33-
      51.

2107 Corrigan, Robert A. "Ezra Pound Criticism, 1904-1917:
      Additions and Corrections," Paideuma, 2, #1 (Spring, 1973),
      115-130.

2108 _____. "The First Quarter Century of Ezra Pound Criti-
      cism" RALS, 2 (Autumn, 1972), 157-207.

2109 _____. "A Yankee in King Edward's Court: The Critical
      Response to Ezra Pound's Early Verse," Paideuma, 1 (Winter,
      1972), 229-260.

2110 _____. "'What Thou Lovest Well Remains,' Ezra Pound and America 1940-1958," DA, 28 (Pennsylvania: 1967), 4985A.

2111 Corsini, Renato. "Ezra Pound economista," Il Secolo d'Italia (Rome: May 4, 1955); repr., "Ezra Pound, Economist: Justice the Final Goal," New Times (Melbourne: December 15, 1955), 7.

2112 Cory, Daniel. Santayana: The Later Years: A Portrait with Letters. New York: Braziller, 1963, pp. 186-188.

2113 Cowley, Malcolm. "The Art of Fiction," ParisR, 24, #84 (Summer, 1982), 53-75.

2114 _____. "Books and People," NR, 109, #1511 (November 15, 1943), 689-690.

2115 _____. "Ezra Pound," After the Genteel Tradition: American Writers Since 1910. New York: W. W. Norton & Co., 1937, passim.

2116 _____. "Laforgue in America: A Testimony," SR, 71 (January-March, 1963), 62-74.

2117 _____. "What the Poets Are Saying: 1941," Think Back on Us. Henry Dan Piper, ed. Carbondale: So. Ill. U. Pr., 1967, II, pp. 372-377.

2118 Cox, Kenneth. "Allen Upward," Agenda, 16, #3-4 (1978-79), 87-107.

2119 Craig, Cairns. "The Continuity of the Associationist Aesthetic: From Archibald Alison to T. S. Eliot (and Beyond)," DR, 60 (1980), 20-37.

2120 _____. Yeats, Eliot, Pound, and the Politics of Poetry: Richest to Richest. (Critical Essays in Modern Literature Set.) Pittsburgh, Pa.; U. of Pittsburgh, 1982.

2121 Craig, David. The Real Foundations: Literature and Social Change. New York: Oxford U. Pr., 1974, pp. 182-184, passim.

2122 Crane, Hart. The Letters of Hart Crane, 1916-1932. Brom Weber, ed. Berkeley and Los Angeles: U. of Calif. Pr., 1965, passim.

2123 Creeley, Robert. "A Note," IJAS, 2, #2 (December, 1972), 15-16.

2124 _____. "A Note on Ezra Pound," A Quick Graph:

Collected Notes and Essays. San Francisco: Four Seasons
Foundation, 1970, pp. 95-98.

2125 _____. "Robert Creeley in Conversation with Charles
Tomlinson," Review, #10 (January, 1964), 24-35.

2126 _____. "Why Pound!?!" Agenda, 17, #3-4; 18, #1 (Aut-
Winter-Spring, 1979-80), 198-199.

2127 Crick, Bernard. "Poets and Partisans," TLS, #3821 (May 30,
1975), 586.

2128 Cronin, Anthony. "A Question of Modernity," XR, 1 (1960),
283-292.

2129 Crosman, Robert. "Do Readers Make Meaning?" The Reader
in the Text: Essays on Audience and Interpretation. Susan
R. Suleiman and Inge Crosman, eds. Princeton U. Pr., 1980,
pp. 151-154.

2130 Crowder, Richard. "Poetry: 1900 to the 1930's," Mon/AmLS,
No. 9 (1971), 277-298.

2131 Cummings, E. E. "Re Ezra Pound," We Moderns. Gothic
Book Mart, 1940, p. 69.

2132 Cunard, Nancy. "The Hours Press," Book Collector, 13, #4
(Winter, 1964), 488-496.

2133 Cunha, Carlos. "Camões num ensaio de Ezra Pound," Coló-
quio, 22 (1963), 65-66.

2134 Cunliffe, Marcus. "Poetry and Criticism Since World War I,"
The Literature of the United States. Baltimore: Penguin Bks.,
Inc., 1955, pp. 321-326, passim.

2135 Curtui, Aurel. "Brancusi as Seen by Ezra Pound," Romanian
Bulletin (New York Romanian Library), (December, 1976),
p. 6.

2136 D'Agostino, Nemi. Ezra Pound. Cf., #519, pp. 315-316.

2137 _____. "La 'fin de siècle' inglese e il giovane Ezra Pound,"
EM, 6 (1955), 135-162.

2138 _____. "La fin de siècle francese e la poesia di Pound e
Eliot," Galleria (Italy), 4 (December, 1954), 327-339.

2139 _____. "La 'poetiche della crisi' in Inghilterra,"
Letteratura (Florence), Nos. 11-12 (sett-dic, 1954), 29-49.

2140 Dahlberg, Edward. The Confessions of Edward Dahlberg.
New York: Geo. Braziller, 1971, passim.

2141 _____. Epitaphs of Our Times: The Letters of Edward
Dahlberg. New York: Geo. Braziller, 1967, pp. 96-99, 275-
278, passim.

2142 Daiches, David. "Literature and Belief," A Study of Literature: For Readers and Critics. New York: Norton, 1964,
pp. 212-226.

2143 _____. "War Poetry, The Imagists, Post-War Satire, The
Sitwells," Poetry and the Modern World: A Study of Poetry
in England Between 1900 and 1939. Chicago: U. of Chicago
Pr., 1940, pp. 61-89.

2144 Dale, Peter. "Some Translations from Jules Laforgue,"
Agenda, 17, #3-4, and 18, #1 (Autumn-Winter-Spring, 1979-
80), 86-102.

2145 Damon, S. Foster. Amy Lowell: A Chronicle. With Extracts
from Her Correspondence. Boston and New York: Houghton
Mifflin Co., 1935, passim.

2146 Daniels, Earl. The Art of Reading Poetry. Cf., #1531, pp.
9, 161.

2147 Danojlić, Milovan. "Poezija Ezre Paunda," LMS, 415 (1975),
639-674.

2148 Dasenbrock, Reed Way. "Dante's Hell and Pound's Paradiso:
'Tutto spezzato,'" Paideuma, 9 (1980), pp. 501-504.

2149 _____. "Literary Vorticism: Painting and the Modernist
Aesthetic of Wyndham Lewis and Ezra Pound," DAI, 42, #9
(Johns Hopkins: 1982), 4005A.

2150 Davenport, Guy. "Ezra Pound," ConL, 11 (1970), 579-585.

2151 _____. "Frobenius and Pounds Sextant," Ezra Pound: 22
Versuche über einen Dichter. Eva Hesse, ed. Cf., #1979,
pp. 186-202.

2152 _____. "The Nuclear Venus: Dr. Williams' Attack upon
Usura," Perspective, 6, #4 (Autumn-Winter, 1953), 183-190.

2153 _____. "The Perpendicular Honeycomb: Pound, De
Gourmont, Frobenius," Meanjin, 14 (December, 1955), 492-
501.

2154 _____. "The Pound Vortex," NatlR, 24 (May 12, 1972),
525-526.

2155 _____. "The Real Lucifer," Paideuma, 8 (1979), 335-336.

2156 _____. "Poet's Romance," NYTBR, 15 (July 12, 1979), 33-34.

2157 Davey, Frank. "Black Days on Black Mountain," Tamarack Rev, 35 (Spring, 1965), 62-71.

2158 Davidson, Peter. "Giulio Romano at the Spring Marriage," Paideuma, 11, #3 (1982), 503-510.

2159 _____. "Heracles & m'la calata," Paideuma, 8 (1979), 413-414.

2160 Davie, Donald. "The Adventures of a Cultural Orphan," Listener, 86 (December 23, 1971), 876-877.

2161 _____. Articulate Energy: An Inquiry into the Syntax of English Poetry. London: Routledge & Kegan Paul, 1955; St. Clair Shores, Michigan: Scholarly Pr., 1971, pp. 154-158, passim.

2162 _____. Ezra Pound. London: Fontana/Collins, 1975; New York: Viking and Penguin, 1976.

2163 _____. "Ezra Pound," Modern Masters: Ezra Pound. Frank Kermode, ed. New York: Viking Pr., 1976.

2164 _____. "Ezra Pound Abandons the English," Poetry Nation, (Manchester, England), No. 4, 1975; repr., in Trying to Explain. Ann Arbor: U. of Michigan Pr., 1979, pp. 114-128.

2165 _____. "Ezra Among the Edwardians," Paideuma, 5, #1 (Spring, 1976), 3-14.

2166 _____. "Ezra Pound and the English," Paideuma, 7 (Spring/Fall, 1978), 297-307; Cf., Trying to Explain, #2164, pp. 150-164.

2167 _____. "Ezra Pound: Der Dichter als Bildhäuer," Ezra Pound: 22 Versuche über einen Dichter. Eva Hesse, Ed. Cf., #1979, pp. 267-279.

2168 _____. "Poetry and the Other Modern Arts," MQR, 7, #3 (Summer, 1968), 193-198.

2169 _____. "A Poetry of Protest," New Statesman, (February 11, 1966), 198-199.

2170 _____. "Pound and Eliot: A Distinction," Eliot in Perspective: A Symposium. Graham Martin, ed. New York: Humanities, 1970, pp. 62-82.

2171 _____. "Pound and Eliot: Eine Unterscheidung," Zur Aktualität T. S. Eliot. Helmut Viebrock and Armin Paul Frank, eds. Frankfort: Suhrkamp, 1975, pp. 118-145.

2172 _____. "Pound and 'The Exile,'" Trying to Explain, Cf., #2164, pp. 128-133.

2173 _____. "Pound and Fascism," NYRB (April 1, 1976), 32-33.

2174 _____. "Davie's Review of The Pound Era," Paideuma, 2, (1972), pp. 263-269; Cf., #732.

2175 _____. "Res and Verba in Rock-Drill and After," Paideuma, 11, (1982), 382-394.

2176 _____. "Six Notes on Pound," Trying to Explain, Cf., #2164, pp. 95-164.

2177 _____. "Two Kinds of Magnanimity," NYRB, 1975; repr., in Trying to Explain, #2164, pp. 143-149.

2178 _____. "The Universe of Ezra Pound," Paideuma, 1 (1972), 263-269; CritQ, 15 (1973), 51-57.

2179 _____. "Yeats and Pound," DublinMag., 30, #4 (October-December, 1955), 17-21.

2180 Davis, Earle. "Ezra Pound: New Emphasis on Economics," Paideuma, 2 (Winter, 1973), 473-478; Cf., Notation by Dennis R. Klinck, Paideuma, 4, #2&3 (Fall-Winter, 1975), 552-553.

2181 Davis, Gary. "Pound's 'Cino' and the Poetics of Process," ContP, 2, #1 (Spring, 1975), 28-39.

2182 Davis, Kay. "Fugue and Canto LXIII," Paideuma, 11 (1982), 15-38.

2183 _____. "Ring Composition, Subject Rhyme, and Canto VI," Paideuma, 11 (1982), 429-439.

2184 Davis, Robert G. "Pound: The Poem and the Poet," New Leader (December 11, 1950), 17-18.

2185 Day, Douglas. "The Background of the New Criticism," Jour. of Aesthetics and Art Criticism, 24, #3 (Spring, 1966), 429-440.

2186 de Bosschère, Jean. "Ezra Pound," Egoist, 4 (1917), 28.

2187 De Campos, Augusto. "Ezra Pound aos oitenta anos," ESPSL (October 30, 1965), 2.

2188   de Chasca, Edmund S. John Gould Fletcher and Imagism.
       London; Columbia: U. of Missouri Pr., 1978, passim.

2189   Dell, Floyd. "To a Poet," Chicago Evening Post, Literary
       Review (April 4, 1913), 4.

2190   Delmer, F. Sefton. "Ezra Pound," Zeitschrift für französis-
       chen und englischen Unterricht, Vol. 29 (1930), 92-110.

2191   de Mailla, Père Joseph. "Histoire Générale de la Chine,"
       Paideuma, 5 (Spring, 1976), 100-121.

2192   Dembo. L. S. The Confucian Odes of Ezra Pound: A Criti-
       cal Appraisal. Berkeley and Los Angeles: U. of California
       Pr., 1963.

2193   _____. "Ezra Pound: Fac Deum," Conceptions of Reality
       in Modern American Poetry. Berkeley and Los Angeles: U.
       of California Pr., 1966, pp. 151-182.

2194   Demetz, Peter. "Ezra Pound's German Studies," GR, 31, #4
       (December, 1956), 279-292.

2195   de Nagy, N. Christoph. "The Place of Laforgue in Ezra
       Pound's Literary Criticism," Jules Laforgue: Essays on a
       Poet's Life and Work. Carbondale: Southern Illinois U. Pr.,
       1969.

2196   Denlin, Vianney M. "In Memoriam Ezra Pound," Greyfriar, 13
       (1972), 42-44.

2197   Dennis, H. M. "A New Approach to the Poetry of Ezra
       Pound through the Medieval Provencal Aspects," DAI, 43, #4
       (1982), 4286C.

2198   de Rachewiltz, Boris. L'Elemento Magico in Ezra Pound.
       Milano: Scheiwiller, 1965.

2199   _____. "Magische und heidnische Symbole in der Dichtung
       Ezra Pounds," Ezra Pound: Versuche über einen Dichtung.
       Eva Hesse, ed. Cf., #1979, pp. 283-301.

2200   de Rachewiltz, Mary. "Fragments of an Atmosphere," Agenda,
       17, #3-4; 18, #1 (Aut-Wntr-Spr., 1979-80), 157-170.

2201   _____. "Pound and Frobenius," KompH, 2 (1980), 92-101.

2202   _____. "Tempus Loquendi," TQ, 10, #4 (Winter, 1967),
       36-39.

2203   _____, and D. S. Carne-Ross. "Pound in Texas," Arion,
       6 (1967), 207-232.

2204 Di Canzio, William. "Pound and the Pateresque Renaissance," DAI, 39, #4 (Johns Hopkins: 1978), 2253A.

2205 Dilworth, Thomas. "Virgil Thomson on George Antheil and Ezra Pound, A Conversation," Paideuma, 12, #2-3 (Fall-Winter, 1983), 349-356.

2206 Dodworth, Edmund. "Ezra Pound in un giudizio di Gino Saviotti," Il Mare, 26 (January 7, 1933), 3.

2207 Donath, Andreas and Hans-Christian Kirsch. "Ezra Pound: ein Proträt in Briefen," Frankfurter Hefte, 9, #5 (May, 1954), 373-379.

2208 Donati, Franco. "Un lottatore stanco," FLe, 15 (March 13, 1960), 3.

2209 Donoghue, Denis. "Ezra Pound," PR, 44, #3 (1977), 452-458. [Review of Ezra Pound by Donald Davie. New York: Viking Pr., 1977.]

2210 _____. "Mediterranean Man," PR, 44, #3 (1977), 452-457.

2211 Doolittle, Hilda. Bid Me to Live. New York: Grove Pr., 1960, passim.

2212 Dos Passos, John, et al. "Aftermath: The Question of Ezra Pound," Esquire, 48 (December, 1957), 12-20.

2213 Drew, Elizabeth. Poetry: A Modern Guide to Its Understanding and Enjoyment. New York: Norton & Co., 1959, passim.

2214 _____, in collaboration with John L. Sweeney. Directions in Modern Poetry. New York: W. W. Norton & Co., 1940, passim.

2215 Drummond, Donald F. "On Ezra Pound," Sou'wester (October 30, 1970), 130.

2216 Drummond, Roberto. "Vicissitudes Vividas por um certo James Joyce," MGSL, 18 (January, 1975), 2-3.

2217 Duberman, Martin. Black Mountain: An Exploration in Community. New York: E. P. Dutton & Co., 1972, passim.

2218 Dudek, Louis. "Lunchtime Reflections on Frank Davey's Defence of the Black Mountain Fort," TamarackRev, 36 (Summer, 1965), 58-63.

2219 _____. "Poetry as a Way of Life," EngQ, 1, #1 (June, 1968), 7-19.

2220 Duffey, Bernard I. "Ezra Pound and the Attainment of Imag-
      ism," Toward a New American Literary History. L. J. Budd,
      E. H. Cady, and C. L. Anderson, eds. Durham, N.C.:
      Duke U. Pr., 1980, pp. 181-194.

2221 _____. "The Whole Poem and the Image: Pound, Williams,
      and Minor Imagists," and "Values in Time: Pound, Eliot,
      Hart Crane," Poetry in America: Expression and Its Values
      in the Times of Bryant, Whitman and Pound. Durham, N.C.;
      Duke U. Pr., 1978, pp. 196-200, 298-305.

2222 Duncan, Robert. "The Lasting Contribution of Ezra Pound,"
      Agenda, Special Issue in Honor of Ezra Pound's Eightieth
      Birthday," 4, ii (October-November, 1965), 23-26.

2223 Duncan, Ronald. "Poet's Poet," An Examination of Ezra
      Pound: A Collection of Essays. Peter Russell, ed. Cf.,
      #114, pp. 154-164.

2224 _____. "Il professore di Rapallo," FLe, 46 (November 16,
      1950), 4.

2225 _____. "Religio," Agenda, 4, #2 (October-November,
      1965), 56.

2226 Duran, Manuel. "Ezra Pound and the Spanish-Speaking
      World," YLM, 126, #5 (December, 1958), 11-16.

2227 Dyson, William. "The Fluctuation of Ezra Pound," B&B, 16,
      #12 (September, 1971), 22-27.

2228 Eastham, Scott Thomas. "Paradise and Ezra Pound: The
      Poet as Psychopomp," DAI, 41, #7 (U. of Calif., Santa
      Barbara: 1979), 3148A.

2229 _____. Paradise and Ezra Pound: The Poet as Shaman.
      Lanham, MD: U. Pr. of America, 1983.

2230 Eckman, Frederick. "Imagism: The Radiant Center,"
      Itinerary 3: Criticism. Frank Baldanza, ed. Bowling
      Green, OH: Bowling Green U. Pr., 1977, pp. 109-119.

2231 Eder, Doris L. Three Writers in Exile: Pound, Eliot, and
      Joyce. Troy, New York: Whitson Pub. Co., 1984.

2232 Edwards, Thomas R. Imagination and Power: A Study of
      Poetry on Public Themes. London: Chatto & Windus, 1971,
      pp. 185, 202.

2233 Egudu, Romanus N. "Ezra Pound in African Poetry: Chris-
      topher Okigbo," CLS, 8, #2 (June, 1971), 143-154.

2234 Ehrenpreis, Irvin. "Love, Hate, and Ezra Pound," NYRB
(May 27, 1976), 6-12.

2235 Eliot, T. S. "American Literature and the American Language," SR, 74, #1 (January-March, 1966), 1-20.

2236 _____. "Clemenza per Ezra Pound: una lettera di T. S.
Eliot," Il Mare, (Rapallo: October 31, 1954), 1.

2237 _____. "Disjecta Membra," Egoist, 5 (April, 1918), 55.

2238 _____. "Ezra Pound," An Examination of Ezra Pound.
Peter Russell, ed., Cf., #114, pp. 25-36.

2239 _____. "Ezra Pound," Poetry, 68 (September, 1946), 326-
328; repr., in New English Weekly (October 31-November 7,
1946).

2240 _____. "Ezra Pound," Ezra Pound: A Collection of Critical Essays. Walter Sutton, ed., Englewood Cliffs, NJ:
Prentice-Hall, Inc., 1963, pp. 17-25.

2241 _____. "Ezra Pound nel 1945," NC, 5-6 (1956), 9-20.

2242 _____. "Five Points on Dramatic Writing," Townsman, I,
#3 (July, 1938), 10.

2243 _____. "The Letters of W. B. Yeats," The Egoist, 4
(July, 1917), 89-90.

2244 _____. "Mr. T. S. Eliot's Quandaries," New English
Weekly, 4 (April 12, 1934), 622-623.

2245 _____. "Mr. Eliot's Virginian Lectures," New English
Weekly, 4 (March 15, 1934), 528.

2246 _____. "Omaggio a Ezra Pound," FLe, 46 (November 16,
1950), 1.

2247 _____. "On a Recent Piece of Criticism," Purpose, 10, #2
(April-June, 1938), 90-94.

2248 _____. "Studies in Contemporary Criticism II," Egoist,
5 (November-December, 1918), 131-133.

2249 _____. "The Three Provincialities," Tyro, #2 (1922), 13.

2250 Elliott, Angela. "Pound's Lucifer: A Study in the Imagery
of Flight and Light," Paideuma, 12, #2-3 (Fall-Winter, 1983),
237-266.

2251 Elliott, George P. "Poet of Many Voices," Carleton Miscellany,
      2, #3 (Summer, 1961), 79-103; repr., in Ezra Pound: A Crit-
      ical Anthology. J. P. Sullivan, ed. Baltimore, Md.: Penguin,
      1970, pp. 251-277.

2252 Ellis, Stephen Paul. "Dante in Pound's Early Career,"
      Paideuma, 8 (1979), 549-561.

2253 Ellmann, Richard. "Gazebos and Gashouses," Eminent Domain:
      Yeats Among Wilde, Joyce, Pound, Eliot, and Auden. New
      York: Oxford U. Pr., 1967, pp. 97-126.

2254 _____. Golden Codgers: Biographical Speculations. Lon-
      don; New York: Oxford U. Pr., 1973, passim.

2255 _____. The Identity of Yeats. New York: Oxford U.
      Pr., 1954, pp. 182-183, 320-321, passim.

2256 _____. James Joyce. New York: Oxford U. Pr., 1959,
      passim.

2257 _____. New Approaches to Ezra Pound. Eva Hesse, ed.,
      Cf., #41, pp. 55-85.

2258 _____. "Two Faces of Edward," Literary Criticism: Idea
      and Act. Ed. with Introd. by W. K. Wimsatt. Berkeley &
      Los Angeles: London: U. of Calif. Pr., 1974, pp. 561-575,
      passim.

2259 _____. Yeats: The Man and the Masks. New York:
      Macmillan, 1948; New York: Norton, 1978, pp. 211-214,
      passim.

2260 Emery, Clark. "Räude und Marasmus: Der wirtschaftpoli-
      tische Angriff," Ezra Pound: 22 Versuche über einen Dichter.
      Eva Hesse, ed., Cf., #1979, pp. 354-375.

2261 Engel, Bernard F. "Ezra Pound, 1885-1972," SSMLN, 3, #1
      (1973), 3-4.

2262 Engel, Carl. "Poet as Prophet," Discords Mingled: Essays
      on Music. New York: A. A. Knopf, 1931, pp. 172-183.

2263 Engel, Ilse. "Story of a Meeting with Ezra Pound," Paideuma,
      8 (1979), 257-260; YULG, 55, #4 (April, 1981), 195-198.

2264 Engelking, Leszek. "Ezra Pound in Poland," Paideuma, 11
      (1982), 105-131.

2265 Enright, D. J. Conspirators and Poets. Chester Springs,
      Pa.: Dufour, 1966; London: Chatto & Windus, 1966, passim.

2266 Eoyang, Eugene. "The Confucian Odes: Ezra Pound's Translations of the Shih Ching," Paideuma, 3, #1 (Spring, 1974),
33-47; Actes du VII congrès de l'Association Internationale de
Littérature Comparée/Proceedings of the 7th Congress of the
International Comparative Literature Association, II: La Littérature comparée aujourd'hui: Théorie et pratique/Compara-
tive Literature Today: Theory and Practice. (Lib. of CRCL
3.) Eva Kushner and Roman Struc, eds. Stuttgart: Bieber,
1979, pp. 637-644.

2267 Epstein, Jacob. Let There Be Sculpture. New York: G. P.
Putnam's Sons, 1940; an extended version: Epstein: An
Autobiography, 2nd ed., Introduction by Richard Buckle.
London: Vista Books, 1963, pp. 44-45, 57-58.

2268 Epstein, Joseph. "The Small-eyed Poet," NR, 160 (June 7,
1969), 23-28.

2269 Eriksson, Pamela. "Pound and Imagism," UES, 15, #2 (1977),
48-51.

2270 Espey, John J. "Das Vermächtlnis von Tó Kalón," Ezra
Pound: 22 Versuche über einen Dichter. Eva Hesse, ed.
Cf., #1979, pp. 90-100.

2271 _____. "Ezra Pound," Fifteen Modern American Authors.
Jackson R. Bryer, ed., Cf., #1433, pp. 323-344.

2272 _____. "Ezra Pound," Sixteen Modern American Authors.
Jackson R. Bryer, ed., Cf., #1434, pp. 445-471.

2273 _____. "The Inheritance of To Kalon," New Approaches
to Ezra Pound. Eva Hesse, ed., Cf., #41, pp. 319-330.

2274 _____. "A Note on 'Nils Lykke,'" Paideuma, 6 (Spring,
1977), 39-40.

2275 _____. "Pound as Subject." Approaches to Twentieth-
Century Literature, 2 (1964), 111-124; Approaches to the
Study of Twentieth Century Literature. East Lansing:
Michigan State U. Pr., 1964.

2276 _____, and William Tay. "Notes and Queries," Paideuma,
4, 2-3 (Winter, 1975), 547, 549.

2277 Espmark, Kjell. "Ezra Pounds 'kejsarsnitt,' Hans roll vid
redigeringen av 'The Waste Land,'" [Pound's 'Caesarean
operation,'], [His role in editing 'The Waste Land,],
Tidskrift for litteratur litteraturvetenskap, 2 (1973), 225-239.

2278 Essary, Loris. "On Language and Visual Language," Visual

Literature Criticism: A New Collection. Carbondale: So.
Ill. U. Pr., 1979, pp. 93-102.

2279   Evans, Oliver W. "Ezra Pound: Poet without a Country,"
Cw, 41 (October 20, 1944), 10-16.

2280   Everett, B. "Eliot's 'Marianne': The Waste Land and Its
Poetry of Europe," RES, 31, #121 (February, 1980), 41-53.

2281   Faas, Egbert. "Formen der Bewusstseinsdarstellung in der
dramatischen Lyrik Pounds und Eliots," Cf., #1368.

2282   Fabiani, Enzo. "Il signore dei monti pallidi," Gente, 6 dic,
(1958), pp. 24-26.

2283   Fabri, Renata. "Un giudizio di Pound su una traduzione
umanistica di Omero," Annali di Ca'Foscari, 12 (1973), 21-44.

2284   Fairchild, Hoxie N. Religious Trends in English Poetry,
1880-1920. Vol. 5, New York: Columbia U. Pr., 1962, pp.
446-456, 551-558; 1920-1965, Vol. 6, 1968, pp. 489-497,
passim.

2285   Fallacara, Luigi. "Il poeta in Prigione," Stagione, 2, #7
(Rome: 1955), 6.

2286   Falqui, Enrico. "Marinetti, Pound e l' ultimissimo," FLe, 19
(1964), 1-2.

2287   Fang, Achilles. "Fenollosa and Pound," HJAS, 20 (June,
1957), 213-238.

2288   _____. "Introduction," The Confucian Odes. The Classic
Anthology Defined by Confucius. (Trans. by Ezra Pound).
New York: New Directions, 1959.

2289   _____. "Some Reflections on the Difficulty of Translation," Studies in Chinese Thought. Arthur F. Wright, ed.
Chicago: U. of Chicago Pr., 1953, pp. 263-285, passim.

2290   Farmer, David R. Ezra Pound: An Exhibition Held in
March, 1967. The Academic Center and Undergraduate Library, U. of Texas, Austin, 1967.

2291   Fauchereau, Serge. "Ezra Pound," QL, 152 (November 16,
1972), 11-12.

2292   _____. "Où Pound et Eliot recontrent Goumilev, Mandel-
stam et Akhmatova," Europe, 601 (1979), 57-73.

2293   _____. "La Prose d'Ezra Pound," Critique (Paris), 30
(February, 1974), 189-190.

2294 Faulkner, Peter. "Yeats, Ireland and Ezra Pound," Threshold, #18 (1963), 58-68.

2295 Feder, Lillian. "Ezra Pound: The Messianic Vision," Ancient Myth in Modern Poetry. Cf., #1369, pp. 293-307.

2296 _____. "Ezra Pound: Rebirth and Reversion," Ancient Myth in Modern Poetry. Cf., #1369, pp. 200-219.

2297 _____. "The Voice from Hades in the Poetry of Ezra Pound," MQR, 10 (Summer, 1971), 167-186.

2298 Fender, Stephen. "Works in Progress in the United Kingdom," Paideuma, 7 (Spring-Fall, 1978), 289-294.

2299 Fenton, Charles. The Apprenticeship of Ernest Hemingway. New York: Farrar, Straus & Young, 1954, p. 227.

2300 Ferkiss, Victor L. "Ezra Pound and American Fascism," Journal of Politics, 17 (May, 1955), 173-197.

2301 Ferlinghetti, Lawrence. "Pound at Spoleto," SatRL, 48, #36 (September 4, 1965), 20.

2302 Ferran, Jaime. "Ezra Pound," Estafeta Literaria, No. 507 (January 1, 1973), 10-11.

2303 Fiedler, Leslie A. The Collected Essays of Leslie Fiedler. New York: Stein & Day, 1971, Vol. II, passim.

2304 _____. An End to Innocence: Essays on Culture and Politics. Boston: Beacon Pr., 1948, 1955, passim.

2305 _____. "Lyrik ist eine sterbende Kunst: Uber den Dichter in der amerikanischen Gesellschaft," DRund, 90, #1 (January, 1964), 34-41.

2306 _____. Waiting for the End: The Crisis in American Culture. New York: Stein & Day, 1964, pp. 184-191, passim.

2307 Fields, Kenneth Wayne. "The Rhetoric of Artifice: Ezra Pound, T. S. Eliot, Wallace Stevens, Walter Conrad Arensberg, Donald Evans, Mina Loy, and Yvor Winters," DA, 28 (Stanford: 1967), 4627A.

2308 Fields, Rick. "'No Oblivion in the Orange Poppy': Ernest Fenollosa and Turn of the Century Orientalism," Zero, 4 (1980), 8-24.

2309 Figgis, Darrell. "Mr. Ezra Pound," New Age, 7 (August 18, 1910), 373-375.

2310 Filler, Louis. "Book Notes," AntiochR, 9 (December, 1949),
      553-555.

2311 Finkelstein, Norman Mark. "The Utopian Invariant: Interior-
      ity and Exteriority in the Twentieth-Century Poetic Conscious-
      ness," DAI, 41, #7 (Emory, 1980), 3104A-05A.

2312 Finkelstein, Sidney. "Ezra Pound's Apologists," Mainstream,
      14, #1 (January, 1961), 19-34.

2313 Firchow, P. E. "Ezra Pound's Imagism and the Tradition,"
      CLS, 18, #4 (September, 1981), 379-385.

2314 Fischer, Walther L. "Ezra Pounds chinesische Denkstruk-
      turen," Ezra Pound: 22 Versuche über einen Dichter. Eva
      Hesse, ed., #1979, pp. 167-181.

2315 Fisher, Esther Safer. "The Pound-Abercrombie Feud," FDP,
      1 (1976), 66-69.

2316 Fitts, Dudley. "O dulce convivium!" Poetry, 79 (December,
      1951), 150-157.

2317 _____. "The Too-Good Friend," NR, 125 (December 10,
      1951), 30.

2318 Fitzgerald, Robert. "Mirroring the Commedia: An Apprecia-
      tion of Laurence Binyon's Version," Paideuma, 10, #3 (Winter,
      1981), 489-508.

2319 Fleming, William. "Ezra Pound and the French Language,"
      Ezra Pound: Perspectives, Essays in Honor of His Eightieth
      Birthday. Noel Stock, ed., #125, pp. 129-150.

2320 _____. "How to Write Poetry, I," Meanjin, 14, #3 (Mel-
      bourne: Spring, 1955), 379-389; II, 14, #4 (Summer, 1955),
      550-564.

2321 _____. "Programme for a Manifesto: Why not imagism?"
      Direction, 1, #2 (Melbourne: December, 1952), 34-37.

2322 Fletcher, John Gould. "'Hard' and 'Soft,'" Poetry, 12 (May,
      1918), 111-112.

2323 _____. Life Is My Song: The Autobiography of John
      Fletcher. New York: Toronto: Farrar & Rinehart, Inc.,
      (1937), pp. 284, passim.

2324 _____. "The Orient and Contemporary Poetry," The Asian
      Legacy and American Life. Arthur Christy, ed. New York:
      John Day, 1942, pp. 152-161, passim.

2325   Flint, F. S. "The History of Imagism," Egoist, 2, #5 (May 1, 1915), 70-71.

2326   _____. "Imagisme," Poetry, 1, #6 (March, 1913), 198-200.

2327   _____. "Letter to Robert Frost," Selected Letters of Robert Frost. New York: Holt, Rinehart & Winston, (1964), 86-87.

2328   _____. "Verse," New Age, 6 (December 9, 1909), 137-138.

2329   Flint, R. W. "Pound and the Lyric," HudR, 4, #2 (Summer, 1951), 293-304.

2330   _____. "Pound, Poetry, and Politics," Commentary, 12, #1 (July, 1951), 85-86.

2331   Flory, Wendy Stallard. "The Pound Problem," Ezra Pound and William Carlos Williams: The University of Pennsylvania Conference Papers. Daniel Hoffman, ed. Philadelphia: U. of Pennsylvania Pr., 1983, pp. 107-127.

2332   _____. "Pound's Prose Works as a Guide to His Thought," DAI, 31 (Austin, Texas: 1971), 6054A.

2333   _____ and Jo Berryman. "Report on the MLS Special Session, 1977," Paideuma, 7 (Spring-Fall, 1978), 317-324.

2334   Ford, Ford Madox. "Enter Ezra Pound ...," Your Mirror to My Times: The Selected Autobiographies and Impressions of Ford Madox Ford. Ed. with Introduction by Michael Killigrew. New York; Chicago: Holt, Rinehart & Winston, 1971, pp. 175-177.

2335   _____. New York Essays. New York: William Edwin Rudge, Inc., 1927, pp. 35-37, passim.

2336   _____. "The Poet's Eye [I II]," New Freewoman, I, #6 (September 1, 1913), 107-110.

2337   _____. "Reviews," Return to Yesterday. New York: Liveright, 1932, pp. 373-375, passim.

2338   _____. Thus to Revisit. London: Chapman & Hall, 1921, passim.

2339   Forde, S. Victoria M. "Basil Bunting's Debt to Ezra Pound and the Classics," CML, 1 (1980), 25-37.

2340   Forgue, Guy J. Letters of H. L. Mencken: Selected and Annotated by Guy J. Forgue. New York: Alfred A. Knopf, 1961, passim.

2341 Forrest-Thomson, Veronica. "The Disconnected Image-
Complex: Pound and Eliot," Poetic Artifice: A Theory of
Twentieth-Century Poetry. New York: St. Martin's Press,
1978, pp. 65-80.

2342 Forsell, Lars. "Ezra Pound," Bonniers Litterära Magasin
(Stockholm), 18 (October, 1949), 608-618.

2343 _____. "Rader från Rapallo," Dagens Nyheter (Stockholm),
(June 2, 1953).

2344 _____. "Sider av Pound," Dagens Nyheter (Stockholm),
(August 9, 1954). 2.

2345 Fraire, Isabel. "Pound and Cardenal," Review, 18 (1976),
36-42.

2346 Franciosa, Massimo. "Ezra Pound, leader di tutti," FLe, 46,
#6 (November 16, 1950), 4.

2347 Franck, J. "Ezra Pound ou la recherche désespérée d'un
monde des bénédictions," RGB (December, 1972), 25-34.

2348 Frankel, Haskell. "The San Francisco Beat," SatRL, 48, #36
(September 4, 1965), 20-21.

2349 Frankenberg, Lloyd. "Ezra Pound," Pleasure Dome: On
Reading Modern Poetry. Boston: Houghton Mifflin Co.,
1949, pp. 273-285.

2350 Fraser, George S. Ezra Pound. Edinburgh and London:
Oliver & Boyd, 1960; New York: Barnes & Noble, 1960.

2351 _____. "The Last English Imagist: On Sir Herbert Read,"
Encounter, 28, #1 (January, 1967), 86-90.

2352 _____. The Modern Writer and His World. London: D.
Verschoyle, Ltd.; New York: Criterion Books & Derek
Verschoyle, 1953, passim.

2353 _____. "Poetic Politics," TSER, 2, #1 (1975), 4-7.

2354 _____. "Pound," Vision and Rhetoric: Studies in Modern
Poetry. New York: Barnes & Noble, 1959, 1960, pp. 84ff.

2355 French, Warren G., ed. The Forties: Fiction, Poetry, Drama.
Deland, Florida: Everett/Edwards, 1969, passim.

2356 _____. The Thirties: Fiction, Poetry, Drama. Deland,
Florida: E. Edwards, 1967, pp. 123-131, passim.

2357   French, William. "For 'Gentle Graceful Dorothy,' a Tardy
       Obit," Paideuma, 12, #1 (Spring, 1983), 89-112.

2358   _____. "'Saint Hilda,' Mr. Pound, and Rilke's Parisian
       Panther at Pisa," Paideuma, 11 (1982), 79-87.

2359   _____, and Timothy Materer. "Far Flung Vortices and
       Ezra's 'Hindoo' Yogi," Paideuma, 11 (1982), 39-53.

2360   Friedman, Melvin J. "The Creative Writer as Polyglot." Wis-
       consin Academy of Sciences, Arts & Letters, 49 (1960), 229-
       236.

2361   Frost, Robert. "To Ezra Pound," Selected Letters of Robert
       Frost. Lawrance Thompson, ed. New York: Holt, Rinehart
       & Winston, 1964. pp. 85-86.

2362   _____. "Letter to John T. Bartlett," Cf., #2361, pp. 69-
       71.

2363   _____. "Letter to Thomas B. Mosher," The New Colophon,
       Part 8 (March, 1950), 316-317; Cf., #2361, pp. 96-97.

2364   _____. "Part of a letter dated December 14, 1932," Thomas
       Madigan's Autograph Album, Vol. 1 (December, 1933), 56.

2365   Froula, Christine. "Ezra Pound: Fragment, 1944," YR, 71,
       #2 (January, 1982), 161-174.

2366   Frye, Northrup. "Phalanx of Particulars," HudR, 4, #4
       (Winter, 1952), 627-631; repr., in Northrop Frye on Culture
       and Literature: A Collection of Review Essays. Robert D.
       Denham, ed. Chicago; London: U. of Chicago Pr., 1978,
       pp. 197-203.

2367   Fuchs, Daniel. "Ernest Hemingway, Literary Critic," Ernest
       Hemingway: Five Decades of Criticism. Linda Welshimer
       Wagner, ed. Michigan State U. Pr., 1974, pp. 40, 44, 56n.

2368   Fukuda, Rikutaro. "Ezra Pound and the Orient: Some
       Oriental Figures behind Ezra Pound," TamkR, 2 (October,
       1971), 61-69; EigoS, 119 (1973), 13-16; Proceedings from the
       International Comparative Literature Conference Held on July
       18-24, 1971 at Tamkang College of Arts and Sciences, Taipei,
       Taiwan, Republic of China. Yen Yuan-Shu, ed. TkR, 2,
       #2-3, i (October, 1971-April, 1972), pp. 61-69.

2369   _____. "Japanese Elements in Western Literature," Year-
       book of Comparative and General Literature, No. 11, Supple-
       ment (1962), 204-210.

2370   Fuller, Buckminster. "Pound, Synergy, and the Great De-
       sign," Agenda, 16, #iii-iv (1978-1979), 130-164.

2371   Fuller, Roy. Owls and Artificers: Oxford Lectures on Po-
       etry. New York: The Library Pr., 1971, pp. 45, 46, 128.

2372   _____. "Philistines and Jacobins," TLS, #3495 (February
       20, 1969), 183-184.

2373   _____. "Poetic Memories of the Thirties," MQR, 12, #3
       (Summer, 1973), 217-231.

2374   Fussell, Edwin. "Ezra Pound: A Note on the International
       Theme," Pound Newsletter, 10 (April, 1956), 1-3.

2375   _____. "From Imagism to 'The Waste Land,'" VWQ, 1, #4
       (1973), 58-68.

2376   Fussell, Paul. Abroad: British Literary Traveling Between
       the Wars. New York: Oxford U. Pr., 1980, passim.

2377   Gage, John T. In the Arresting Eye: The Rhetoric of
       Imagism. Baton Rouge: La. St. U. Pr., 1981, passim.

2378   _____. "Paradoxes of Objectivity and Argument in Imagist
       Theory," P&R, 12 (1979), 153-175.

2379   Gall, Sally M. "Domestic Monologues: The Problem of Voice
       in Contemporary American Poetry," MR, 23 (1982), 489-503.

2380   Gallup, Donald. "'Boobliography,' and Ezra Pound," TQ, 10,
       #4 (Winter, 1967), 80-92.

2381   _____. "The Search for Mrs. Wood's Program," Ezra
       Pound: Perspectives, Cf., #125, pp. 78-85.

2382   _____. "Some Notes on Ezra Pound and Censorship,"
       YLM, 126 (December, 1958), 37-41.

2383   _____. "T. S. Eliot and Ezra Pound: Collaborators in
       Letters," AtlM, 225, #1 (January, 1970), 48-62; repr., Poetry
       (Australia), 32 (February, 1970), 58-80.

2384   Gardner, Helen. "The Waste Land: Paris, 1922," Eliot in
       His Times: Essays on the Occasion of the Fiftieth Anniver-
       sary of 'The Waste Land.' Princeton, N.J.: Princeton U.
       Pr., 1973, pp. 67-94.

2385   Garelick, Judith Spritzer. "Marianne Moore, Modern Poet:
       A Study of Miss Moore's Relationships with William Carlos
       Williams, E. E. Cummings, T. S. Eliot, Wallace Stevens, and
       Ezra Pound," Diss., Harvard U., 1972.

1386 Geisheker, Mary Rose. "Des Imagistes: Toward a Poetic
Revolution," DAI, 33 (Milwaukee, Wisconsin: 1973), 3644A-
45A.

2387 Geltman, Max. "The Poetry and Politics of Hate," Midstream,
22, #6 (1976), 57-68.

2388 _____. "Pound and/or Mussolini," Quadrant, 16 (November-
December, 1972), 55-64.

2389 _____. "The Real Ezra Pound," Quadrant, 18 (January-
February, 1974), 39-46.

2390 Gibbons, Reginald. "Pound and the Gods," Agenda, 17,
#3-4, and 18, #1 (Autumn-Winter-Spring, 1979-80), 239-255.

2391 Gibson, Mary Ellis. "Browning and Pound: 'Pourquoi nier
son pere?'" BSNotes, 10, ii (1980), 1-10.

2392 Gifford, Henry. "Pound, Mayakovsky and the Defence of
Human Nature," PNR, 6 (1977), 15-18.

2393 Gil de Biedma, Jaime. "Postrera imagen de Ezra Pound,"
Plural, 18 (1973), 10-11.

2394 Gilkes, Martin. "Discovery of Ezra Pound," English, II, #8
(1938), 74-83.

2395 Ginsberg, Allen. "Encounters with Ezra Pound," Composed
on the Tongue. Donald Allen, ed. Bolina, Calif.: Grey Fox
Pr., 1980, pp. 1-17.

2396 Giuliani, Alfredo. "Ezra Pound e I colori della ta velezza,"
La Parrucca, III, #3 (Milan), (May 18, 1955), 32-33.

2397 _____. "The Metrical Recherche of Ezra Pound," [the
Problem of the Lyre], Italian Images of Ezra Pound. Angela
Jung and Guido Palandri, eds. Cf., #510, pp. 87-92.

2398 _____. "Le ragioni metriche di Ezra Pound (Il problema
della cetra)," NC, Nos. 5-6 (genn.-giugno, 1956), 105-111.

2399 Goacher, Denis. "BBC Third Program: Ezra Pound--
Translations from the Chinese," Cf., #125, pp. 210-219.

2400 _____. "Dr. Leavis or Mr. Pound," The European, #1
(March, 1953), 41-51.

2401 Godden, Richard. "Icons, Etymologies, Origins and Monkey
Puzzles in the Languages of Upward and Fenollosa," Ezra
Pound: Tactics for Reading. Ian F. A. Bell, ed., Cf.,
#449, pp. 221-244.

2402 Goekjian, Gregory F. "The Function and Effect of Rhyme,"
      DAI, 31, #9 (Pittsburgh: 1970), 4714A.

2403 Going, William T. "A Peacock Dinner: The Homage of
      Pound and Yeats to Wilfrid Scawen Blunt," JML, 1, #3 (1971),
      303-310.

2404 Goldman, Arnold. "Ezra Pound (1885-1972)," American Liter-
      ature in Context, IV: 1900-1930. New York: London:
      Methuen, 1982, pp. 75-87.

2405 Goldring, Douglas. The Last Pre-Raphaelite: A Record of
      the Life and Writings of Ford Madox Ford. London: Macdonald
      & Co., Ltd., 1948, passim.

2406 _____. People and Places. Boston: Houghton Mifflin &
      Co., 1929, p. 264.

2407 _____. South Lodge. London: Constable & Co., Ltd.,
      1943, pp. 48-49, passim.

2408 _____. Trained for Genius: The Life and Writings of
      Ford Madox Ford. New York: E. P. Dutton & Co., Inc.,
      1949, passim.

2409 Goldsmith, Arnold L. "The Influence of Hulme, Richards,
      and Pound," American Literary Criticism: 1905-1965. Vol.
      III. Boston: G. K. Hall, 1979, pp. 103-104.

2410 Golffing, Francis, and Barbara Gibbs. "The Public Voice:
      Remarks on Poetry Today," Commentary, 28, #1 (July, 1959),
      63-69.

2411 Goodwin, K. L. "Ezra Pound's Influence on Literary Criti-
      cism," MLQ, 29, #4 (December, 1968), 423-438.

2412 _____. "Some Corrections to Standard Biographies of
      Yeats," N&Q, 12, #5 (May, 1965), 260-262.

2413 Gordon, Ambrose, Jr. The Invisible Tent: The War Novels
      of Ford Madox Ford. Austin: U. of Texas Pr., 1964, pp.
      29-30, passim.

2414 Gordon, David. "Academia Bulletin," Paideuma, 3 (Winter,
      1974), 381-384.

2415 _____. "Ezra Pound Translating a Li Po Poem," Paideuma,
      3, #1 (Spring, 1974), 55-59.

2416 _____. "From the Blue Serpent to Kati," Paideuma, 3, #2
      (Fall, 1974), 239-244.

2417 _____. "Notes and Observations: The Pith of Del Mar,"
     Paideuma, 6 (Spring, 1977), 41-42.

2418 _____. "'Root/Br./By Produce' in Pound's Confucian Ode,
     166," Paideuma, 3, #1 (Spring, 1974), 13-32.

2419 Gordon, Robert. "'Old Yeats,' Young Willie, and 'this queer
     creature Ezra Pound,'" MJSS, 2, #1 (Summer, 1973), 68-73.

2420 Gorlier, Claudio. "Poesia e Civilta," NC, Nos. 5-6 (genn.-
     giugno, 1956), 112-122; "Poetry and Civilization," Italian
     Images of Ezra Pound, Angela Jung and Guido Palandri, eds.,
     and trs., Cf., #518, pp. 93-101.

2421 _____. "Riflessioni su Ezra Pound," Approdo, 59-60
     (1972), 51-56.

2422 Gorman, H. S. "Bolingbroke of Bards," NAR, 219 (June,
     1924), 855-865.

2423 Grant, Joy. Harold Monro and the Poetry Bookshop.
     Berkeley and Los Angeles: U. of Calif. Pr., 1967, passim.

2424 Graves, Robert. The Common Asphodel: Collected Essays
     on Poetry: 1922-1949. London: H. Hamilton, 1949, passim.

2425 _____. "Dr. Syntax and Mr. Pound," The Crowning
     Privilege: The Clark Lectures, 1954-1955. London:
     Cassell & Co., c1955, pp. 212-214.

2426 _____. "Dr. Syntax and Mr. Pound," On Poetry: Col-
     lected Talks and Essays. New York: Doubleday, 1969.

2427 _____. "Letter to Editors of the Yale Literary Magazine,"
     YLM, 127, #6 (January, 1959), 10.

2428 _____. "These Be Your Gods, O Israel!" EIC, 5 (April,
     1955), 129-150; NR, 134 (February 27, 1956), 16-18; (March
     5, 1956), 17-18.

2429 _____. "Working Models for Young Poets," TLS (October
     29, 1954), 689.

2430 Greenbaum, Leonard. "The Hound & Horn Archive," YULG,
     39, #3 (January, 1965), 137-146.

2431 Greene, Elizabeth. "Ezra Pound and Francois Villon: A
     Solution in Lyric Sequence," DAI, 32 (Toronto: 1969), 430A.

2432 Gregory, Horace. "The London Adventures," Amy Lowell:
     Portrait of the Poet in Her Time. Edinburgh; New York:
     Thomas Nelson & Sons, 1958, pp. 93-131.

2433 _____. "Pound's Sterling Age," NYT (July 9, 1950), 7.

2434 Griffin, Ernest. "'E. P. Ode Pour L'Election de Son Sepul-
chre' and Max Plowman's Pamphlet, 'The Right to Live,'"
Paideuma, 5, #2 (Fall, 1976), 269-274.

2435 _____. "Pound in Perspective," TSEN, 1, #2 (1974), 13-15.

2436 Grigson, Geoffrey. "From Imagists to the Black Mountain,"
The Contrary View: Glimpses of Fudge and Gold. Rowman &
Littlefield, 1974, pp. 221-229.

2437 Grillandi, Massimo and Lina Amgioletti. "Una poesia ardua e
chiara," FLe, 48:46 (1972), 6-8.

2438 Gross, Dalton. "Ezra Pound's Early Literary Reputation:
George Sterling's Dissent," Paideuma, 2, #2 (Fall, 1973), 203-
204.

2439 Gross, Harvey S. "The 'Celebrated Metric' of Ezra Pound,"
Sound and Form in Modern Poetry: A Study of Prosody from
Thomas Hardy to Robert Lowell. Ann Arbor, Mich: U. of
Michigan Pr., 1964, pp. 130-168.

2440 _____. "The Contrived Corridor: A Study in Modern
Poetry and the Meaning of History," DA, 15 (Michigan:
1955), 583.

2441 Grubb, Frederick. A Vision of Reality: A Study of Liberal-
ism in Twentieth-Century Verse. London: Chatto & Windus,
1965; New York: Barnes & Noble, 1965, passim.

2442 Gugelberger, Georg M. Ezra Pound's Medievalism. (EurH,
XVIII, 17). Frankfort: Lang, 1979.

2443 _____. "Medium Aevum Novum: Medieval European Literature and Ezra Pound," DAI, 33 (Iowa U.: 1972), 1724A.

2444 _____. "The Secularization of 'Love' to a Poetic Metaphor:
Cavalcanti, Center of Pound's Medievalism," Paideuma, 2, #2
(Fall, 1973), 159-173.

2445 _____. "Zum Mittelaltereinfluss in der modernen Dichtung:
Ezra Pounds Chaucerbild," OL, 35 (1980), 220-234.

2446 Guglielmi, Joseph E. "Pound ou la saturation livresque,"
CdS, 53 (July-September, 1966), 122-125.

2447 Guidacci, Margherita. "Ezra Pound," Stagione, 2, #7 (Rome:
1955), 7.

2448 _____. "Saggi, letteria di Ezra Pound," Humanitas, 4
(1975), 277-284.

2449 Guimond, James. The Art of William Carlos Williams: A
Discovery and Possession of America. Urbana and Chicago:
U. of Illinois Pr., 1968, passim.

2450 Gutchess, Elizabeth Denver. "Four Translators 'after' Pound:
Studies of Richard Wilbur, Robert Lowell, Robert Bly and
Galway Kinnell," DAI, 44, #3 (Notre Dame: 1983), 752A.

2451 Haas, Rudolf. "Ein erstes Modell: Masefields 'Cargoes' und
Pounds 'melopoeia,' 'phaenopoeia,' 'logopoeia,' " Theorie und
Paris der Interpretation: Modellanalysen englischer und
amerikanischer Texte. (Grundlagen der Anglistik und
Amerikanistik 5.) Berlin: Schmidt, pp. 68-83.

2452 Haase, Camilla Bunker. "Serious Artists: The Relationship
between Ford Madox Ford and Ezra Pound," DAI, 45, #12,
Part 1 (Harvard: 1984), 3635A.

2453 Haeusermann, H. W. "W. B. Yeats's Criticism of Ezra
Pound," SR, 57 #3 (July-September, 1949), 437-455.

2454 Hagemann, E. R. " 'Dear Folks ... Dear Ezra,' Hemingway's
Early Years and Correspondence, 1917-1924," CollL, 7 (1980),
202-212.

2455 Hagenbüchle, Roland, ed. "Pound's Imagist Alba: Myth as
Cognitive Method," Poetic Knowledge: Circumference and
Center. Joseph Swann, ed. Bonn: 1980, n.p.

2456 Hall, Donald. "Poets Aloud," Poetry, 139, #5 (February,
1982), 297-305.

2457 _____. "The Poet's Place," Goatfoot, Milktongue Twinbird:
Interviews, Essays, and Notes on Poetry, 1970-1976. Ann
Arbor: U. of Michigan Pr., 1978, pp. 205, 208.

2458 _____. "Ezra Pound," Writers at Work: The Paris Review
Interviews. 2nd ser. [Prepared for book publication by
George Plimpton], Introduction by Van Wyck Brooks. Viking
Pr., 1963, pp. 35-59.

2459 Halper, Nathan. "How Simple: A Tale of Joyce and Pound,"
PR, 44, #3 (1977), 438-446.

2460 Halperen, Max. "Ezra Pound: Poet-Priest, Poet-Propagandist,"
Warren French, ed. The Thirties: Fiction, Poetry, Drama.
Cf., #2356, pp. 123-131.

2461 Hamburger, Michael. A Mug's Game: Intermittent Memoirs,
      1924-1954. Cheadle: Carconet Pr., 1973, pp. 245, 247, 265.

2462 _____. The Truth of Poetry: Tensions in Modern Poetry
      from Baudelaire to the 1960's. New York: Harcourt, Brace
      & World, 1969, passim.

2463 Hamilton, Alastair. The Appeal of Fascism: A Study of In-
      tellectuals and Fascism, 1919-1945. New York: Macmillan,
      1971, passim.

2464 Hamilton, Ian. "A Conversation with Robert Lowell," MoOc,
      2, #1 (Winter, 1972), 28-48.

2465 Hand, Alonzo. "Talk of the Town," New Yorker, 19 (August
      14, 1943), 16-17.

2466 Hand, Claudius A. "Grow old along with me," Hamilton
      Alumni Review (July, 1955), 181-183.

2467 Hannah, J. M. "Ezra Pound," Manuscripts, No. 7 (Mel-
      bourne), (November, 1933), 33-40.

2468 Hansen, Miriam. Ezra Pounds frühe Poetik und Kulturkritik
      zwischen Aufklärung und Avantgarde. (SAVL, 16), Stutt-
      gart: Metzler, 1979.

2469 Hargreaves, Frederic Kline, Jr. "The Concept of Private
      Meaning in Modern Criticism," DAI, 38, #12, Pt. I (Boston
      U.: 1978), 7324A.

2470 Harmer, J. B. Victory in Limbo: Imagism, 1908-1917.
      London: Secker & Warburg, 1975; New York: St. Martin's
      Pr., 1975, p. 76.

2471 Harmon, William R. "Ideas of Time in Ezra Pound's Work,"
      DAI, 31 (Cincinnati: 1970), 3548A.

2472 Harper, Michael Frederick. "Beyond Romanticism: The
      Poetry of Ezra Pound," DAI, 34 (Pennsylvania: 1973), 5173A.

2473 Harris, Frank. "H. L. Mencken, Critic," Contemporary Por-
      traits. 4th Series. New York: Brentano's Publishers, 1923,
      p. 149.

2474 Harris, Natalie Beth. "Aesthetics and/or Politics: Ezra
      Pound's Late Critical Prose," CentR, 23 (Winter, 1979), 1-19.

2475 _____. "A Map of Ezra Pound's Literary Criticism," SoR,
      19 (1983), 548-572.

2476   _____. "New Pound Holdings at the Lilly Library,"
          Paideuma, 8 (1979), 141-146.

2477   _____. "The Patterned Energy of Ezra Pound's Criticism,"
          DAI, 38 (Indiana: 1977), 5478A.

2478   Harrison, Keith. "No Things But in Ideas: Doctor Williams
          and Mr. Pound," DR, 47, #4 (Winter, 1967-68), 577-580.

2479   Hart, Lawrence. "The New Face of Conformity," Works, I,
          #3 (Spring, 1968), 106-113.

2480   Hartman, Charles O. "Condensation: The Critical Vocabulary
          of Pound and Eliot," CE, 39 (October, 1977), 179-190.

2481   _____. "Some Notes on Poetic Value," ConP, 2, #3 (1977),
          24-50.

2482   Hartman, Geoffrey. "The Maze of Modernism," Beyond For-
          malism: Literary Essays, 1958-1970. New Haven: Yale U.
          Pr., 1970, pp. 258ff, passim.

2483   Haruyama, Yukio. "Ezura Paundo," [Ezra Pound], Joisu
          Chushin no Bungaku Undo [The Joyce-Centered Literary
          Movement], December 15, 1933, pp. 21-50.

2484   _____. 20 Seiki Ei Bungaku Shin Undo, [New Develop-
          ments in Twentieth Century English Literature], Tokyo:
          Daiichi Shobo, 1935.

2485   Hasbany, Richard. "The Shock of Vision: An Imagist Read-
          ing of In Our Time," Ernest Hemingway: Five Decades of
          Criticism. Linda Welshimer Wagner, ed. Michigan State U.
          Pr., 1974, pp. 224-240.

2486   Hassall, Christopher. A Biography of Edward March. New
          York: Harcourt, Brace & Co., 1959, p. 82.

2487   Hatlen, Burton. "Report on Work in Progress," Paideuma, 3,
          #2 (Fall, 1974), 275-277.

2488   _____. "Report on Work in Progress," Paideuma, 5, #3
          (Winter, 1976), 469-470.

2489   Hattersley, Michael Elkins. "Poets of Light: Ezra Pound,
          William Carlos Williams, and Wallace Stevens," DAI, 37, #7
          (Yale: 1976), 4353A.

2490   Hattum, Marinus van. "Der Pound-Text im Requiem," ABnG,
          5 (1976), 103-109.

2491   Häusermann, H. W. "W. B. Yeats' Criticism of Ezra Pound,"
       English Studies, 29, #4 (August, 1948), 97-109; SR, 57, #3
       (1949), 437-455.

2492   Hayman, David. "Pound at the Wake or the Uses of a Con-
       temporary," JJQ, 2 (Spring, 1965), 204-216.

2493   _____. "Tristan and Isolde in Finnegans Wake: A Study
       of the Sources and Evolution of a Theme," CL, 1, #2 (1964),
       94-112.

2494   Healey, Eleanor Claire. "Ezra Pound: Poet in Rebellion,"
       MJSS, 2, #1 (1973), 56-67.

2495   _____. "Imagist Dialogue," DAI, 29, #10 (Columbia:
       1968), 3612A.

2496   Healy, J. V. "Addendum," Poetry, 68 (September, 1946),
       347-349.

2497   Heap, J. "Ezra Pound's Critics," and "Pounding Ezra,"
       The Little Review Anthology. Margaret Anderson, ed. New
       York: Hermitage House, Inc., 1953, pp. 211-212, 272-273.

2498   Heath-Stubbs, John. "The Last Humanist," Ezra Pound: A
       Collection of Essays. Peter Russell, ed. Cf., #114, pp. 249-
       256.

2499   _____. "Michael Alexander's The Poetic Achievement of
       Ezra Pound," Agenda, 17, #3-4; 18, #1 (Aut-Wntr-Spr.,
       1979-80), 278-280.

2500   Heinzelman, Kurt. "'Getting It' in Paterson: The Increment
       Defended," The Economics of the Imagination. Amherst: U.
       of Mass. Pr., 1980, pp. 234-275.

2501   Helmling, Steve. "A Homemade World by Hugh Kenner,"
       Paideuma, 4, #1 (Spring, 1975), 171-173.

2502   Helwig, Werner. "Wesen, Werk und Wege des Ezra Pound,"
       FH, 28 (1973), 49-56.

2503   Hemingway, Ernest. "Homage to Ezra," An Examination of
       Ezra Pound. Rev. & Enl. Peter Russell, ed. Cf., #114,
       pp. 73-76; This Quarter (Paris), I, 1 (Spring, 1925), 221-
       225.

2504   _____. "Hüldigung an Ezra," Ezra Pound: 22 Versuche
       über einen Dichter. Eva Hesse, ed., #1979, pp. 398-400.

2505   _____. "I sessantacinque anni di un significativo poeta,
       Ezra Pound," FLe, 46, #3 (November 19, 1950), 3.

2506 _____. "A Note on Ezra Pound," Ezra Pound: Perspectives. Noel Stock, ed., Cf., #125, pp. 151-153.

2507 _____. "The Soul of Spain, Part I," Der Querschmitt, (October, 1924); repr., in Sou'wester (October 30, 1970), p. 71.

2508 Henderson, Alice Corbin. Review: "Des Imagistes: An Anthology," Poetry, 5, #1 (October, 1914), 38-40.

2509 Henderson, Archibald, III. "Pound and Music: The Paris and Early Rapallo Years," DAI, 44, #1 (Los Angeles: 1983), 169A.

2510 Hendrickson, John R. "An Exchange on Pound," Poetry, 91, #3 (December, 1957), 209-211.

2511 Henn, T. R. The Lonely Tower: Studies in the Poetry of W. B. Yeats. London: Methuen & Co., Ltd., 1950, p. 97; New York: Barnes & Noble, 1965.

2512 Hesse, Eva. Ezra Pound: von Sinn und Wahnsinn. Münich: Kindler Verlag, 1978, pp. 414-415.

2513 _____. "Ezra Pounds ABC des Lesens," Dichten und Trachten, 9 (1957), 70-75.

2514 _____. "Mythopoiós," Paideuma, 8 (1979), 293-295.

2515 _____. "Pound oder der Verlangerte Konflikt," Diagonale, 5 (1967), 26-29.

2516 _____. "Schiavoni: 'That Chap on the Wood Barge,'" Paideuma, 4, #1 (Spring, 1975), 101-104; "Schiavoni: Or: When St. Hieronymus Turned His Back," Paideuma, 4, #1 (Spring, 1975), 105-110.

2517 _____. "Von der Nationalität des Dichters," Akzente, 15 (August, 1968), 354-382.

2518 _____. "The Vortex: On the Source of Pound's 'Vortex,'" Paideuma, 9 (1980), 329-331.

2519 _____ [a]; Dorothy Pound [b]; William Howell [c], "Notes and Queries/Letters to the Editor," Paideuma, 1, #2 (Winter, 1972), 271-277, 281-282.

2520 Heyen, William. "Toward the Still Point: The Imagistic Aesthetic," BSUF, 9, #1 (Winter, 1968), 44-48.

2521 Heymann, C. David. "Ezra Pound: A Portrait of the Artist as an Old Man," UDQ, 6 (Autumn, 1971), 1-12.

2522 _____. "The Pound Files," NYTB, VII (April 21, 1974), 47.

2523 Highet, Gilbert. "Homage to Ezra Pound," Nation, 154 (February 21, 1942), 228-230.

2524 Hillyer, Robert. "The Crisis in American Poetry," AmMercury, 70 (January, 1950), 65-71.

2525 _____. In Pursuit of Poetry. New York; London: McGraw-Hill Bk. Co., Ltd., 1960, pp. 187-190, 193-195, passim.

2526 Hindus, Milton. "Philip Rahv: The Critic and the Man," Images and Ideas in American Culture: The Functions of Criticism. Essays in Memory of Philip Rahv. Arthur Edelstein, ed. Hanover, New Hampshire: Pub. by Brandeis U. Pr., distributed by U. Pr. of Brandeis, New England, 1979, pp. 182-183.

2527 Hobhouse, Janet. Everybody Who Was Anybody: A Biography of Gertrude Stein. New York: G. P. Putnam's Sons, 1975, pp. 116, 125.

2528 Hobsbaum, Philip. "The Growth of English Modernism," WSCL, 6, #1 (Winter-Spring, 1965), 97-105.

2529 Hoffman, Daniel. "Old Ez and Uncle William," The Reporter, 37 (November 2, 1967), 59-63.

2530 Hoffman, Frederick John. The Imagination's New Beginning: Theology and Modern Literature. Notre Dame, Indiana; London: U. of Notre Dame Pr., 1967, passim.

2531 Hogg, Robert. "The Open Universe of Modern Poetry," Brave New Universe: Testing the Values of Science and Society. Tom Henighan, ed. Ottawa: Tecumseh: 1980, pp. 125-139.

2532 Holaday, Woon-Ping Chin. "From Ezra Pound to Maxine Hong Kingston: Expressions of Chinese Thought in American Literature," MELUS, 5, ii (1978), 15-24.

2533 _____. "Pound and Binyon: China via the British Museum," Paideuma, 6 (Spring, 1977), 27-36.

2534 Hölderlin, Friedrich. "Three Poems Translated by Richard Sieburth," Agenda, 17, #3-4; 18, #1 (Aut-Wntr-Spr., 1979-80), 118-121.

2535 Hollander, John, ed. "Ezra Pound: A Retrospect," Modern

Poetry: Essays in Criticism. London; New York: Oxford U. Pr., 1968, pp. 3-14.

2536 Holmes, John. "Pound Wise, Pound Foolish," Audience, 8, #3 (January, 1962), 109-112.

2537 Homberger, Eric. The Art of the Real: Poetry in England and America since 1939. London: Rowman & Littlefield, 1977, passim.

2538 _____. "Pound, Ford and 'Prose': The Making of a Modern Poet," JAmS, 5, #3 (December, 1971), 281-292.

2539 _____. "The Uncollected Plath," New Statesman, 84, #2166 (September 22, 1972), 404-405.

2540 Honig, Edwin. "That Mutation of Pound's," KR, 17, #3 (Summer, 1955), 349-356.

2541 Hough, Graham. "Imagism and Its Consequences," Image and Experience: Studies in a Literary Revolution. London: Duckworth, 1960; Lincoln: U. of Nebraska Pr., 1960, passim.

2542 Houserman, H. W. "W. B. Yeats' Criticism of Ezra Pound," ES, 29 (August, 1948), 97-109.

2543 Howarth, Herbert. Notes on Some Figures Behind T. S. Eliot. Boston: Houghton, Mifflin, 1964, pp. 216-222, passim.

2544 Howarth, R. G. "Ezra Pound," Southerly, 4 (Sidney: 1955), 237-238.

2545 _____. "Ezra Pound," Some Modern Writers. Australia: Extension Board of the University of Sydney, 1940, pp. [7]-31.

2546 _____. Two Modern Writers: Ezra Pound and Edith Sitwell. Cape Town: U. of Cape Town Editorial Board, 1963.

2547 Howe, Susan and Charles Ruas. "New Directions: An Interview with James Laughlin," The Art of Literary Publishing: Editors on Their Craft. Bill Henderson, ed. Yonkers, New York: Pushcart Pr., 1980, pp. 13-48.

2548 Hubbell, Jay B. "Ezra Pound," Who Are the Major American Writers? A Study of the Changing Canon. Durham, N.C.: Duke U. Pr., 1972, pp. 192-195, passim.

2549 Hubbell, L. W. "The Age of Pound," EigoS, 117 (1972), 670-673.

2550 Hubbell, Lindley. "Yeats, Pound, and Nō Drama," EWR, 1
      (Spring, 1964), 70-78.

2551 Hume, Robert. "The Contribution of Ezra Pound," English,
      8 (Summer, 1950), 60-65.

2552 Hummel, John. "The Provençal Translations," TQ, 10, #4
      (Winter, 1967), 47-51.

2553 Hunting, Robert. "A Woodnote Wild," Paideuma, 6 (Fall,
      1977), 177-179.

2554 Huntley, Carter. "The Imagistes," Poetry and Drama, I
      (June, 1913), 127-128.

2555 Hurtado, Gerardo César, ed. Ezra Pound. (Pensamiento de
      Amér. 12.) San José, Costa Rica: Ministerio de Cultura,
      Juventud y Deportes, 1978.

2556 Hurwitz, Harold M. "Ezra Pound and Rabindranath Tagore,"
      AL, 36, #1 (March, 1964), 53-63.

2557 _____. "Hemingway's Tutor, Ezra Pound," MFS, 17, #4
      (Winter, 1972), 469-482; Ernest Hemingway: Five Decades of
      Criticism. Linda Welshimer Wagner, ed. East Lansing:
      Michigan State U. Pr., 1974, pp. 8-21.

2558 Hutchins, Patricia. "Ezra Pound in Kensington," New World
      Writing. (11th Mentor Selection.) New York: New American
      Library of World Lit. (1957), pp. 203-213.

2559 _____. "Fifty Years of Ezra Pound," Time & Tide, 40
      (May 23, 1959), 599-600.

2560 _____. James Joyce's World. London: Methuen & Co.,
      Ltd., 1957, pp. 110-113, passim.

2561 Hynes, Samuel, ed. Introduction. Further Speculation by
      T. E. Hulme. Minn.: U. of Minnesota Pr., 1955; repr.,
      Lincoln, Nebr., 1962, pp. xviiff.

2562 _____. "Some Views of the Village Explainer," SR, 69, #3
      (Summer, 1961), 468-476.

2563 Ivănescu, Mircea. "'Il miglior Fabbro,'" SXX, 15, ix (1972),
      38-46.

2564 Izubuchi, Hiroshi. "Kankei e no Shokushu--Pound no Giho,"
      EigoS, 119 (1973), 5-6. [Feeling for relations--Pound's
      skill.]

2565 Izzo, Carlo. "Ezra Pound: 'Il miglior fabbro,'" Paragone,
      280 (1973), 88-96.

2566 _____. "Ezra Pound," Storia della letteratura nord-
      americana. 2nd ed. Milan: Nuova accademia, 1958, pp.
      584-590.

2567 Jackaman, Rob. "The Early and the Late Ezra Pound," SoRA,
      12 (1979), 76-87.

2568 Jackson, Brendan. "'The Fulsomeness of her Prolixity':
      Reflections on H. D., 'Imagiste,'" SAQ, 83, #1 (Winter,
      1984), 91-102.

2569 _____. "A Reluctant American: Pound's Response to
      Whitman, Whistler, and Henry James," Paideuma, 11 (1982),
      326-334.

2570 Jackson, Thomas Herbert. The Early Poetry of Ezra Pound.
      Diss. Yale U., 1960; Harvard U. Pr., 1969.

2571 _____. "Herder, Pound, and the Concept of Expression,"
      MLQ, 44, #4 (December, 1983), 374-393.

2572 _____. "The Poetic Politics of Ezra Pound," JML, 3
      (April, 1974), 987-1011.

2573 Janssens, G. A. M. The American Literary Review: A
      Critical History, 1920-1950. Paris: The Hague-Mouton,
      1968, passim.

2574 _____. "Perspectives on Pound," DQR, 3 (1973), 11-17.

2575 Jarrell, Randall. "Fifty Years of American Poetry."
      PrairieSch, 37, #1 (Spring, 1963), 1-27.

2576 Jeffares, Alexander Norman. W. B. Yeats: Man and Poet.
      London: Routledge & Kegan Paul, Ltd., 1040, pp. 176-177,
      passim.

2577 Jenkins, Alan. "Strange Correspondences: On Ezra Pound,"
      Encounter, 58, #1 (January, 1982), 40-49.

2578 Jennings, Elizabeth. "Idea and Expression in Emily Dickin-
      son, Marianne Moore and Ezra Pound," AmP, 31 (1965), 97-
      113; American Poetry. Ervin Ehrenpreis, ed. New York:
      St. Martin's Pr., 1965.

2579 Johnson, Carol. "The Translator as Poet," ArtInt, 16, #8
      (October, 1972), 129-121.

2580 Johnson, Geoffrey. "English Poetry Today," LHY, 6, #1
      (January, 1965), 30-35.

2581 Johnson, Scott. "The 'Tools' of the Ideogramic Method,"
      Paideuma, 10, #3 (Winter, 1981), 525-532.

2582 Jones, A. R. "Notes Toward a History of History of Imagism:
      An Examination of Literary Sources," SAQ, 60 (Summer, 1961),
      262-285.

2583 Jones, Dan Lewis. "The Poetics of Ezra Pound and T. S.
      Eliot," DAI, 34 (Utah: 1973), 777A.

2584 Jones, David. "Extract from a Letter to Father Desmond
      Chute," Agenda, 17, #3-4; 18, #1 (Aut-Wntr-Spr., 1979-80),
      273-277.

2585 Joost, Nicholas. Ernest Hemingway and 'The Little Maga-
      zines': The Paris Years. Barre, Mass.: Barre Pubs.,
      1968, passim.

2586 _____. "Ezra Pound and The Dial--And a Few Transla-
      tions," Sou'wester, Special Ezra Pound No., (October 30,
      1970), 59-71.

2587 _____, and Alvin Sullivan. D. H. Lawrence and 'The
      Dial', Carbondale and Edwardsville: So. Ill. U. Pr., 1970,
      passim.

2588 Jordan, Barbara Scott. "Viola Jordan and Ezra Pound:
      Some Notes on Their Friendship," YULG, 51, #2 (1976), 98-
      103.

2589 Joseph, Terri Brint. "'Near Perigord': A Perplexity of
      Voices," Paideuma, 11 (1982), 93-98.

2590 Joyce, James. "Letter on Pound," Critical Writings of James
      Joyce. Ellsworth Mason and Richard Ellmann, eds. New
      York: Viking Pr., 1959, pp. 253-254.

2591 _____. "Letter to Ernest Walsh," This Quarter. Paris, I,
      i (Spring, 1925), 219.

2592 _____. The Letters of James Joyce. Stuart Gilbert, ed.
      New York: The Viking Pr., Ltd., 1957, pp. 23-24, passim.

2593 Juhasz, Suzanne H. "Patterns of Metaphor: Their Function
      in Some Modern Long Poems--Studies in Williams, Pound,
      Stevens, and Eliot," DAI, 32 (Calif., Berkeley: 1971), 920-
      21A.

2594 _____. "Williams, Pound, Stevens, and the Imagist Movement," Cf., #724, pp. 13-39.

2595 Jung, Angela Chih-ying. "Ezra Pound and China," DA, 15 (Seattle, U. of Washington: 1955), 2208-09. Ann Arbor, Univ. of Microfilms, 1955.

2596 _____, and Guido Palandri. "Uncle Ez," IQ, 64 (1973), 23-29.

2597 Junkins, Donald. "Mountain Interval: A Visit with Robert Frost in Ripton, Vermont," IndianLit (New Delhi), III (September, 1960), 30-37. [Frost's reminiscences of Pound.]

2598 Just, Klaus G. "Zur amerikanischen Literaturkritik: Ezra Pound und R. P. Blackmur," Merkur, 10 (December, 1956), 1230-1233.

2599 Kanaseki, Hisao. "Pound to Modernism--Passionate Simplicity," EigoS, 119 (1973), 7-8.

2600 Kappel, Andrew J. "Ezra Pound in Heaven," HudR, 35, #1 (Spring, 1982), 73-86.

2601 _____. "Ezra Pound, Thomas Carter, and the Making of an American Literary Magazine," Shenandoah, 31, #3 (1980), 3-22.

2602 _____. "Perception's Champion: The Affirmation and Refinement of Value in the Poetry of Ezra Pound," DAI, 39, #3 (Rice U.: 1978), 1550A.

2603 _____. "The Reading and Writing of a Modern Paradiso: Ezra Pound and the Books of Paradise," TCL, 27, #3 (Fall, 1981), 223-246.

2604 Karpinski, Joanne B. "Poetics and Polemics: Strategies of Ezra Pound and Vladimir Mayakovsky," DAI, 41, #8 (U. of Colorado at Boulder: 1980), 3566A.

2605 Kayman, Martin A. "A Contest for Hart's 'Complex': A Contribution to a Study of Pound and Science," Paideuma, 12, #2-3 (Fall-Winter, 1983), 223-235.

2606 _____. "Ezra Pound and the Phantasy of Science: An Investigation into the Relation Between Pound's Poetic Techniques and His Political Ideology, through the Image and Its Scientific Background," DAI, 39, #3119C.

2607 _____. "Report on the Ezra Pound Conference Held at the

University of Keele, September 20-23, 1976," Paideuma, 5, #3 (1976), 461-467.

2608   Kazin, Alfred. "Language as History: Ezra Pound's Search for the Authority of History," The Problem of Authority in America, Mark E. Kann, ed. Philadelphia: Temple U. Pr., 1981, pp. 113-125.

2609   _____. "The Writer as Political Crazy," Playboy, 20 (1973), pp. 207-8, 136, 206-9.

2610   Keller, David Michael. "Ezra Pound and Guido Cavalcanti: The Poetics of Translation," DAI, 35, #5 (Wisconsin: 1974), 2993A-94A.

2611   Kelly, Robert G. "The Premises of Disorganization: A Study of Literary Form in Ezra Pound, T. S. Eliot, James Joyce, and Dorothy Richardson," Diss. (Stanford: 1952), pp. 226-228.

2612   Kempf, Roger. "James Job Joyce," CritP, 24, #251 (April, 1968), 368-379.

2613   Kennedy, George. "Fenollosa, Pound, and the Chinese Character," YLM, 126 (December, 1958), 24-36.

2614   Kenner, Hugh. The Art of Poetry. New York: Holt, Rinehart & Winston, 1959.

2615   _____. "'As of Wings and of Water,'" Poetry, 85 (December, 1954), 159-165.

2616   _____. "Baker Street to Eccles Street: The Odyssey of a Myth," HudR, 1, #4 (Winter, 1949), 483.

2617   _____. Bucky: A Guided Tour of Buckminster Fuller. New York: Morrow, 1973, pp. 83-84, 152-153, passim.

2618   _____. "Dante tra Pound ed Eliot," Verri, #18 (1964), 35-40.

2619   _____. Review: Dichtung und Prosa of Ezra Pound, Trans. by Eva Hesse, Die Tat, #304 (Zurich: November 7, 1953), 11; and in Poetry, 83, #6 (March, 1954), 357-366.

2620   _____. "Douglas," Sou'wester (So. Ill. U.), Special Ezra Pound Number (Fall, 1970), 6-20.

2621   _____. "An Exchange on Ezra Pound," Poetry, 91, #3 (December, 1957), 210-221.

2622 _____. "Ezra Pound, RIP," NatlRev, 24, #43 (November 24, 1972), 1289.

2623 _____. "Ezra Pound and Chinese," Agenda, Special Issue in Honor of Ezra Pound's Eightieth Birthday, 4, #2 (October-November, 1965), 38-41.

2624 _____. "Ezra Pound and the Light of France," YFS, 10 (1953), 54-64; repr., and "Faces to the Wall," Gnomon: Essays on Contemporary Literature. New York: McDowell, Obolensky, 1958, pp. 80-100; 263-279.

2625 _____. "Ezra Pound and Provision of Measures," Poetry, 83, #1 (October, 1953), 29-35.

2626 _____. "Ezra Pound und das Geld," NDH, 114 (1967), 22-40.

2627 _____. "Ezra Pound und das Licht der Aufklarung," Ezra Pound: 22 Versuche über einen Dichter. Eva Hesse, ed., Cf., #2504, pp. 149-162.

2628 _____. "Faces to the Wall," Shenandoah, 6, #1 (Winter, 1954), 39-51.

2629 _____. "The Five Laws and Che Funge," Paideuma, I, #1 (Spring-Summer, 1972), 83-85.

2630 _____. "From a Lost World," NatlR, 20 (February 27, 1968), 195-197.

2631 _____. "Ghosts and Benedictions," Poetry, 113, #2 (November, 1968), 109-121.

2632 _____. A Homemade World: The American Modernist Writers. New York: Alfred A. Knopf, 1975, pp. 3-6, 8-12, passim.

2633 _____. "Horizontal Chords," Sumac, 2 (Winter-Spring, 1970), 227.

2634 _____. "The Invention of China," Spectrum, 9, #1 (Spring, 1967), 21-54.

2635 _____. "Leucothea's Bikini: Mimetic Homage," Ezra Pound: Perspectives in Honor of His Eightieth Birthday. Noel Stock, ed. Cf., #125, pp. 25-40.

2636 _____. "The Magic of Place: Ezra Pound," IQ, 16, #64 (1973), 5-10.

2637   _____. "MAO^4 or Presumption," Shen, 21, #3 (Spring, 1970), 84-93.

2638   _____. "The Muse in Tatters," Agenda, 6, #2 (Summer, 1968), 212-233; also in Arion, 7 (1968), 212-233.

2639   _____. "A Note on CX/778," Paideuma, 8 (1979), 51-52.

2640   _____. "The Persistent Past," Spectrum, 10 (Spring, 1969), 5-13.

2641   _____. "The Poetics of Error," TkR, 6, #2-7, #1 (1975-76), 89-98.

2642   _____. "Poets at the Blackboard," YR, 71 (Winter, 1982), 173-184.

2643   _____. "The Possum in the Cave," Allegory and Representation. Stephen Jay Greenblatt, ed. Johns Hopkins U. Pr., (Selected Papers from the English Institute [1979-1980], New Series, #5.)

2644   _____. "Pound and Around," Review, 3 (1981), 25-44.

2645   _____. "Pound on Joyce," Shenandoah, 3, #3 (Autumn, 1952), 3-8.

2646   _____. "The Rope in the Knot," KyR, 2, #3 (1968), 10-29.

2647   _____. "To the Editor of Poetry," Poetry, 91, #3 (December, 1957), 210-211; [Reply to John R. Hendrickson, Poetry, 91, #3 (1957), 209-210.]

2648   _____, ed. Introduction by Hugh Kenner. The Translations of Ezra Pound. London: Faber; New York: 1953. Review: NR, 130 (January 4, 1954), 18-19.

2649   _____. Ulysses. London; Boston: Geo. Allen & Unwin, 1980, pp. 2, 169, 170.

2650   Kent, Jay. "Der Fall Ezra Pound," Wort und Wahrheit (Vienna), VII, (1952), 880-882.

2651   Kereaski, Rodica. "Incercare de caracterizare a criticii lui Ezra Pound," AUB-LG, 22 (1973), 93-104.

2652   Kermode, Frank. "The New Apocalyptists," PR, 33, #3 (Summer, 1966), 339-361.

2653   _____. The Romantic Image. New York; London: Macmillan, 1957, passim.

2654 Ketchiff, David. "William James and/or Ezra Pound: Percep-
tions of Reality," DAI, 39 (North Carolina, Chapel Hill:
1978), 6757A.

2655 Kidney, Jennifer. "An American Prelude: Nostalgia and the
Sense of Death in American Poetry," DAI, 36 (Yale: 1974),
275A.

2656 Kimpel, Ben D., and T. C. Duncan Eaves. "Ezra Pound on
Hitler's Economic Policies," AL, 55, #1 (March, 1983), 48-54.

2657 _____, and _____. "Ezra Pound's Anti-Semitism," SAQ,
81, #1 (Winter, 1982), 56-69.

2658 _____, and _____. "Ezra Pound's Use of Sources as
Illustrated by His Use of Nineteenth-Century French History," MP, 80 (August, 1982), 35-52.

2659 _____, and _____. "Herbert Hoover and the London
Judge," Paideuma, 9 (1980), 505-507.

2660 _____, and _____. "The Intentional-Fallacy Fallacy and
Related Contemporary Orthodoxies," SAQ, 83, #1 (Winter,
1984), 103-113.

2661 _____, and _____. "Note on 'e li mestriers ecoutes,'"
Paideuma, 9 (1980), 311-312.

2662 _____, and _____. "Pound and Pumpelly," ELN, 17
(June, 1980), 293-294.

2663 King, Michael John. "An ABC of Ezra Pound's Library,"
LCUT, 17 (1981), 30-45.

2864 _____. "'Go, Little Book': Ezra Pound, Hilda Doolittle
and 'Hilda's Book,'" Paideuma, 10, #2 (Fall, 1981), 347-360.

2665 Kirk, Russell. Eliot and His Age: T. S. Eliot's Moral
Imagination in the Twentieth Century. New York: Random
House, 1971, passim.

2666 _____. "Personality and Medium in Eliot and Pound," SR,
82 (Fall, 1974), 698-705.

2667 Kirstein, Lincoln. "Ezra Pound and the Visual Arts," NYTBR,
28 (April 20, 1982), 18.

2668 Klarman, Adolf D. "The Age of Abstraction in Modern European Literature," Four Quarters, 14, #4 (May, 1965), 19-29.

2669 Klein, Marcus. Foreigners: The Making of American

Literature, 1900-1940. Chicago: U. of Chicago Pr., 1981,
passim.

2670 Klinck, Dennis R. "Pound, Social Credit, and the Critics,"
Paideuma, 5, #2 (Fall, 1976), 227-240.

2671 _____. "Pound's 'Economist Consulted of Nations,'"
Paideuma, 5, #1 (Spring, 1976), 67-68.

2672 _____. "Pound's 'Gods': The Many and the One," SoRA,
11 (1978), 296-315.

2673 Knapp, James F. Ezra Pound. Boston: Twayne, 1979.

2674 Knoerle, Sister Jeanne. "Ezra Pound and the Literature of
China," TamkR, 4, #1 (1973), 53-62.

2675 Kobayashi, Manji. "Marie Stopes to Pound," EigoS, 123
(1977), 397-399.

2676 Kodama, Jitsuei. "Pound no Naso to Fenollosa MSS no Hak-
ken," EigoS, 115 (1969), 234-237.

2677 Kodama, Sanehide. "The Chinese Subject in Ezra Pound's
Poetry," SELit, [Eng. No.], No. 37-62 (1970).

2678 _____. "Cosmopolitanism in Ezra Pound," Doshisha
Women's College of Liberal Arts. Annual Reports of Studies.
Vol. 24. Kyoto: Doshisha Women's College, 1973, pp. 125-137.

2679 _____. "Dappi no Itami--Shoki Shihen o megutte," EigoS,
119 (1973), 11-12.

2680 _____. "Ezra Pound," America Bungaku no Jiko Keisel:
20 seiki America Bungaku I. Toshihiko, Agata, ed. Kyoto:
Yamaguchi, 1981, pp. 337-382.

2681 _____. "Persona, Pound, His Poetry," Doshisha Literature, (Kyoto), 22 (January, 1962), 9-19.

2682 _____. "The Road to Cathay: Ezra Pound's Experiments
in Translation," AnRS, 28 (1977), 201-229.

2683 Kodoma, Sanchiko. "Swords and Aether: A Study on the
Management of Tone in the Poetry of Ezra Pound," Gakujutsu
Kenkyu Nempo, No. 11 (December, 1960), 47-58.

2684 Koehler, Stanley. "The Art of Poetry, VI," ParisR, 8, #32
(Summer-Fall, 1964), 111-51.

2685 Köhring, Klaus H. "The American Epic," SHR, 5, #3 (Summer, 1971), 265-280.

2686 Kojecky, Roger. T. S. Eliot's Social Criticism. London:
      Faber & Faber, 1971; New York: Farrar, Straus & Giroux,
      1971, passim.

2687 Korg, Jacob. "Hulme and Pound," Language in Modern Lit-
      erature Innovation and Experiment. New York: Barnes &
      Noble; Sussex: The Harvester Pr., 1979, pp. 84-92.

2688 _____. "T. S. Eliot," CLit, 13, #4, (Autumn, 1972), 535-
      540.

2689 Korn, Marianne. Ezra Pound: Purpose/ Form/ Meaning.
      London: Pembridge Pr., publ. for Middlesex Polytechnic
      Pr., 1983.

2690 _____. "Truth Near Perigord," Paideuma, 10, #3 (Winter,
      1981), 571-579.

2691 Kostelanetz, Richard. "Reactions and Alternatives: Post-
      World War II American Poetry," Chelsea, 26 (May, 1969),
      7-34.

2692 Kramer, Jane. "Paterfamilias--I," NY, 44, #26 (August 17,
      1968), 32-73.

2693 Kreymborg, Alfred. "E. P.," The Little World, 1914 and
      After. New York: Coward-McCann, Inc., 1932, p. 141.

2694 _____. A History of American Poetry: Our Singing
      Strength. New York: Tudor Pub. Co., 1934, pp. 294-296,
      333-347, passim.

2695 _____. Troubadour: An Autobiography. New York:
      Liveright, Inc., 1925, pp. 369-370.

2696 Kriegel, Leonard. "Poetry and Politics," PR, 42 (1975),
      287-290.

2697 Kroll, Ernest. "With Ezra Pound before Rapallo," CimR, 2
      (1973), 7-17.

2698 Kuberski, Philip. "Ezra Pound and the Calculations of
      Interest," NOR, 10, #2-3 (Summer-Fall, 1983), 69-74.

2699 Kumashiro, Sobu. Ezra Pound to T. S. Eliot. Tokyo:
      Hokuseido, 1970.

2700 Kunitz, Stanley J., and Howard Haycraft. "Ezra Pound,"
      Twentieth Century Authors. New York: H. W. Wilson Co.,
      1942, pp. 1121-1123.

2701 Kwan-Terry, John. "Ezra Pound and the Invention of China,"
      TkR, 10 (1979), 127-144.

2702 _____. "The Prosodic Theories of Ezra Pound," PLL, 9,
      #1 (Winter, 1973), 48-64.

2703 Laing, Alexander. "The Nation and Its Poets," Nation, 201,
      #8 (September 20, 1965), 212-218.

2704 Lander, Jeannette. Ezra Pound. New York: Ungar Pub.
      Co., 1971.

2705 Langbaum, Robert. "Ezra Pound's Dramatic Monologues,"
      The Poetry of Experience. New York: Random House, 1957;
      repr., in Critics on Ezra Pound. E. San Juan, Jr., ed.
      Coral Gables, Fla.: U. of Miami Pr., 1972, pp. 47-48.

2706 _____. The Modern Spirit: Essays on the Continuity of
      Nineteenth and Twentieth Century Literature. New York:
      Oxford U. Pr., 1970, passim.

2707 _____. The Mysteries of Identity: A Theme in Modern
      Literature. New York: Oxford U. Pr., 1977, passim.

2708 Languasco, Nardo. "L'attésa di Pound," FLe, 47 (November
      20, 1955), 6.

2709 _____. "Ezra Pound non scrive più versi," FLe, 8
      (October 4, 1953), 5.

2710 Langumier, Eric. "Scarabs and Gold," Paideuma, 8 (1979),
      57.

2711 Lattès, Jean-Claude. "Les silences d'Ezra Pound," NL
      (November 11, 1965), 3.

2712 Laughlin, James. "Gists and Piths: From the Letters of
      Pound and Williams," Poetry, 139, #4 (January, 1982), 229-
      244.

2713 _____. "A Portrait of Ezra Pound," UR, 6, #2 (December,
      1939), 111-119.

2714 _____. "Pound the Teacher: The Ezuversity," StAR, 1,
      #1 (Fall-Winter, 1970), 17-18.

2715 _____. "Pound's Prose," New Democracy, 5 (December 1,
      1935), 120.

2716 Laurie, Peter Hamilton. "Peacocks in Kore's House: A Note
      on Pound's Alchemy," Paideuma, 9 (1980), 333-337.

2717 _____. "The Poet and the Mysteries: Pound's Eleusis,"
DAI, 37 (Brown Univ.: 1975), 309A.

2718 Lawrence, D. H. The Letters of D. H. Lawrence. James T.
Boulton, ed. New York; London: Cambridge U. Pr., 1979,
passim.

2719 _____. D. H. Lawrence: A Composite Biography. Edward Nehls, ed. Madison: Wisconsin U. Pr., 1957-59, passim.

2720 Layton, Irving. "Shaw, Pound and Poetry," CIV/n, 7 (Montreal), 19-20.

2721 Leavis, Frank Raymond. "The Americanness in American
Literature," Commentary, 14 (November, 1952), 466-474.

2722 _____. "Eliot and Pound," TLS, #3574 (August 28, 1970),
950; #3576 (September 11, 1970), 998.

2723 _____. "Ezra Pound: The Promise and the Disaster," PR,
18, #6 (November-December, 1951), 727-733; also in The
Partisan Review Anthology. William Phillips and Philip Rahv,
eds. New York: Holt, Rinehart & Winston, 1962, pp. 440-
443.

2724 Le Breton, Eileen. "Ezra Pound," TLS, #3891 (October 8,
1976), 1280.

2725 Lechlitner, Ruth. "The Poetry of William Carlos Williams,"
Poetry, 54, #6 (September, 1939), 326-335.

2726 Ledbetter, Jack Tracy. "Modern Poetry and the American
Idiom," Cresset, 32, #3 (January, 1969), 8-10.

2727 Lee, Pen-Ti, and Donald Murray. "The Quality of Cathay:
Ezra Pound's Early Translations of Chinese Poems," LE&W, 10
(September, 1966), 264-277.

2728 Lehmann, John, ed. The Craft of Letters in England: A
Symposium. London: Cresset, 1956; Boston: Houghton
Mifflin Co., 1957.

2729 Lemaire, Marcel. "Some Recent American Novels and Essays,"
RLV, 28 (1962), 70-78.

2730 Lensing, George S. "Review: Ezra Pound: An Introduction
to the Poetry by Sister Bernetta Quinn," Paideuma, 2 (1973),
327-329. Cf., #876.

2731 Leonello, Claudio. "Pound e la Cina," Galleria, 26 (1976),
17-21.

2732 Lesemann, Maurice. "Mr. Pound and the Younger Genera-
      tion," Poetry, 30, #4 (July, 1927), 216-222.

2733 Levenson, Harry Michael. "A Genealogy of Modernism: Con-
      stituents of a Literary Doctrine, 1908-1922," DAI, 41, #8
      (Stanford, 1980), 3573A.

2734 Levertov, Denise. "Grass Seed and Cherry Stones," AntigR,
      8 (Winter, 1972), 29-33; repr., in The Poet in the World.
      New Directions, 1973, pp. 249-253.

2735 Levi, Albert W. "Three," [Poetics of Stevens, Pound, and
      T. S. Eliot], The Hidden Harmony: Essays in Honor of
      Philip Wheelwright. Oliver Johnson, David Harrah, Peter
      Fuss, and Theodore Guleserian, eds. New York: Odyssey,
      1966, pp. 73-91.

2736 Levin, Gail. "Wassily Kandinsky and the American Literary
      Avant-Garde," Criticism, 21 (1979), 347-361. [Influence on
      Stein, Pound, and Williams].

2737 Levin, Harry. "Ezra Pound, T. S. Eliot, and the European
      Horizon," first presented as the Taylorian Special Lecture,
      1974, at Oxford University; republished as pamphlet by
      Clarendon Pr., 1975; and in Memories of the Moderns. New
      York: New Directions, 1980, pp. 13-34.

2738 _____. "Ezra Pound, T. S. Eliot, and the Idea of Com-
      parative Literature," Actes du VIIe congres de l'Association
      Internationale de Litterature Comparee/Proceedings of the 7th
      Congress of the International Comparative Literature Associa-
      tion. Milan V. Dimic, and Juan Ferrate, eds. (Lib. of CRCL
      2.) Stuttgart: Bieber, 1979, pp. 545-552.

2739 _____. Grounds for Comparison. Cambridge, Mass.:
      Harvard U. Pr., 1972, pp. 280-282, 297, passim.

2740 _____. "Literature and Exile," Listener, 62 (1959), 613-
      617.

2741 _____. "Unfrocked Professor," YR, 43, #4 (Summer, 1954),
      602-604.

2742 Levy, Alan. "Ezra Pound's Voice of Silence," NYTMS (Janu-
      ary 9, 1972), 14-15, 59, 61-65, 68; Pub.: Ezra Pound: The
      Voice of Silence. Sag Harbor, NY: Permanent Pr., 1983.

2743 Lewis, John S. "Ezra Pound," TLS, (July 14, 1961), 433.

2744 Lewis, Roger. "Most Friendship Is Feigning," EIC, 34, #2
      (April, 1984), 169-175.

2745   Lewis, Wyndham. "Early London Environment," T. S. Eliot:
       A Symposium from Conrad Aiken and Others. Richard March
       and M. J. Tambimuttu, eds. Chicago: Regnery, 1949, pp.
       24-32.

2746   _____. "First Meeting with Ezra Pound," Blasting and
       Bombardiering. London: Eyre & Spottiswoode, 1937; Berke-
       ley and Los Angeles: U. of Calif. Pr., 1967, pp. 271-281.

2747   _____. "To Ezra Pound," The Letters of Wyndham Lewis.
       W. K. Rose, ed. Norfolk, Conn.: New Directions, 1963,
       passim.

2748   Linati, Carlo. "Eliot e Pound," Letteratura (Florence), #7
       (genn.-febb, 1954), 60-61.

2749   _____. "Ezra Pound," Scrittori anglo-americani d'oggi,
       Milan: Corticelli, 1944, pp. 87-98.

2750   Lindberg, Kathryne Victoria. "Reading, Writing, and Rheto-
       ric: Nietzschean Traces in the Later Criticism of Ezra
       Pound," DAI, 45, #5 (Victoria: 1984), 1395A.

2751   Lindberg-Seyersted, Brita, ed., with Introduction, Commen-
       tary, and Notes. Pound/Ford: The Story of a Literary
       Friendship. Norfolk, Conn.: New Directions, 1982.

2752   Lindstrom, Naomi. "Ezra Pound: Creation and Play in Crit-
       ical Discourse," BRMMLA, 35, #4 (1981), 291-303.

2753   Link, Franz H. "Mythos und Image in der frühen Dichtung
       Ezra Pounds," LJGG, 20 (1979), 209-260.

2754   _____. "Pound's 'A Girl' and Ovid's Metamorphoses, I,
       547-555," Paideuma, 8 (1979), 409-410.

2755   Lipke, William C., and Bernard W. Rogran. "Ezra Pound and
       Vorticism: A Polite Blast," WSCL, 7 (Summer, 1966), 201-210.

2756   _____, and Walton Litz, eds. Modern Literary Criticism:
       1900-1970. New York: Atheneum, 1972, passim.

2757   Lipman, Samuel. "Forms and Decorations," TLS, #3967
       (April 14, 1978), 415-416.

2758   Lippincott, Henry F., Jr. "Pound, Richard Lattimore and
       Odyssey IX," Sou'wester (So. Ill. U.), Ezra Pound Birthday
       Issue (October 30, 1970), 36-45.

2759   Little, Matthew. "Corrections to Gallup's Pound and Some
       History of Pound's Essays on the Jefferson-Adams Letters,"
       BSAP, 74, #3 (1980), 270-272.

2760 _____. "Pound and ylh: Bishop Carame's Translation of
Avicenna as Background," Paideuma, 12, #1 (Spring, 1983),
33-40.

2761 _____. "Pound's Use of the Word Totalitarian," Paideuma,
11, #1 (Spring-Summer, 1982), 147-156.

2762 Litz, A. Walton. "Literary Criticism," Harvard Guide to
Contemporary American Writing. Daniel Hoffman, ed. Cambridge, Mass., and London: Harvard U. Pr., 1979, pp. 79-
80.

2763 _____. "Pound and Eliot on Ulysses: The Critical Tradition," JJQ, 10 (1972), 5-18; repr., Germanistische Streifzuge.
Gert Mellbourn, et al., eds. Stockholm: Almqvist & Wiksell,
1974, pp. 5-18; Ulysses: Fifty Years. Thomas F. Staley,
ed. Bloomington: Indiana U. Pr., 1974, pp. 5-18.

2764 Llona, Victor. "With Ezra Pound before Rapallo," CimR, 22
(1973), 7-17.

2765 Lloyd, Margaret Glynne. William Carlos Williams' Paterson:
A Critical Appraisal. Rutherford and Madison, N.J.:
Fairleigh Dickinson U. Pr., 1980, pp. 35-36, 39-41, passim.

2766 Logu, Pietro de. "Ezra Pound," Il Messaggero (Rome: July
19, 1954).

2767 Lombardo, Agostino. "Ezra Pound: The Last Decadent," Lo
Spettatore Italiano, 8 (1955), 471-475; Realismo e simbolismo:
saggi di letteratura americana contemporanea. Rome: Edizioni
di storia e letteratura, 1957, pp. 75-84; Italian Images of Ezra
Pound: Twelve Critical Essays. Angela Jung and Guido
Palandri, eds. #518, pp. 16-25.

2768 _____. "Introduction," SR, 68, #3 (July-September, 1960),
353-374.

2769 _____. La poesia inglese dall estetismo al simbolismo.
Roma: 1950, passim.

2770 Lopez, Enrique Hank. Conversations with Katherine Anne
Porter: Refugee from Indian Creek. Boston: Little, Brown
& Co., 1981, pp. 132-133, 268-269, passim.

2771 Lowell, Amy. A Fable for Critics. Boston; New York:
Houghton Mifflin Co., 1922; repr., A Critical Fable. New
York: AMS Pr., 1981, passim.

2772 _____. "The Imagists: 'H. D.' and John Gould Fletcher,"
Tendencies in Modern American Poetry. Boston; New York:
1917, 236, 251-254.

2773 Lowell, Robert. "Ezra Pound," [Poem], History. New York:
      Farrar, Straus & Giroux, 1973, p. 140; also in Notebook:
      1967-1968, passim, p. 71.

2774 Luckett, Richard. "'Meaning Motion': Old Music and Some
      Modern Writers," E&S, 30 (1977), 88-97.

2775 Ludwig, Richard M. "Ezra Pound's London Years," Aspects
      of American Poetry: Essays Presented to Howard Mumford
      Jones. Richard Milton, ed. Columbus: Ohio U. Pr., 1962,
      pp. 99-119; Modern American Poetry: Essays in Criticism.
      Guy Owen, ed. Deland, Florida: Everett/Edwards, 1972,
      pp. 81-97.

2776 Lund, Mary Graham. "The Eliotian Cult of Impersonality,"
      TexQt, 9 (Spring, 1966), 164-167.

2777 Lunkvist, Arthur. "Ezra Pound," Morgen-Tidningen (Stock-
      holm), (October 17, 1953).

2778 MacAfee, Norman. "'I am a free man': Pasolini's Poetry in
      America," IQ, 21-22 (Fall-Winter, 1982-83), 99-105.

2779 McAfee, Thomas. "On Reading an Anthology of 'Most of the
      Boys Who Have ...,'" Sou'wester (October 30, 1970), p. 131.

2780 McAlister, Floyd L. "Milton and the Anti-Academics," JEGP,
      61, #4 (October, 1962), 779-787.

2781 McCarthy, Dermot. Social Theory and Criticism of Ezra
      Pound. Diss., Queen's University, Kingston, Ontario, 1974-
      1975.

2782 Maccoby, Hyam. "The Jew as Anti-Artist: The Anti-
      Semitism of Ezra Pound," Midstream, 22, #3 (1976), 59-71.

2783 McCormick, John. "Poets," The Middle Distance: A Compara-
      tive History of American Imaginative Literature: 1919-1932.
      New York: Free Pr., 1971, 111-161.

2784 McCuaig, Ronald. "Ezra Pound," Bulletin (N.Y.P.L.), 72, #2
      (April, 1951), 2.

2785 McDougal, Stuart Y. Ezra Pound and the Troubadour Tradi-
      tion. London; Princeton, N.J.: Princeton U. Pr., 1972.

2786 _____. "A Parnassian in Provence: Ezra Pound and the
      Troubadour Tradition," DAI, 31, #10 (Pennsylvania: 1970),
      5415A.

2787 MacDougall, Allan Ross. "Orpheus in Paris: Ida Rubenstein,

Ezra Pound and Much Gaiety," Arts and Decoration, 25 (October, 1926), 69, 98, 114.

2788   McFarland, Ronald E. "A Note on Monsieur Verog," Paideuma, 11 (1982), 446–448.

2789   McInnes, Marion Kaighn. "'The Discontinuous Gods' in the Poetry of Ezra Pound," DAI, 45, #4 (Yale: 1984), 1115A–1116A.

2790   MacKendrick, Louis K. "T. S. Eliot and the Egoist: The Critical Preparation," DR, 55 (1975), 140–154.

2791   McKeown, Thomas Wilson. "Ezra Pound's Early Experiments with Major Forms, 1904–1925," DAI, 44, #5 (U. of British Columbia: Canada, 1983), 1454A.

2792   Macksey, R. A. "The Old Poets," Johns Hopkins Mag, 19 (1968), 42–48.

2793   McLachian, W. I. "Translation and Critical Judgment: A Comparative Study of Ezra Pound and Gavin Douglas," DilR, 14, #2 (April, 1966), 166–191.

2794   MacLeish, Archibald. "Archibald MacLeish: Selected Letters," ParisR, 24, #84 (Summer, 1982), 104–144.

2795   _____. "In Praise of Dissent," NYTBR, 61, #51 (December 16, 1956), 5.

2796   _____. "The Most Compelling Acts of Love to Touch My Life," Today's Health, 51 (February, 1973), 40.

2797   _____. Poetry and Experience. Cambridge: Riverside Pr., 1961, passim.

2798   _____. "Poetry and the Public World," AtlM, 163 (1939), 829–830.

2799   _____. "Public Speech and Private Speech in Poetry," A Time to Speak. Boston: Houghton Mifflin Co., 1941, pp. 59–69.

2800   _____. "There Was Something about the Twenties," SatRL, 49 (December 31, 1966), 10–13.

2801   _____. "The Venetian Grave," SatRWorld, I, ii (February 9, 1974), 26, 28–29; repr., in Riders on the Earth: Essays and Recollections. Boston: Houghton Mifflin, 1978, pp. 115–122.

2802 _____. "Why Can't They Say What They Mean?" A Con-
tinuing Journey. Boston: Houghton Mifflin, 1968, pp. 194-
195, passim.

2803 McLuhan, Marshall. "Pound, Eliot, and the Rhetoric of The
Waste Land," NLH, 10 (Spring, 1979), 557-580.

2804 _____. "Pound's Critical Prose," An Examination of Ezra
Pound: A Collection of Essays. Peter Russell, ed., Cf., #
114, pp. 165-171; also in The Interior Landscape: The Lit-
erary Criticism of Marshall McLuhan, 1943-1962. (Selected,
Compiled and edited by Eugene McNamara.) New York:
McGraw-Hill, 1969, pp. 75-81.

2805 MacShane, Frank. "The English Review," SAQ, 60 (Summer,
1961), 311-320.

2806 _____. The Life and Work of Ford Madox Ford. New
York: Horizon Pr., 1965, passim.

2807 MacSween, R. J. "Yeats and His Language," AntigR, 14
(Summer, 1973), 17-24.

2808 McVeagh, John. Tradeful Merchants: The Portrayal of the
Capitalist in Literature. Boston: Routledge & Kegan Paul,
1981, passim.

2809 Makin, Peter. "The American Poet, Ezra Pound, and
Mediaeval Provençal Poetry," Diss. (London U.: 1972).

2810 _____. "Ezra Pound and Scotus Erigena," CLS, 10, #1
(March, 1973), 60-83.

2811 _____. "Ezra Pound's Abilities as a Translator of Provençal," Poetica (Tokyo), 4 (Autumn, 1975), 111-132.

2812 _____. "Kennedy, Fenollosa, Pound and the Chinese
Character," Agenda, 17, #3-4; 18, #1 (Autumn-Winter-Spring,
1980), 220-237.

2813 _____. "Pound's Provence and the Medieval Paideuma: An
Essay in Aesthetics," Ezra Pound: The London Years: 1908-
1920. Philip Grover, ed. Cf., #52, pp. 31-60.

2814 _____. Provence and Pound. Berkeley and Los Angeles,
U. of Calif. Pr., 1978.

2815 Malanga, Gerard. "Interview of Charles Olson," ParisR, 49
(Summer, 1970), 177-204.

2816 Malof, Joseph Fetler. "Ez Pound, Inc.," Ezra Pound: Perspectives.... Noel Stock, ed., Cf., #125, pp. 204-206.

2817   Mancuso, Girolamo. <u>Pound e la Cina</u>. Milan: Feltrinelli,
       1974.

2818   Manganaris-Decavalles, Andonis.   "Ezra Pound and the Medi-
       terranean World," DA, 21 (Northwestern: 1961), 3770.

2819   Manganiello, Dominic.   "Dante Among the Moderns," Selecta,
       1 (1980), 15-18.

2820   Margolis, John D.   <u>T. S. Eliot's Intellectual Development:</u>
       <u>1922-1939</u>. London; Chicago: U. of Chicago Pr., 1972, pp.
       197-198, passim.

2821   Mariani, Paul.   "Two Essays on Ezra Pound," MassR, 14
       (Winter, 1973), 118-129.

2822   Marin Morales, José A.   "Radiografia epistolar: Joyce-Pound,"
       Arbor, 318 (1972), 93-98.

2823   Mariorana, M. T., and M. C. Rezzano de Martini.   "Un poema
       de Ezra Pound," Sur, #242 (1956), 22-30.

2824   Marschall, Hiltrud, et al.   "Biographische Zeittafel," <u>Ezra</u>
       <u>Pound: 22 Versuche über einen Dichter</u>.   Cf., #503, pp.
       427-434.

2825   Marsh, Edward.   <u>A Number of People</u>. London: W. Heine-
       mann, Ltd.-H. Hamilton, Ltd., 1939, p. 82.

2826   Martin, Loy Davis.   "The Literary Style of Robert Browning
       and Ezra Pound," DAI, 35, #5 (Virginia: 1974), 2947A.

2827   _____.   "Pound and Fenollosa: The Problem of Influence,"
       CritQ, 20, #1 (Spring, 1978), 48-60.

2828   Martin, Wallace.   "Freud and Imagism," N&Q, 8, #12 (Decem-
       ber, 1961), 470-471, 474.

2829   _____.   "The Literary Significance of <u>The New Age</u> under
       the Editorship of A. R. Orage, 1907-1922," Diss., University
       of London, 1961.

2830   _____.   <u>The New Age under Orage: Chapters in English</u>
       <u>Cultural History</u>. New York: Manchester U. Pr.; Barnes &
       Noble, Inc., 1967, pp. 151-154, passim.

2831   _____.   "The Sources of the Imagist Aesthetic," PMLA, 85
       (March, 1970), 196-204.

2832   Martz, Louis L.   <u>The Poem of the Mind: Essays on Poetry,</u>
       <u>English and American</u>. New York: Oxford U. Pr., 1966,
       pp. 143-146, 147-153, passim.

2833 Materer, Timothy. "Doppelganger: Ezra Pound in His Let-
      ters," Paideuma, 11, #2 (1983), 241-256.

2834 _____. "The English Vortex: Modern Literature and the
      'Pattern on Hope,'" JML, 3 (July, 1974), 1123-1139.

2835 _____. "Pound's Vortex," Paideuma, 6, #2 (Fall, 1977),
      175-176.

2836 _____. "The Value of a Pound," Cw, 96 (July 28, 1972),
      409-410.

2837 _____. Vortex: Pound, Eliot, and Lewis. London;
      Ithaca: Cornell U. Pr., 1979, passim.

2838 Matthiessen, F. O. The Achievement of T. S. Eliot. Boston;
      New York: Oxford U. Pr., 1935, passim.

2839 _____. "American Poetry, 1920-40," SR, 55, #1 (1947),
      24-55.

2840 _____. American Renaissance. Art and Expression in the
      Age of Emerson and Whitman. New York: Oxford U. Pr.,
      1941, passim.

2841 Matz, C. A. "Menotti and Pound," OperaN, 30 (November 20,
      1965), 14-15.

2842 Maxwell-Mahon, W. D. "Ezra Pound: Critical and Creative
      Influences," UES, 15, #2 (1977), 8-14.

2843 May, Henry F. The End of American Innocence: A Study of
      the First Years of Our Own Time, 1912-1917. New York:
      Alfred A. Knopf, 1959, pp. 269-277, passim.

2844 Mazzaro, Jerome. "Fusions," FarP, #5 (Winter-Spring, 1971),
      70-73.

2845 _____. "The Legacy of Modernism," Salmagundi, Nos. 31-
      32 (Fall, 1975-Winter, 1976), pp. 303-308.

2846 _____, ed. Modern American Poetry: Essays in Criticism.
      New York: McKay, 1970, passim.

2847 _____. Postmodern American Poetry. Urbana: U. of Ill.
      Pr., 1980, passim.

2848 Mei, Francesco. "Il mito di Ezra Pound," FLe, 17 (November
      12, 1962), 5.

2849 Meixner, John A. Ford Madox Ford's Novels: A Critical
      Study. Minneapolis: U. of Minn. Pr., 1962, passim.

2850 Melchiori, Giorgio. The Tightrope Walkers: Studies of Man-
      nerism in Modern English Literature. New York: Macmillan,
      1936; London: Routledge & Kegan Paul, 1956, pp. 176-177,
      passim.

2851 Mellow, James R. Charmed Circle: Gertrude Stein and Com-
      pany. New York: Praeger Pubs., Inc., 1974, passim.

2852 Melote Castro, E. M. "Ezra Pound: Da obra," Coloquio, 11
      (1973), 51-53.

2853 Mendes, Murilo. "Cocteau, Jouve, Pound," Coloquio, 12
      (1973), 18-24.

2854 Menides, Laura Jehn. "The Use of the Past in Modern Amer-
      ican Poetry: Eliot, Pound, Williams, Crane, Berryman, Olson,
      Lowell," DAI, 39, #6 (New York U.: 1978), 3583A.

2855 Merchant, W. Moelwyn. "Agenda," YLM, 126, #5 (December,
      1958), 3-9.

2856 _____. "Ezra Pound," CritQ, 1 (Winter, 1959), 277-287.

2857 Meyer, G. P. "The Sage of Rapallo," SatRL, 33 (December 2,
      1950), 24-25.

2858 Meyer, Peter. Die Finanz und wirtschaftspolitische Auffassung
      Ezra Pounds und ihre Bedeutung für seine Dichtung. Diss.
      Freiburg, [1959?].

2859 Meyerson, Edward L. The Seed Is Man: A Collection of
      Poetry and an Essay on Ezra Pound. New York: William-
      Frederick Pr., 1967, pp. 33-54.

2860 Michaels, Walter B. "Pound and Erigena," Paideuma, I, #1
      (Spring and Summer, 1972), 37-54.

2861 Michelena, Margarita. "Breve nota sobre Pound y la epopeya,"
      El Libro y el Pueblo, III (April-September, 1960), 75-77.

2862 Michelson, Max. "The Independents," Poetry, 8 (May, 1916),
      94-96.

2863 Middleton, Christopher. "Documents on Imagism from the
      Papers of F. S. Flint," Review: A Magazine of Poetry and
      Criticism, 15 (April, 1965), 35-51.

2864 Miller, James E., Karl Shapireo, and Bernice Slote. Start
      with the Sun: Studies in Cosmic Poetry. Lincoln: Nebraska
      U. Pr., 1960, pp. 207-225, passim.

2865 Miller, Liam. "W. B. Yeats and Stage Design at the Abbey
Theatre," MalR, #16 (October, 1970), 50-84.

2866 Miller, Vincent. "Eliot's Submission to Time," SR, 84 (Summer, 1976), 448-464.

2867 Mills, Ralph J., Jr. Cry of the Human: Essays on Contemporary American Poetry. Urbana; Chicago: U. of Ill. Pr.,
1975, passim.

2868 Milner, Philip. "Life at All Its Points: An Interview with
Robert Creeley," AntigR, #26 (Summer, 1976), 37-47.

2869 Miner, Earl. "Pound, Haiku, and the Image," HudR, 9
(Winter, 1956-57), 570-584.

2870 _____. "Pound's Debt to Japan," PoundN, #6 (April,
1955), 13-15.

2871 _____. "Vom Image zum Ideogram," Ezra Pound: 22
Versuche über einen Dichter. Eva Hesse, ed. Cf., #1979,
pp. 104-124.

2872 Miyake, Akiko. "Ezra Pound's Vorticism," SEL, 52 (December, 1975), 49-66.

2873 _____. "A Note on So-shu," Paideuma, 6 (Winter, 1977),
325-328.

2874 _____. "Pound and Confucianism," St. AndrewsRev
(Special Pound Issue), I, i (Fall-Winter, 1970), 45-47.

2875 Molesworth, Charles. "Frightful Fashions and Compulsive
Occasions," Salmagundi, 50-51 (1980-81), 322-339.

2876 _____. The Fierce Embrace: A Study of Contemporary
American Poetry. Columbia: U. of Missouri Pr., 1979,
passim.

2877 Monk, Donald. "Pound: A Divergent Influence," CritQ, 25,
#3 (Autumn, 1983), 29-34.

2878 Monro, Harold. Some Contemporary Poets. London: Leonard
Parsons, 1920, pp. 87-93.

2879 Monroe, Harriet. "Ezra Pound," The New Poetry. New York:
Macmillan, 1932, pp. 744-746.

2880 _____. "Miss Monroe re Ezra Pound," EJ, 20, #1 (January,
1931), 86-87.

2881 _____. "Notes and Announcements," Poetry, 1, #1 (October, 1912), 31; 1, #2 (November, 1912), 64.

2882 _____. "Some Imagist Poets--An Anthology," Poetry, 6, #3 (June, 1915), 150-153.

2883 Montale, Eugenio. "Se i biglietti da mille fossero quelli di Ezra Pound," Corriere d'informazione (Milan), (November 18-19, 1955). 3.

2884 _____. "Selva," Corriere della sera (Milan), Genn. 9, (1952), 3.

2885 _____. "The Second Life of Art," and "Voluntary Exile in Italy," The Second Life of Art: Selected Essays. Ed. & Trans. by Jonathan Gallassi. New York: Ecco Pr., 1982, pp. 203-208, 283-285.

2886 Montgomery, Marion. "Beyond Pound's Quarrel with Eliot's Text," GaR, 2 (1972), 415-425.

2887 _____. "Eliot and 'Il Miglior Fabbro,'" SCR, 6, i (November, 1973), 7-13.

2888 _____. "Eliot and the Particle Physicist: The Merging of Two Cultures," SoR, 10, #3 (July, 1974), 583-589.

2889 _____. Ezra Pound. (CWCP). Grand Rapids: Mich.: 1970.

2890 _____. "Ezra Pound's Angry Love Affair with America," JPC, 2 (Winter, 1968), 361-369.

2891 _____. "Ezra Pound's Arrogance," Sou'wester (So. Ill. U.), (Special Ezra Pound No.), (October 30, 1970), 46-54.

2892 _____. "Ezra Pound's Problems with Penelope," SHR, 3, #2 (Spring, 1969), 114-123.

2893 Moody, A. D. "Broken Images/Voices Singing," CamQ, 6 (1973), 45-56.

2894 Moore, Marianne. "Ezra Pound," QRL, 5, #2 (1949), 146.

2895 _____. "Marianne Moore on Ezra Pound, 1905-1915," MMN, 3, #2 (1979), 5-8.

2896 _____. "Teach, Stir the Mind, Afford Enjoyment," Ezra Pound: A Collection of Criticism. Grace Shulman, ed. Cf., #1084, pp. 39-44.

2897 _____. "The Ways Our Poets Have Taken in Fifteen Years Since the War," NY Herald Tribune Bk. Rev., (June 26, 1960), pp. 1, 11.

2898 Moramarco, Fred S. Edward Dahlberg. New York: Twayne Pub., Inc., 1972, passim.

2899 Morgan, Edwin. "Provenance and Problematics of 'Sublime and Alarming Images' in Poetry," PBA, 63 (1977), 293-313.

2900 Morgan, Frederick. "A Note on Ezra Pound," HudR, 4 (Spring, 1951), 156-160.

2901 Morrison, Blake. The Movement: English Poetry and Fiction of the 1950's. New York: Oxford U. Pr., 1980, passim.

2902 Motsch, Monika. Ezra Pound und China. Heidelberg: Winter, 1976.

2903 Mottram, Eric. "Pound, Merleau-Ponty and the Phenomenology of Poetry," Ezra Pound: Tactics for Reading. Ian F. A. Bell, ed. Cf., #449, pp. 121-147.

2904 _____. "Sixties American Poetry, Poetics and Poetic Movements," American Literature Since 1900. Marcus Cunliffe, ed. London: Barrie & Jenkins, 1975, pp. 271-311.

2905 Movius, Geoffrey H. "Caviar and Bread: Ezra Pound and William Carlos Williams, 1902-1914," JML, 5 (September, 1976), 383-406.

2906 Mowrer, Deane. "The Cracked Mirror and the Brazen Bull," NMQ, 20 #2 (Summer, 1950), 233-247.

2907 Munsi, Pradeep. "Prastutiparve Ejra Paund," Uttarasuri, 24 (1976-1977), 237-250.

2908 Munson, Gorham B. Robert Frost: A Study in Sensibility and Good Taste. New York: George H. Doran & Co., 1927; Haskell House, Pubs., 1967, passim.

2909 Murray, David. "Pound-signs: Money and Representation in Ezra Pound," Ezra Pound: Tactics for Reading. Ian F. A. Bell, ed., Cf., #449, pp. 50-78.

2910 Myake, Akiko. "Contemplation East and West: A Defense of Fenollosa's Language and Its Influence on Ezra Pound," Paideuma, 10, #3 (Winter, 1981), 533-570.

2911 Namjoshi, Suniti. "Ezra Pound and the Hex Hoax," AntigR, 23 (1975), 65-83.

2912   Nänny, Max. "Ezra Pound and the Menippean Tradition,"
       Paideuma, 11 (1982), 395-405.

2913   _____. "Ezra Pounds letzte Texte," NZZ (November, 1976),
       41.

2914   _____. "Ezra Pound's Visual Poetry and the Method of
       Science," ES, 43 (Autumn, 1962), 426-430.

2915   _____. "The Oral Roots of Ezra Pound's Methods of Quota-
       tion and Abbreviation," Paideuma, 8 (Winter, 1979), 381-387.

2916   Nathan, Leonard. "The Private 'I' in Contemporary Poetry,"
       Shen, 22, #4 (Summer, 1971), 80-99.

2917   Nelson, F. William. "The Waste Land Manuscript," Wichita
       State U. Bulletin. University Studies #86, Vol. XLVII (Feb-
       ruary, 1971), #1, passim.

2918   Niikura, Shunichi. "Pound to Eliot--Arechi-teki naru mono,"
       EigoS, 119 (1973), 9-10.

2919   Niikura, Toshikazu. "The American Identity of Ezra Pound,"
       American Literature in the 1950's. Annual Report, 1976 (Tokyo
       Chap.,) American Lit. Soc. of Japan, pp. 105-110.

2920   Nims, Bruce Gladden. "Life-Powered Poetry: The Narration
       of Perception Processes in the Early Poetry of Ezra Pound and
       Wallace Stevens," DAI, 38 (Florida: 1977), 6717A.

2921   Nist, John. "Ezra Pound: Young Poets, Beware!" Approach,
       38 (Winter, 1961), 5-9.

2922   Nolde, John J. "The Literary Revolutions of Hu Shih and
       Ezra Pound," Paideuma, 9 (Fall, 1980), 235-248.

2923   Nolte, William H., ed. "Ezra Pound," H. L. Mencken's Smart
       Set. Sel., and ed. by Wm. H. Nolte. Ithaca, New York:
       Cornell U. Pr., 1968, pp. 76-78, passim.

2924   North, Michael. "The Architecture of Memory: Pound and
       the Tempio Malatestiano," AL, 55, #3 (October, 1983), 366-
       387.

2925   Oakes, Randy Wayne. "The Discovery of Myth: Joyce,
       Pound, and Eliot, 1918-1923," DAI, 43, #6 (Georgia: 1982),
       1969A.

2926   Oberg, Arthur. Modern American Lyric: Lowell, Berryman,
       Creeley, and Plath. New Brunswick, New Jersey: Rutgers
       U. Pr., 1978, passim.

2927 O'Connor, William Van. An Age of Criticism (1900-1950).
      Chicago: H. Regnery Co., 1952, pp. 68-69.

2928 _____. Sense and Sensibility in Modern Poetry. Chicago:
      U. of Chicago Pr., 1948, passim.

2929 Oderman, Kevin M. "'Calvalcanti': That the Body Is Not
      Evil," Paideuma, 11 (1982), 257-279.

2930 _____. "The Servants of Amor in Pound's Early Poems,"
      Paideuma, 8 (1979), 389-403.

2931 Odlin, Reno. "Kati and Antef," Paideuma, 6 (1977), 181-182.

2932 O'Grady, Desmond. "Versions from Greek," Agenda, 17,
      #3-4; 18, #1 (Aut-Wntr-Spr., 1979-80), 187-192.

2933 [Olson, Charles]. "The Art of Poetry XII: Charles Olson,"
      ParisRev, 13, #49 (Summer, 1970), 177-204.

2934 Oppenheim, Lois. "An Inheritance of Poetic Referentiality,"
      CLS, 20, #3 (Fall, 1983), 329-345.

2935 Orsini, G. N. G. "Ezra Pound, critico letterario," Lettera-
      ture moderne, VII (1957), 34-51.

2936 _____. "Ezra Pound and Italian Literature (1957)," SR,
      68, #3 (July-September, 1960), 465-472.

2937 Orsini, Napoleone. "Ezra Pound, critico letterario,"
      Letterature moderne, 7 (January-February, 1957), 34-51.

2938 Otto, Lon Jules. "Medieval Prosody and Four Modern Poets:
      The Accentual Poetry of Hopkins, Hardy, Pound, and Auden,"
      DAI, 35, #7 (Indiana: 1974), 4447A.

2939 Owen, Guy, ed. Modern American Poetry: Essays in Criti-
      cism. Deland, Fla.: Everett/Edwards, 1972, pp. 254-255.

2940 Pack, Robert. "The Georgians, Imagism and Ezra Pound: A
      Study in Revolution," ArQ, 12 (Autumn, 1956), 250-265.

2941 Paden, William D., Jr. "Pound's Use of Troubadour Manu-
      scripts," CompLit, 32 (Fall, 1980), 402-412.

2942 Paechter, Heinz. "Verrat der Intellektuellen?" Wirtschafts-
      Seitung (Stuttgart), 4, #41 (1949), 15.

2943 Paige, D. D. "Introductory Note," QRL, 5, #2 (November 2,
      1949), 103-104.

2944 Palandri, Angela Jung. "Ezra Pound and His Italian Critics,"
      TkR, 3, #2 (1972), 41-57.

2945 _____. "Ezra Pound Revisited," West Coast Review, 2
      (Winter, 1968), 5-8.

2946 _____. "'La pietra mi è viva nella mano.' Le traduzioni
      dal cinese di Pound," Il Verri, 27 (1968), 3-19.

2947 _____. "'The Stone Is Alive in My Hand'--Ezra Pound's
      Chinese Translations," LE&W, 10 (September, 1966), 278-291.

2948 _____. "Le traduzioni dal cinese di Pound," Verri, 27
      (1968), 3-19.

2949 Palm, Göran. "Tva bilder av Ezra Pound," BLM, 32 (Febru-
      ary, 1963), 121-139.

2950 Panichas, George A. "Politics and Literature," Modern Age,
      12, #1 (Winter, 1967-68), 84-89.

2951 Paolucci, Anne. "Ezra Pound and D. G. Rossetti as Trans-
      lators of Guido Cavalcanti," RR, 51, #4 (December, 1960),
      256-267.

2952 _____. "Benn, Pound, and Eliot: The Monologue Art of
      German Expressionism and Anglo-American Modernism," RNL,
      9 (1978), 10-24.

2953 Parisi, Joseph. "Miss Monroe, Mr. Pound and the Boorzoi,"
      Poetry, 131 (October, 1977), 39-51.

2954 Parisoff, Myra Jane Heinz. "A Study of the Relative Mode of
      Mind in Pound, Eliot, Stevens, and Williams," DAI, 41, #8
      (Tulsa, Okla. U.: 1981), 3574A-75A.

2955 Parker, Andrew. "Ezra Pound and the 'Economy' of Anti-
      Semitism," Boundary, 11, #1-2 (Fall-Winter, 1982-83), 103-128.

2956 Parkinson, Thomas. "Pound among the Artists and Pound in
      His Later Years," OhR, 19, #1 (1978), 115-126.

2957 _____. "Yeats and Pound: The Illusion of Influence,"
      CompLit, 6 (Summer, 1954), 256-264.

2958 Pasquier, Marie-Claire. "L'Ancien et le nouveau dans l'oeuvre
      poétique d'Ezra Pound," CRB, 94 (1977), 90-99.

2959 Pasquini, Luigi. "Incontro con Ezra Pound," Martinella, 21
      (1967), 222-224.

2960 Patnaik, Deba P. "Ezra Pound and Naresh Guha," Paideuma, 3 (Spring, 1974), 67-68.

2961 _____. "Ezra Pound and Rabindranath Tagore," IJAS, 2, #2 (December, 1972), 53-69.

2962 _____. "Only the Quality of the Affection Endures," Paideuma, 3, #3 (Winter, 1974), 313-318.

2963 Patterson, Gertrude. "'The Waste Land' in the Making," CritQ, 14, #3 (Autumn, 1972), 269-283.

2964 Pattinson, John Patrick. "A Study of British Poetic Criticism between 1930 and 1965 as Exemplified in the Critics of Yeats, Pound, and Eliot," DAI, 30 (New York U.: 1970), 4460A-61A.

2965 Pea, Enrico. "Grazie, Ezra Pound," Stagione, 2, #7 (Rome: 1955), 3-4.

2966 Pearce, Roy Harvey. "Ezra Pound's Appraisal of Walt Whitman: Addendum," MLN, 74, #1 (January, 1959), 23-28.

2967 _____. "Pound and the New Poetry," and "Pound, Whitman and the American Epic," The Continuity of American Poetry. Cf., #857, pp. 163-177, 293-296.

2968 Pearlman, Daniel. "The Anti-Semitism of Ezra Pound," ConL, 22, #1 (Winter, 1981), 104-115.

2969 Peck, John. "Arras and Painted Arras," Paideuma, 3, #1 (Spring, 1974), 61-66.

2970 _____. "Pound and Hardy," Agenda, 10, ii-iii (Spring-Summer, 1972), 3-10.

2971 _____. "Pound's Idylls with Chapters on Catullus, Landor, and Browning," DAI, 34 (Stanford, 1973), 1290A.

2972 Peper, Jürgen. "Das imagistische 'Ein-Bild-Gedicht': Zwei Bildauffassungen," GRM, 22 (1972), 400-418.

2973 Pérez, Louis C. "Observations by Ezra Pound on the Dramatic Quality of Lope de Vega," Bulletin of the Comediantes, 7 (1955), 19-21.

2974 Peri, Jeffrey Michael. "The Return: Ideologies of 'Nostos' and the Nature of Modernism," DAI, 41, #4 (Princeton: 1980), 1581.

2975 Perkins, David. "Ezra Pound: The Early Career," A History

of Modern Poetry: From the 1890's to the High Modernist
Mode. Cambridge, Mass., and London: Belknap Pr., of
Harvard U. Pr., 1976, pp. 449-489.

2976 Perlès, Alfred. My Friend Henry Miller. London: Neville
      Spearman, Ltd., 1955, pp. 32, 83-84, passim.

2977 Perloff, Marjorie G. "Charles Olson and the 'Inferior Prede-
      cessors': 'Projective Verse' Revisited," ELH, 40 (Summer,
      1973), 285-306.

2978 _____. "A First Textbook," NR, 171, #26 (December 28,
      1974), 21-22.

2979 _____. "'No Edges, No Convexities': Ezra Pound and
      the Circle of Fragments," The Poetics of Indeterminacy: Rim-
      baud to Cage. Princeton, New Jersey: Princeton U. Pr.,
      1981, pp. 155-199.

2980 _____. "The Poet and His Politics," NR, 170, #11 (March
      16, 1974), 21-23.

2981 _____. "Pound and Rimbaud: The Retreat from Symbol-
      ism," IowaR, 6, #1 (1975), 91-117.

2982 _____. "Pound/Stevens: Whose Era?" NLH, 13 (Spring,
      1982), 485-514.

2983 Permoli, Piergiovanni. "Appunti sull'imagismo in America e in
      Russia," NC, Nos. 5-6 (January-June, 1956), 155-164.

2984 Perrine, Laurence, and James M. Reid. 100 American Poems
      of the Twentieth Century. New York: Harcourt, Brace &
      World, Inc., 1966, pp. 82-83.

2985 Pettersson, Gunnar. "Ezra Pound, Il Miglior fabbro--Ezra
      Pound, Il fascista?" MSpr, 72 (1978), 15-18.

2986 Pinto, Vivian de Sola. "Imagists and D. H. Lawrence," Cri-
      sis in English Poetry, 1880-1940. London: Hutchinson U.
      Library, Rev. ed., 1961, pp. 153-155, passim.

2987 Pisanti, Tommaso. "Ezra Pound e Dante," Dante e l'Italia
      meridionale. Atti del Congresso nazionale di studi danteschi
      di Caserta. Florence: Olschki, 1966, pp. 329-336.

2988 _____. "Ezra Pound lettore di Dante," NA, 517:2066
      (1973), 243-240.

2989 Pleynet, Marcelin. "La compromission poétique," Tel Quel,
      70 (1977), 11-26.

2990   Poirier, Richard. "The Art of Poetry II," ParisR, 6, #24
        (Summer-Fall, 1960), 89-120.

2991   Poli, Bernard J. Ford Madox Ford and the Transatlantic
        Review, Syracuse, New York: Syracuse U. Pr., 1967,
        passim.

2992   Pondrom, Cyrena N. "The Book of the Poets' Club and
        Pound's 'School of Images,'" JML, 3 (1973), 100-102.

2993   _____. "Modern French Poetry: Pound's First Important
        View," The Road from Paris: French Influence on English
        Poetry, 1900-1920. Cambridge: Cambridge U. Pr., 1974,
        pp. 172-174.

2994   Popescu, Adrian. "Duminica fără Ezra Pound," ["Sunday
        without Ezra Pound,"], Sreaua (n.s.), 23, #22 (November,
        1972).

2995   Popescu, Petru. "Řeflectie unui poet după stingere,"
        ["Thoughts for a poet after his death"], Cronica, 8, #1
        (January 12, 1973).

2996   Porter, Katherine Anne. "From the Notebooks of Katherine
        Anne Porter--Yeats, Joyce, Eliot, Pound," SoR, 1, #3 (Sum-
        mer, 1965), 570-573.

2997   _____. "It is hard to stand in the middle," The Days Be-
        fore. New York: Harcourt, 1952, pp. 74-81; The Collected
        Essays and Occasional Writings of Katherine Anne Porter.
        New York: Delacorte Pr., 1970, pp. 40-46.

2998   Porteus, Hugh Gordon. "Ezra Pound and His Chinese Char-
        acter," An Examination of Ezra Pound. Peter Russell, ed.,
        Cf., #114, pp. 203-217.

2999   _____. "The Pound Errata," Encounter, 40 (June, 1973),
        66-68.

3000   Pottorf, Michael. "The Great Gatsby: Myrtle's Dog and Its
        Relation to the Dog-God of Pound and Eliot," AN&Q, 14, #5
        (1976), 88-90.

3001   Potts, P. "Poem about Ezra Pound," Commentary, 26 (Novem-
        ber, 1958), 410.

3002   Pound, Dorothy Shakespear, ed. Etruscan Gate. Exeter:
        Rougemont Pr., 1971.

3003   _____, et al. "Notes and Queries--Letters to the Editor,"
        Paideuma, 1, #2 (Winter, 1972); b, 271-277, 281-282.

3004 Pound, Omar, and A. Walton Litz, eds. Ezra Pound and
      Dorothy Shakespear: Their Letters: 1909-1914. New York:
      New Directions, 1984.

3005 Pratt, William C. "Imagism and Irony: The Shaping of the
      International Style," SAQ, 83, #1 (Winter, 1984), 1-17.

3006 _____. "Revolution without Betrayal: James, Pound, Eliot
      and the European Tradition," DA, 17 (Vanderbilt: 1957),
      2600.

3007 Praz, Mario. "Gli scrittori e la tecnica," Tempo (Rome), 6
      dic. 1954, p. 3.

3008 _____. "La critica americana d'oggi," Prospetti, #4 (1955).

3009 _____. Mnemosyne: The Parallel between Literature and
      the Visual Arts. Princeton: Princeton U. Pr., 1970, passim.

3010 _____. "T. S. and Dante," SoR, 2, #3 (Winter, 1937),
      525-548; (Pound passim).

3011 _____. "Two Notes on Ezra Pound," Cronache letterarie
      anglosassoni. Rome: Edizioni di storia e letterature, 1950-
      1951, Vol. I, pp. 175-183.

3012 Precosky, Donald A. "'Make Ezra Pound and the Whole
      Caboodle of Them Sit Up': Florence Ayscough and the
      Lowell-Pound Feud," Four Decades of Poetry, 1890-1930, II
      (July, 1979), 204-209.

3013 Press, John. The Chequer'd Shade: Reflections on Obscur-
      ity in Poetry. London: Oxford U. Pr., 1958, passim.

3014 _____. "Ezra Pound, 1909-1919," A Map of Modern English
      Verse. London; New York: Oxford U. Pr., 1969, pp. 53-69.

3015 _____. The Fire and the Fountain: An Essay on Poetry.
      London: Oxford U. Pr., 1955, passim.

3016 _____. The Lengthening Shadows. London: Oxford U.
      Pr., 1971, passim.

3017 _____. Rule and Energy: Trends in British Poetry since
      the Second World War. London; New York: Oxford U. Pr.,
      1963, passim.

3018 Prestin, J. H. "Three American Poets," VQR, 3, #3 (July,
      1927), 450-462.

3019 Prezzolini, Giuseppe. "Ezra Pound e il fascismo," Nazione,
      2, #3 (1973).

3020 _____. "In attesta del risvogliamonte Ezra Pound sta in manicomie," Il Tempo (November 13, 1950), 3.

3021 _____. "Note Americane," Il Borghese, VI (Milan: February 10, 1956), 208.

3022 _____. "La polemica su Ezra Pound," America: con gli stivali. Firenze: Valecchi Editore, 1954, pp. 621-631.

3023 Pricop, Constantin. "Sisteme lirice [Lyrical Systems], ConvLit, 6 (1975), 14.

3024 Pritchard, William H. "Ezra Pound: Persistent Explorer," Lives of the Modern Poets. Cf., #1160, pp. 141-170.

3025 _____. "On Wyndham Lewis," PR, 35, #2 (Spring, 1968), 253-267.

3026 _____. "Paradise Lost," HudR, 25, #2 (Summer, 1972), 316-322.

3027 _____. Wyndham Lewis. New York: Humanities Pr., 1972, passim.

3028 _____. Seeing Through Everything: English Writers, 1918-1940. New York: Oxford U. Pr., 1977, passim.

3029 Pritchett, V. S. "Public Eye," NSt, 74 (July 28, 1967), 119-120.

3030 Puckett, Harry Thomas. "Encounter with the Gods: Form and Style in the Poetry of Ezra Pound," DAI, 32 (Indiana: 1971), 4630A.

3031 Puckett, Walter Edward. "The Nineteenth-Century Foundations of the Robert Browning-Ezra Pound Bridge to Modernity in Poetry," DA, 22, #9 (St. Louis: 1961), 3205.

3032 Puknat, E. M., and S. B. Puknat. "Goethe and Modern American Poets," GQ, 42 (1969), 21-36.

3033 Pulik, Ruth. "Pound and The Waste Land," UES, 15, #2 (1977), 15-24.

3034 Putnam, Samuel. "Ezra Pound: Cracker-barrel 'Revolutionist,'" Mosaic, 1, #5 (November-December, 1934), 3-8.

3035 _____. Paris Was Our Mistress. New York: Viking Pr., (1947), passim.

3036 Putz, Manfred. "A Conversation with William C. Chace," Occident, 8 (Spring, 1974), 51-65.

3037 Quartermaine, Peter. "'To Make Glad the Heart of Man':
      Bunting, Pound, and Whitman," Basil Bunting: Man and Poet.
      Carroll F. Terrell, ed. Orono, ME: National Poetry Founda-
      tion: 1981, pp. 145-158.

3038 Quinn, Mary Bernetta. "Ezra Pound and the Metamorphic
      Tradition," WR, 15 (Spring, 1951), 169-181.

3039 _____. Metamorphic Tradition in Modern Poetry: Essays
      on the Work of Ezra Pound, Wallace Stevens, William Carlos
      Williams, T. S. Eliot, Hart Crane, Randall Jarrell and William
      Butler Yeats. New Brunswick, N.J., Rutgers U. Pr., 1955;
      New York: Gordian Pr., 1966.

3040 Racey, Edgar F., Jr. "Pound and Williams: The Poet as
      Renewer," BuR, 11, #2 (March, 1963), 21-30.

3041 Raffel, Burton. Ezra Pound: Prime Minister of Poetry.
      Hamden, Conn.: Shoe String Pr., 1984.

3042 _____. Possum and Ole Ez: Contemporaries and Peers on
      T. S. Eliot and Ezra Pound. Hamden, Conn.: The Shoe
      String Pr., 1985.

3043 Rago, Henry. "Faith and the Literary Imagination: The
      Vocation of Poetry," Adversity and Grace: Studies in Re-
      cent American Literature. Nathan A. Scott, Jr., ed.
      Chicago; London: U. of Chicago Pr., 1968, pp. 249-252ff.

3044 Raine, Kathleen. "Besök i tjugonde seklet," BLM, 21 (Octo-
      ber, 1952), 599-600.

3045 _____. "Il Miglior Fabbro," NS&N, 40 (November 25,
      1950), 510-512.

3046 Ramsey, Warren. Jules Laforgue and the Ironic Inheritance.
      New York: Oxford U. Pr., 1953, passim.

3047 _____. "Pound, Laforgue, and Dramatic Structure," CL,
      3 (Winter, 1951), 47-56.

3048 Rattray, David. "Der rapelköpfige Anhang," Ezra Pound:
      22 Versuche über einen Dichter. Eva Hesse, ed. Cf.,
      #1979, pp. 401-412.

3049 Ray, David. "Dealing with Mambrino's Helmet," The Art of
      Literary Publishing: Editors on Their Craft. Bill Henderson,
      ed. Yonkers, New York: Pushcart Pr., 1980, p. 267.

3050 Raymond, Marcel. From Baudelaire to Surrealism. New
      York: Wittenborn, Schultz, Inc., 1950, passim.

3051 Read, Forrest. "Pound, Joyce, and Flaubert: The Odys-
      seans," New Approachs to Ezra Pound: A Coordinated In-
      vestigation of Pound's Poetry and Ideas. Eva Hesse, ed.
      Cf., #41, pp. 125-144.

3052 _____, ed. Pound/Joyce: Letters and Essays. With
      Introduction and Commentary. New York: New Directions,
      1967.

3053 _____. "Storicamente Joyce, 1930: Ezra Pound's First
      Italian Essay, " TriQ, 15 (Spring, 1969), 100-107.

3054 _____. "'When will they ever learn': Sho-shu Again,"
      Paideuma, 9 (1980), 327-328.

3055 Read, Herbert. "Révolte et réaction dans la poésie anglaise
      moderne," Présence, Geneva (April, 1946), 56.

3056 Reed, John. "A Word to Mr. Pound," Poetry, 2, #3 (June,
      1913), 112-113.

3057 Reedy, William Marion. "What I Have Been Reading," Reedy's
      Mirror, 25 (July 14, 1916), 462-463; repr., in Ezra Pound:
      The Critical Heritage. Eric Homberger, ed., Cf., #1545,
      pp. 117-118.

3058 Rees, Thomas. "Ezra Pound and the Modernization of Yeats,"
      JML, 4 (Fall, 1975), 574-592.

3059 Reeves, Gareth. "Obstetrics of The Waste Land," CritQ, 17
      (Spring, 1975), 33-53.

3060 Regier, Willis G. "The Allusive Fabric of 'Apparuit,'"
      Paideuma, 9 (1980), 319-322.

3061 _____. "Ezra Pound and E. E. Cummings: Confrontations
      between Tradition and the Avant-Garde," DAI, 39 (Lincoln,
      Nebraska: 1978), 6766A.

3062 Reid, Benjamin L. "Four Winds," SR, 87 (Spring, 1979),
      273-288.

3063 Reid, David, and Mark Turner. "A Conversation with Hugh
      Kenner," Occident, 7, #1 (1973), 18-48.

3064 Reid, Richard. "Pound's Radio Speeches," Agenda, 17, #3-4;
      18, #1 (Aut-Wntr-Spr., 1979-80), 171-186.

3065 Rexroth, Kenneth. American Poetry in the Twentieth Cen-
      tury. New York: Herder & Herder, 1971, pp. 39-44.

3066 Rhys, Ernest. Everyman Remembers. London: J. M. Dent
& Sons, Ltd., and Cosmopolitan Bk. Co., 1931, passim.

3067 _____, ed. The Prelude to Poetry: The English Poets in
Defence and Praise of Their Own Art. New York: Dutton,
Everyman Series, No. 789, 1970, passim.

3068 Ricciardi, Caterina. "La cosmologia della luce nel sincretismo
poundiano," L'esotismo nella letteratura angloamericana.
Elémire Zola. (Studi di Lett. Angloamer. 2.), Rome: Luca-
rini, 1979, pp. 83-119.

3069 Rich, W. "Ezra Pound and Poetry," Dial, 54 (May 1, 1913),
370-371.

3070 Richardson, Jack. "Looking Back at 'The Waste Land,'"
Commentary, 60, #2 (August, 1975), 65-69.

3071 Ricks, Christopher. "Davie's Pound," New Statesman, 69
(April 16, 1965), 610.

3072 Riddel, Joseph N. "Decentering the Image: The 'Project' of
'American' Poetics?" Textual Strategies: Perspectives in Post-
Structuralist Criticism. Josue V. Harai, ed. Ithaca, NY:
Cornell U. Pr., 1979, pp. 322-358.

3073 _____. "'Neo Nietzschean Clatter'--Speculation and/on
Pound's Poetic Image," Boundary, 2, IX, #3 (Spring, 1981);
Ezra Pound: Tactics for Reading. Ian F. A. Bell, ed.
London Vision Pr.; Noble Pr., 1982; Totowa, N.J.: Barnes &
Noble, 1982, pp. 187-220.

3074 Ridge, Lola. "Ezra's Mind," Little Review Anthology. Margaret Anderson, ed. New York: Horizon Pr., 1953, pp.
273-274.

3075 Ringer, Gordon. "Notes on the Present State of Pound
Studies," Shenandoah, 6, #3 (Summer, 1955), 64-66.

3076 Rizzardi, Alfredo. La condizione americana. Studi su poeli
nord-americani. Bologna: Capelli, 1959, passim.

3077 _____, ed. "Inchiesta su Ezra Pound e la poesia americana," Studi e Opinioni su Ezra Pound, NC, Nos. 5-6 (1956),
205-236.

3078 _____. "Molte pagine per Pound," FLe, 3 luglio, 1955,
p. 2.

3079 _____. "Una mostra bibliografica e iconografica di Ezra
Pound," Conv, 27 (1959), 249-251.

3080   _____. "'Saeve indignatio' di Ezra Pound," NC, Nos. 5-6
(genn.-giugno, 1956), 1-8.

3081   Roberts, Michael. Critique of Poetry. London: Jonathan
Cape, 1934, pp. 162-166.

3082   Robinson, James K. "Terror Lumped and Split: Contemporary British and American Poets," SoR, 6, #1 (January,
1970), 216-228.

3083   Robinson, Janice S. H. D.: The Life and Work of an
American Poet. Boston: Houghton Mifflin, 1982, passim.

3084   Rodgers, Frederick George. "The Literary Background of
Brazilian Concrete Poetry: The Impact of Pound, Mallarmé
and Other Major Writers of the 'Noigandres' Group," DAI,
35, #12 (Indiana: 1974), 7922A.

3085   Roditi, Eduard. "Der Fall Ezra Pound oder Die Grenzen der
esthetischen Wertschätzung," Der Monat (München), I, #10
(Munich: July, 1949), 107-113.

3086   Rorem, Ned. "Ezra Pound as a Musician," LonM, 7, #10
(January, 1968), 10, 27-41.

3087   Rose, W. K. "Ezra Pound and Wyndham Lewis: The Crucial
Years," SoR, 4, #1 (January, 1968), 72-89; Agenda, 7, #3-4
(Autumn-Wntr, 1969-70), 117-132.

3088   Rosen, David Matthew. "Art and Economics in Pound,"
Paideuma, 9 (1980), 481-497.

3089   Rosenberg, Harold. "Sanity, Individuality and Poetry," The
New Act, Vol. 2 (June, 1933), 59-75.

3090   Rosenthal, M. L. "Ezra Pound: The Poet as Hero," ForumH,
3 (1960), 29-32.

3091   _____. "New Works on Ezra Pound," Poetry, 106, #5
(August, 1965), 361-365.

3092   _____. "Volatile Matter: Humor in Our Poetry," MassR,
22 (Winter, 1981), 807-817.

3093   Rosmarin, Adena Margaret. "The Historical Imagination:
Browning to Pound," VN, 61 (1982), 11-17.

3094   _____. "Lyric and Ironic Speakers in Modern Poetry:
An Inquiry into the Modes and Methods of Our Literary
Understanding," DAI, 39 (Berkeley: 1978), #5531.

3095   Ross, Robert H. The Georgian Revolt, 1910-1922: Rise and
       Fall of a Poetic Ideal. Carbondale: So. Ill. U. Pr., 1965,
       passim.

3096   Rossi, Aldo. "Ezra Pound," Paragone, #116 (Agosto, 1959),
       pp. 91-94.

3097   Rowe, Hershel Dale. "Basic Elements in the Criticism of
       Ezra Pound," DA, 20 (Florida: 1960), 2807-2808.

3098   Rubin, Louis D., Jr. The Curious Death of the Novel: Es-
       says in American Literature. Baton Rouge: La. St. U.,
       1967, passim.

3099   Runte, Hans R. "Symbolist and Imagist Poetic Processes:
       Comparing Stéphane Mallarmé and Ezra Pound," Dimic, Milan
       V., and Juan Ferraté, eds. Actes du VII congres de l'As-
       sociation Internationale de Litterature comparée/Proceedings
       of the 7th Congress of the International Comparative Litera-
       ture Association, I: Litteratures americaines: .... (Lib.
       of CRCL 2.) Stuttgart: Bieber, 1979, pp. 173-177.

3100   Russell, Peter. "The Decay of Poetry," NatlRev, 17, #20
       (May 18, 1965), 428-430.

3101   _____. "P, Q, and R," MalaR, 19 (July, 1971), 5-23.

3102   Ruthven, Greystiel. "Charles Tomlinson--An Introduction,"
       Gemini/Dialogue, 3 (January, 1960), 30-33.

3103   Ruthven, K. K. "The Composite Mistress," AUMLA, #26
       (November, 1966), 198-214.

3104   _____. "Ezra Pound, Alice Kenny, and the Triad,"
       Landfall, 23 (1969), 73-84.

3105   _____. "The Poet as Etymologist," CritQ, 2 (Spring, 1969),
       9-37.

3106   _____. "Some New Approaches to Ezra Pound," SoRA, 4,
       #4 (1971), 308-315.

3107   Ryan, Judith. "Ezra Pound und Gottfried Benn: Avant-
       garde, Faschismus und asthetische Autonomie," Faschismus
       und Avantgarde. Grimm, Reinhold, and Jost Hermand, eds.
       Königstein: Athenäum, 1980, pp. 29-34.

3108   Sahal, K. L. "The Objective Correlative and the Theory of
       Rasa," CalcR, 2, #2 (October-December, 1970), 237-240.

3109   Sala, Annamaria. "Some Notes on Vorticism and Futurism,"
       Agenda, 7, #3-4/ 8, #1 (Autumn-Winter, 1969-70), 156-162.

3110 Saloman, Louis B. "The Pound-Ruskin Axis," CE, 16 (February, 1955), 270-276.

3111 Saltin, Myles. "More by Ezra Pound," YLG, 30 (October, 1955), 74-80.

3112 Salvalaggio, Nantas. "Ezra Pound sano di mente è tuttora in un manicomie," Il Giornale d'Italia (Rome: July 28, 1955), 1-2.

3113 Sanavio, Piero. Ezra Pound. Venezia, 1977.

3114 _____. "Politik-Gegebenheit oder Traum," Ezra Pound: 22 Versuche über einen Dichter. Eva Hesse, ed., Cf., #1979, pp. 378-386.

3115 Sandburg, Carl. "Poets Major and Minor," Home Front Memo. New York: Harcourt, 1943, pp. 258-260.

3116 _____. "The Work of Ezra Pound," Poetry, 7, #5 (February, 1916), 249-257.

3117 Sanders, Frederick K. "The View Beyond the Dinghey," SR, 79, #3 (Summer, 1971), 433-460.

3118 Satin, Joseph. "Ballatetta," Reading Poetry [Part Four of Reading Literature]. Boston: Houghton Mifflin Co., 1964, pp. 497-498.

3119 Schafer, R. Murray. "Der absolute Rhythmus," Ezra Pound: 22 Versuche über einen Dichter. Eva Hesse, ed. Cf., #1979, pp. 72-86.

3120 _____. "The Developing Theories of Absolute Rhythm and Great Bass," Paideuma, 2, #1 (Spring, 1973), 23-35.

3121 Schiffer, Reinhold. "Der zweimal verwandelte Dionysos: Zur Mythenrezeption bei Ovid und Pound," Arcadia, 8, #3 (1973), 235 247.

3122 Schiralli, Martin Guy. "Education and the Experience of Poetic Meaning," DAI, 39, #5 (Urbana-Champaign, Ill.: 1978), 2813A.

3123 _____. "The Educational Significance of Ezra Pound," JAE, 9, #3 (1975), 41-59.

3124 Schlauch, Margaret. Modern English and American Poetry: Techniques and Ideologies. London: Watts, 1956, passim.

3125 Schleppenbach, Barbara Aschemann. "Irony and Beyond:

The Mythic Method in Conrad, Eliot, and Pound," DAI, 38 (Stanford: 1977), 5467A.

3126 Schmidt, Gerd. "Conversations in Courtship: Ezra Pound als Ubersetzer altagyptischer Liebeslieder," Arcadia, 5 (1970), 296-302.

3127 _____. "'Et Vera Incessu Patuit Dea': A Note on Eliot, Pound, and the Aeneid," TSEN, 1, ii (Fall, 1974), 4-6, (#2-74).

3128 _____. "'I am thy soul, Nikoptis': Pound's The Tomb at Akr Caar," Archiv, 212 (1975), 127-129.

3129 Schmied, Wieland. "T. S. Eliot und Ezra Pound als Kritiker," WZ, V, xi (1959), 44-46.

3130 Schneditz, Wolfgang. Begegnung mit Zeitgenossen. Bilder und Berichte. München: Prestel, 1959.

3131 Schneeman, Peter Henry. "Ezra Pound and the Act of Translation," DAI, 33 (Minnesota: 1972), 6373A-74A.

3132 _____. "Pound's 'Englischer Brief': A Look Toward Germany," Paideuma, 7 (Spring-Fall, 1978), 309-316.

3133 Schneidau, Herbert Newton. "Ezra Pound's Criticism and the Influence of His Literary Relationships in London, 1908-1920," DA, 24 (Princeton: 1963), #1177.

3134 _____. "Pound and Wordsworth on Poetry and Prose," Romantic and Modern: Revaluations of Literary Tradition. George Bornstein, ed. Pittsburgh: U. of Pittsburgh Pr., 1977, pp. 133-145.

3135 _____. "Pound and Yeats: The Question of Symbolism," ELH, 32 (June, 1965), 220-237.

3136 _____. "Pound, Olson, and Objective Verse," Paideuma, 5 (Spring, 1976), 15-30.

3137 _____. "Pound's Book of Cross-Cuts," Genre, 11, #4 (Winter, 1978), 505-521.

3138 _____. "Pound's Poetics of Loss," Ezra Pound: Tactics for Reading. Ian F. A. Bell, ed. Cf., #449, pp. 103-120.

3139 _____. "Vorticism and the Career of Ezra Pound," MP, 65, #3 (February, 1968), 214-227.

3140 _____. "Wisdom Past Metaphor: Another View of Pound,

Fenollosa, and Projective Verse," Paideuma, 5, #1 (Spring, 1976), 15-29.

3141 Schobert, Timothy. Review: "Pound, Ezra: 'Ezra Pound Speaking': Radio Speeches of WW.II," LibJ, 103, #16 (September 15, 1978), p. 1750.

3142 Schroth, Randall. "A Primer for Some of Pound's Chinese Characters," Paideuma, 9 (Fall, 1980), 271-288.

3143 Schulte, Edvige. "Omaggio a Ezra Pound," AION, SG, 1 (1958), 203-238.

3144 _____. "Ritmi Vecchi e nuovi nella poesia inglese moderna," AION, SG, 2 (1959), 191-238.

3145 Schultz, Robert Dale. "Ezra Pound's Developing Poetics: 1908-1915," DAI, 41, #12 (Cornell: 1981), 5103A.

3146 Schutz, Alexander H. "Pound as Provencalist," RomN, 3, #2 (Spring, 1962), 58-63.

3147 Schwartz, Delmore. "Graves in Dock--The Case for Modern Poetry," NR, 134 (March 19, 1956), 20-21.

3148 Schwartz, Sanford Ray. "The Relative Sublime: Pound, Eliot, Richards, and the Making of Modern English Poetics," DAI, 38 (Princeton: 1977), 4186A-87A.

3149 Schwartz, William Leonard. "L'Appel de l'extreme-orient dans la poesie des Etats-Unis," RLC (January, 1928), 113-126.

3150 Scott, Nathan A., Jr., ed. Adversity and Grace: Studies in Recent American Literature. Chicago: U. of Chicago Pr., 1968, passim.

3151 _____. The Broken Center: Studies in the Theological Horizon of Modern Literature. London; New Haven: Yale U. Pr., 1966, passim.

3152 Scott, Tom. "An Appreciation," Ezra Pound Perspectives: Essays in Honor of His Eightieth Birthday. Noel Stock, ed. Cf., #125, pp. 182-197.

3153 Scully, James. "A Prefatory Note," Modern Poetics. James Scully, ed. New York: McGraw-Hill Bk. Co., 1965, pp. 9ff.

3154 _____, ed. Modern Poets on Modern Poetry. London: Collins, 1966, passim.

3155 Sechi, Giovanni. " 'Decadenza' e 'avanguardia' in Ezra

Pound," NC, Nos. 5-6 (genn.-giugno, 1956), 184-196; Cf.,
#518, pp. 26-36.

3156   Seed, David. "The Ezra Pound Conference at Sheffield University," Paideuma, 5, #2 (Fall, 1976), 339-342.

3157   Seidel, Frederick. "The Art of Poetry III," ParisR, 7
(Winter-Spring, 1961), 57-95.

3158   Sell, Frederick C. "The Fusion of Languages," MinnR, 4, #1
(Fall, 1963), 51-59.

3159   Senior, John. "E. P. Pour L'Erection," [poem], QRL, 5, #2
(1949), 145-146.

3160   Sergeant, Elizabeth Shepley. Robert Frost: The Trial by
Existence. New York: Holt, Rinehart & Winston, 1960, pp.
101-112, passim.

3161   Seyersted, Brita L., ed. Pound-Ford: The Story of a Literary Friendship. New York: New Directions, 1982.

3162   Shaheen, Mohammed Y. "Pound and Blunt: Homage for
Apathy," Paideuma, 12, #2-3 (Fall-Winter, 1983), 281-287.

3163   _____. "Pound in Arabic," Paideuma, 6 (1977), 399-410.

3164   Shapiro, Karl. "Ezra Pound: The Scapegoat of Modern
Poetry," In Defense of Ignorance. New York: Random
House, 1960, pp. 61-85; The Poetry Wreck: Selected Essays; 1950-1970. New York: Random House, 1975, pp.
29-54.

3165   _____. "Modern Poetry as a Religion," ASch, 28, #3
(Summer, 1959), 259-305.

3166   _____. Prose Keys to Modern Poetry. New York: Harper
& Row, 1962, pp. 104, 136-137.

3167   _____. Trial of a Poet, and Other Poems. New York:
Reynal & Hitchcock Pr., 1947.

3168   Sharp, Frederick Thomas. "'Objectivists' 1927-1934: A
Critical History of the Work and Association of Louis Zukofsky, William Carlos Williams, Charles Reznikoff, Carl Rakosi,
Ezra Pound, George Oppen," DAI, 43, #8 (Stanford: 1982),
2663A.

3169   Shaw, Peter. "Pound's Quantities and Absolute Rhythm,"
ELWIU, 4 (1977), 95-109.

3170 Shaw, Robert B., ed. American Poetry Since 1960: Some
Critical Perspectives. Chester Springs, Pa.: Dufour, 1974;
Cheadle: Carcanet Pr., 1973, passim.

3171 Sieburth, Richard Raymond. "Dada Pound," SAQ, 93, #1
(Winter, 1984), 44-68.

3172 _____. "Ezra Pound," American Writers in Paris: 1920-
1939. Karen Lane Rood, ed. Detroit, Michigan: Gale Research Co., 1980, pp. 315-333.

3173 Simpson, David. "Pound's Wordsworth; or Growth of a Poet's
Mind," ELH, 45 (Winter, 1978), 660-686.

3174 Simpson, Louis. "The California Poets," LonM, 11 (February-
March, 1972), 56-63.

3175 Sinclair, Upton. "Ezra Pound," My Lifetime in Letters.
Columbia: Missouri U. Pr., 1960, pp. 368-376.

3176 Singh, G. "Pound's Critical Credo," AJES, 6, #1 (1981),
48-75.

3177 Sisson, Charles Hubert. The Avoidance of Literature: Collected Essays. Michael Schmidt, ed. Manchester: Carcanet
Pr., 1979.

3178 _____. "Ezra Pound," English Poetry, 1900-1950: An Assessment. London; New York: Methuen, 1971, pp. 96-124.

3179 _____. "Ezra Pound," Ishmael, 1, #2 (Summer, 1971),
49-74.

3180 _____. "Pound's Literary Programmes," Agenda, 17, #3-4;
18, #1 (Aut-Wntr-Spr., 1979-80), 200-207.

3181 Sitwell, Edith. "Yeats e la soluzione di Pound," FLe, No. 46
(November 16, 1950), 3.

3182 Skorina, Violet Cameron. "Leaving 'Wardour Street': An
Examination of the Relationship between Ford Madox Ford and
Ezra Pound during Their Years Together in London c. 1908-
1915 and the Influence of Ford's Theory of the 'Prose Tradition' upon Pound's Verse Style," DAI, 40, #8 (Connecticut:
1979), 4592A-93A.

3183 Slatin, Myles. "'Mesmerism': A Study of Ezra Pound's Use
of the Poetry of Robert Browning," DA, 29 (Yale: 1957),
1234A-35A.

3184 _____. "More by Ezra Pound," Yale U. Library Gazette,
30, #2 (October, 1955), 74-80, passim.

3185   Smith, Bernard. Forces in American Criticism: A Study in
       the History of American Literary Thought. New York:
       Harcourt, Brace & Co., 1939, pp. 351-352, passim.

3186   Smith, Chard P. "Semi-Classical Poetry and the Great Tra-
       dition," MassR, 3 (Autumn, 1961), 41-61.

3187   Smith, Lewis Worthington. "The New Naiveté," AtlM, 117
       (April, 1916), 487-492.

3188   Smith, Paul. "Pound/Zukofsky," DR, 61, #2 (Summer, 1981),
       356-362.

3189   Smith, Ray. Permanent Fires: Reviews of Poetry, 1958-1973.
       Metuchen, NJ: Scarecrow Pr., 1975, passim.

3190   Smith, Richard Eugene. Richard Aldington. Boston: Twayne
       Pub. Co., 1977, pp. 19-24, passim.

3191   Sokol, B. J. "What Went Wrong between Robert Frost and
       Ezra Pound," NEQ, 49, #4 (1976), 521-541.

3192   Sonne, Jørgen. "Ezra Pounds ideer," Horisonter. Intro-
       duktioner og essays. Copenhagen: Munksgaard, 1973, pp.
       96-108.

3193   Soper, Brian. "Ezra Pound: Some Notes on His Philosophy,"
       An Examination of Ezra Pound. Peter Russell, ed., Cf.,
       #114, pp. 229-248.

3194   Sorda, Enrique. "Otra muerte en Venecia," Estafeta Literaria,
       #507 (January 1, 1973), 9-10.

3195   Sorrentino, Gilbert. The Sullen Art: Interviews by David
       Ossman with Modern American Poets. New York: Corinth
       Books, 1963, pp. 54-55.

3196   Southworth, James Granville. "Ezra Pound," More Modern
       American Poets. Freeport, New York: Bks. for Libraries
       Pr., 1954; repr., 1964; pp. 18-34.

3197   Spears, Monroe K. "The Beginnings of Modernism in English
       Verse," Dionysus and the City: Modernism in Twentieth-
       Century Poetry. New York: Oxford U. Pr., 1970, pp. 105-
       152, passim.

3198   Spector, Robert Donald. "Eliot, Pound, and the Conservative
       Tradition," HINL, 3, ii (April, 1957), 2-5.

3199   _____. "Pound as Pound," HINL, 4 (January, 1958),
       9-10.

3200 Spencer, Benjamin T. "Eight Ways to Nationality," Patterns
      of Nationality: Twentieth-Century Literary Versions of Amer-
      ica. New York: (American Cultural Heritage Series 7), Burt
      Franklin, 1981, passim.

3201 _____. "Pound: The American Strain," PMLA, 81, #7
      (December, 1966), 457-466.

3202 Spender, Stephen. "Ebb Tide in England: The American
      Visitors," Love-Hate Relations: English and American Sensi-
      bilities. New York: Random House, 1974, pp. 149-163.

3203 _____. "On Literary Movements," Encounter, I, #2
      (November, 1953), 66-68.

3204 _____. World Within World: The Autobiography of Stephen
      Spender. London: Hamish Hamilton, 1951, pp. 95, 164-165.

3205 _____. "Writers and Politics," PR, 34, #3 (Summer, 1967),
      359-381, passim.

3206 Spiller, Robert E. The Cycle of American Literature: An
      Essay in Historical Criticism. New York: Macmillan, 1955,
      passim.

3207 _____, et al. Literary History of the United States.
      Vol. 2. New York: Macmillan Pub. Co., 1946, passim.

3208 _____. The Third Dimension: Studies in Literary History.
      London: Collier-Macmillan; New York: Macmillan, 1965,
      p. 146, passim.

3209 Stafford, Jack R. "Ezra Pound and Segregation," LonM, 9,
      #6 (September, 1969), 60-72.

3210 Stancioff, Marion Mitchell. "How I Remember Ezra Pound,"
      America, 128, #10 (March 17, 1973), 240-241.

3211 Stanford, Ann. "Ezra Pound--Poetry 1910-1930," American
      Literary Scholarship: An Annual, 1964. Durham, N.C.:
      Duke U. Pr., 1966, pp. 184-186.

3212 Stanford, Donald E. "Elizabeth Daryush (1887-1977) and Ezra
      Pound (1885-1972)," SoR, 13, #4 (Autumn, 1977), 641-645.

3213 _____. Revolution and Convention in Modern Poetry:
      Studies in Ezra Pound, T. S. Eliot, Wallace Stevens, Edwin
      Arlington Robinson, and Yvor Winters. East Brunswick,
      N.J.: U. of Delaware Pr., 1983.

3214 _____. "Thoughts on the Pound Era," SoR, 9, #1 (Winter,
      1973), viii-xv.

3215 Starkie, Enid. From Gautier to Eliot: The Influence of
France on English Literature, 1851-1939. Hutchinson of
London: Repub., 1971 by Scholarly Pr., 1971, pp. 155-161,
passim.

3216 Stearns, Harold E., ed., with Introd. America Now: An
Inquiry into Civilization in the United States. London; New
York: Chas. Scribner's Sons, 1938, pp. 50-53, 56-58, pas-
sim.

3217 Stegman, Michael O. "William Carlos Williams and Paterson:
An Exorcism of Pound and Eliot; Wallace Stevens at the
Harmonium; Wallace Stevens and Music," DAI, 39, #6 (New
York at Stony Brook: 1978), 3587A.

3218 Steiner, Francis George. "An Essay on the Situation of
Modern Verse," Rivista di Letterature Moderne (Italy), I
(July, 1950), 57-64.

3219 _____. "Cruellest Months," NY, 48 (April 22, 1972), 134ff.

3220 Stern, Richard. "Extracts from a Journal," Triquarterly,
#50 (Winter, 1981), 261-273.

3221 Stewart, Mairi. "Ezra Pound," Poetry Review, 33, #5
(September-October, 1942), 285-289.

3222 Stewart, Peter. "Browning and Pound," BSNotes, 10, #3
(1980), 11-16.

3223 Stock, Noel. "Balancing the Books," PoetA, 30 (October,
1969), 42-52.

3224 _____. "Ezra Pound and an American Tradition," Agenda,
2, #4 (June, 1961), 4-10.

3225 _____. "Ezra Pound's Central Judgments on Contemporary
Literature," Quadrant (Sydney), 6 (Winter, 1962), 5-17.

3226 _____. "Innovation Through Translation," TQ, 10, #4
(Winter, 1967), 40-46.

3227 _____. "Modern Poetry and the Norm of Language," TQ,
4, #4 (Winter, 1961), 134-144.

3228 _____. "Pound der Historiker," Ezra Pound: 22 Versuche
über einen Dichter. Eva Hesse, ed., Cf., #1979, pp. 336-348.

3229 _____. "Thrones 1959," Reading the Cantos: A Study of
Meaning in Ezra Pound. Cf., #954, pp. 104-117.

3230   _____. "The Young Poet," PoetA, 12 (October, 1966),
        36-40.

3231   Stoenescu, Stefan. "Secretul celebrarii perpetue," SXX, 15,
        #9 (1972), 30-37.

3232   Stonier, G. W. "The Mystery of Ezra Pound," Purpose, 10,
        #1 (January-March, 1938), 21-26.

3233   Stough, Christina Carolina. "The Literary Relationship of
        T. S. Eliot and Ezra Pound after The Waste Land," DAI, 41,
        #4 (U. of So. Calif.: 1980), 1601A.

3234   Stovall, Floyd. American Idealism. Norman, Okla.: U. of
        Oklahoma Pr., 1943, passim.

3235   _____, ed. The Development of American Literary Criticism.
        Chapel Hill, NC: North Carolina U. Pr., 1955, passim.

3236   Strickland, G. R. "Flaubert, Pound and Eliot," CamQ, 2
        (Summer, 1967), 242-263.

3237   Strough, Christina C. "The Skirmish of Pound and Eliot in
        The New English Weekly: A Glimpse at Their Later Literary
        Relationship," JML, 10, #2 (June, 1983), 231-246.

3238   Stuart, Duane R. "Modernistic Critics and Translators,"
        PULC, 11 (Summer, 1950), 177-198.

3239   Sühnel, Rudolf. "Die Literarischen Voraussetzungen von
        Joyce's Ulysses," Germanisch-Romanische Monatsschrift, N.S.,
        XII, #2 (April, 1962), 202-211.

3240   _____. "Ezra Pound und die homerische Tradition," Ezra
        Pound: 22 Versuche über einen Dichter. Eva Hesse, ed.
        Cf., #1979, pp. 206-210.

3241   Sullivan, J. P., ed. Preface and Introduction. Ezra Pound:
        A Critical Anthology. Harmondsworth: Penguin, 1970, pp.
        11-13, 200-207.

3242   _____. "Ezra Pound as a Latin Translator," Arion, III, #3
        (Autumn, 1964), 100-111.

3243   _____. "Ezra Pound on Classics and Classicists," Arion,
        3, #1 (Spring, 1964), 9-22.

3244   Surette, Philip Leon. "Also Sprach Ezra: Pound Exposed,"
        Mosaic, 15, #2 (June, 1982), 57-62.

3245   _____. "A Case for Occam's Razor: Pound and Spengler,"
        Paideuma, 6 (Spring, 1977), 109-113.

3246 Sutherland, Donald. "What of Ezra Pound?" DenverQ, 8, #1
      (Spring, 1973), 1-9.

3247 Swabey, Henry. "A Page without Which ...," Paideuma, 5,
      #2 (Fall, 1976), 329-337.

3248 _____. "Towards an A.B.C. of History," Ezra Pound: A
      Collection of Essays. Peter Russell, ed., Cf., #114, pp. 186-
      202.

3249 Sweeney, Richard Monnett. "'Editur Ez' and 'Old Hugger-
      Scrunch': The Influence of Ezra Pound on the Poems of
      William Carlos Williams," DAI, 31, #1 (Brown: 1970), 404A-
      405A.

3250 Symons, W. T. "A Public Scandal," New English Weekly, 7
      (May 16, 1935), 100.

3251 Szasz, Thomas. "Ezra Pound," TLS, #3892 (October 15,
      1976), 1306.

3252 Taggart, John Paul. "Intending a Solid Object: A Study of
      Objectivist Poetics," DAI, 36 (Syracuse: 1974), 332A.

3253 Tagliaferri, Aldo. "Ezra Pound's Jefferson and/or Musso-
      lini," IQ, 16, #64 (1973), 109-115.

3254 Tagore, Rabindranath. "A Bundle of Letters," Ezra Pound:
      Perspectives. Noel Stock, ed., Cf., #125, pp. 109-110.

3255 Takada, Tomiichi. "'Kotoba' no Buto: Fenollosa-Pound no
      Baai," Phoenix o Motomete: Eibei Shosetsu no Yukue.
      Tokyo: Nan'undo, 1982, pp. 429-443.

3256 Takayanagi, Shunichi. "T. S. Eliot to Ezra Pound--The
      Waste Land no Seiritsu wo megutte," ELLS, 9 (1972), 100-144.

3257 Takuwa, Shinji. "The Difficulties of Ezra Pound," KAL, 5
      (April, 1962), 42-47.

3258 Tanner, Tony. "Pound Revalued," Spectator, 223 (1969),
      406-407.

3259 Tate, Allen. "Ezra Pound," The Man of Letters in the Mod-
      ern World. Selected Essays. London: Meridian Bks., 1957,
      pp. 257-263.

3260 _____. "Ezra Pound: 1931," On the Limits of Poetry:
      Selected Essays, 1928-1949. New York: The Swallow Pr.,
      and Wm. Morrow Co., 1948, pp. 350-357.

3261 _____, ed. Introduction by Allen Tate. Six American
Poets from Emily Dickinson to the Present. Minneapolis:
Minn. U. Pr., 1969, pp. 3-8.

3262 _____. "Ezra Pound," Sixty American Poets, 1896-1944.
Selected with Preface and Critical Notes by Allen Tate. Library of Congress, General Reference and Bibliography Divi-
sion, Washington, D.C., 1945, pp. 115-122; Rev. ed., 1954,
pp. 93-101.

3263 Tatlow, Anthony. "Stalking the Dragon: Pound, Waley and
Brecht," CL, 25 (Summer, 1973), 193-211.

3264 Taupin, René. "The Example of Remy de Gourmont," Criterion, 10 (July, 1931), 617-620.

3265 _____. "La poésie d'Ezra Pound," RAA, 8 (February,
1931), 221-236.

3266 Tay, William. "Fragmentary Negation: A Reappraisal of
Ezra Pound's Ideogrammic Method," Chinese-Western Comparative Literature Theory and Strategy. John J. Deeney, ed.
Chinese U. Pr., Distributed by University of Washington Pr.,
1981, pp. 129-153.

3267 Taylor, Daniel William. "The Great London Vortex: Art as
Patterned Energy," DAI, 35 (Emory: 1974), 4564A.

3268 Taylor, James. "The Difficult Individual," [poem], Sou'
wester (October 30, 1970), p. 132.

3269 _____. "The Typical Critic of Pound," Sou'wester, Special Ezra Pound Number, (October 30, 1970), 118-123.

3270 Taylor, Mark. "The Value of Pound," Cw, 97, #10 (December 8, 1972), 226-227.

3271 Taylor, Thomas. "The Eleusinian and Bacchic Mysteries,"
Paideuma, 7 (Spring-Fall, 1978), 155-179.

3272 Taylor, Walter Fuller. The Story of American Letters.
Chicago: Henry Regnery Co., Rev. ed., 1956, pp. 407-408,
passim.

3273 Teele, Roy E. "Ezra Pound," TexQt, 10, #4 (Winter, 1967),
34-35.

3274 _____. Through a Glass Darkly: A Study of English
Translations of Chinese Poetry. Ann Arbor: 1949. (Thesis:
Columbia U.)

3275 Teodorescu, Virgil. "Ezra Pound," Secolul, 20, #7 (1969),
      34-35.

3276 Terramagnino, Geronimo. "Kafka e Pound," Novite (Milan),
      (January, 1954).

3277 Terrell, Carroll F. "Conversations with Celia," Paideuma, 7
      (1978), 585-600.

3278 _____. "A Couple of Documents," Paideuma, 6 (Winter,
      1977), 359-361.

3279 _____. "John Adams Speaking: Some Reflections on
      Technique," Paideuma, 4, #2 (Fall-Winter, 1975), 533-538.

3280 _____. "K.R.H. [Katherine Ruth Heyman] and the
      Young E. P.," Paideuma, 2 (Spring, 1973), 49-51.

3281 _____. "Mang-Tsze, Thomas Taylor, and Madam YAH,"
      Paideuma, 7 (Spring-Fall, 1978), 141-175.

3282 _____. "Meeting E. P. and Then....," Paideuma, 3, #3
      (Winter, 1975), 343-360.

3283 Thatcher, David S., ed. "Richard Aldington's Letters to
      Herbert Read," MalR, 15 (July, 1970), 5-44.

3284 Theall, Donald F. "Communication Theories in Modern Poetry:
      Yeats, Pound, Eliot, Joyce," Diss., U. of Toronto, 1955.

3285 Thomas, C. T. "Link's 'Honey-Comb': A Rejoinder,"
      Paideuma, 8 (1979), 541-542.

3286 Thomas, Ronald Edward. "Armstrong, Pound and Browning,
      or the Mystery of the Missing Bookcase," SBHC, 8, #1 (1980),
      61-64.

3287 _____. "The Catullan Landscape in Pound's Poetry," ConP,
      4, #1 (1981), 66-78.

3288 _____. "'Ere He His Goddis Brocht in Latio': On Pound's
      Appreciation of Gavin Douglas," Paideuma, 9 (1980), 509-517.

3289 _____. "The Latin Masks of Ezra Pound," DAI, 38 (Michi-
      gan: 1977), 6731A; Pub., UMI Research Pr., Ann Arbor,
      Michigan, 1983.

3290 Thompson, Douglas. "Pound and Brazilian Concretism,"
      Paideuma, 6 (Winter, 1977), 279-294.

3291 Thompson, Harold. "Ezra Pound," Hamilton Alumni Review,
      I, #3 (March, 1936), 82-90.

3292 Thompson, Lawrance, ed. Selected Letters of Robert Frost.
      New York; Chicago: Holt, Rinehart & Winston, 1964, passim.

3293 _____, and R. H. Winnick. Robert Frost: The Later
      Years, 1938-1963. New York: Holt, Rinehart & Winston,
      1976, passim.

3294 Thorp, Willard. "Make It New, 1920-1950," American Writing
      in the Twentieth Century. Cambridge, Mass.: Harvard U.
      Pr., 1960, pp. 198-203, passim.

3295 Thorwall, John C. "The Quality of Mercy Not Strained,"
      Pound Newsletter, No. 8 (October, 1955), 22-23.

3296 Thurley, Geoffrey. The American Moment: American Poetry
      in the Mid-Century. New York: St. Martin's Pr., 1978,
      pp. 128-132, passim.

3297 _____. "The New Phenomenalist Poetry in the U.S.A.,"
      SoRA, 4, #1 (1970), 15-28.

3298 Tierney, Bill. "Ezra Pound: State of the Poet," AntigR, 12
      (Winter, 1973), 85-96.

3299 Tietjens, Eunice. "The End of Ezra Pound," Poetry, 60, #1
      (April, 1942), 38-40.

3300 Todd, Olivier. "Pound in Paris," NSt, 70 (November 19,
      1965), 801.

3301 Tolley, A. T. "Rhetoric and the Moderns," SoR, 6, #2
      (April, 1970), 380-397.

3302 Tomlinson, Charles. "Dove sta memoria: In Italy," HudR,
      33, #1 (Spring, 1980), 13-34.

3303 _____. "The Tone of Pound's Critics," Agenda (London),
      4, #2 (October-November, 1965), 46-49.

3304 Torres, Aldo. "El reto de Ezra Pound," Atenea (Concepcion,
      Chile), 135 (December, 1959), 90-94.

3305 Trotter, David. The Making of the Reader: Language and
      Subjectivity in Modern American, English and Irish Poetry.
      New York: St. Martin's Pr., 1984.

3306 Tryford, John. "Wallace Stevens: John Tryford's Random
      Notes," Trace, 66 (Fall, 1967), 339-344.

3307 Tsukui, Nobuko. Ezra Pound and Japanese Noh Plays.
      Washington, D.C.: U. Pr. of America, 1983.

3308 Tucker, John Joseph. "Pound, Vorticism, and the New
      Esthetic," Mosaic, 16, #4 (Fall, 1983), 83-96.

3309 _____. "A Reading of Ezra Pound's Criticism, 1910-1920;
      The Fulcrums of Revolution," DAI, 39, #4 (Toronto: 1976),
      2266A.

3310 Tucker, William P. "Ezra Pound, Fascism, and Populism,"
      RPol, 18 (February, 1956), 105-107.

3311 Turco, Lewis. "The Age of Pound," ConP, 4, #3 (1982),
      33-46.

3312 Turner, Mark. "Pound and Provence," Occident, 7, #1
      (Berkeley, Calif.: 1973), 54-63.

3313 Uchino, Takako. "The Confucian Odes as a Case Study of
      Problems in Translating Oriental Classics into English," KAL,
      11 (1968), 77-86.

3314 Uedo, Makoto. "Zeami, Basho, Yeats, Pound: A Study in
      Japanese and English Poetics," DA, 22 (U. of Washington:
      1961), 4007-4008.

3315 _____. Zeami, Bashō, Yeats, Pound: A Study in Japanese
      and English Poetics. The Hague: Mouton, 1965.

3316 Uejio, Clifford Kiyoshi. "Romanticism to Modernism: The
      Force of the Personae-Self Relationship in the Poetry of
      Wordsworth, Pound, and Williams," DAI, 37 (State U., Buf-
      falo, New York: 1976), 5100A-01A.

3317 Unger, Leonard, ed. "Ezra Pound," Seven Modern American
      Poets: An Introduction. Minneapolis: U. of Minnesota Pr.,
      1969, pp. 119-154.

3318 Untermeyer, Jean Starr. "Ezra Pound: The Mosaic of a
      Mandarin," Private Collection. New York: Alfred A. Knopf,
      1965, pp. 208-217.

3319 Untermeyer, Louis. Bygones: The Recollections of Louis
      Untermeyer. New York: Harcourt, Brace & World, 1965,
      pp. 46, 61, 93-97.

3320 _____. "Ezra Pound," American Poetry Since 1900. New
      York: Henry Holt & Co., 1923, pp. 157-169.

3321 _____. "Ezra Pound," Makers of the Modern World. New
      York: Simon & Schuster, 1955, pp. 643-649.

3322 _____. "Ezra Pound," Modern American Poetry. New

York: Harcourt, Brace & Co., c1919; repub., Scholarly Pr.,
1970, pp. 201-214.

3323 _____. "Ezra Pound," The New Era in American Poetry.
New York: Henry Holt, 1919; repub., Scholarly Pr., 1970,
pp. 201-214.

3324 _____. "Ezra Pound--Proseur," NR, 16 (August 17, 1918),
83-84.

3325 _____. "Ezra Pound," A Treasury of Great Poems. New
York: Simon & Schuster, 1955, p. 1123, passim.

3326 Urdanivia-Bertarelli, Eduardo. "La poesía de Ernesto Cardenal: Fe cristiana y compromiso político," DAI, 44, #2
(August, 1983), 497A (Section A).

3327 Uribe Arce, Armando. Pound. Santiago de Edit (Chile):
Editione Universitaria, 1963.

3328 Vallette, Jacques. "Ezra Pound," MdF, #1025 (January,
1949), 160-163.

3329 _____. "Faut-il lire Ezra Pound Essayiste?" MdF, 322
(October, 1954), 320-322.

3330 Valsecchi, Marco. "Si vuole liberare Ezra Pound," Tempo
(Milan: November 17, 1955), 17-18.

3331 Van Doren, Mark. "The Garden," Introduction to Poetry.
New York: Holt, Rinehart & Winston, 1951, pp. 46-49.

3332 Vázquez Amaral, José. "La poesía de los trovadores y Ezra
Pound," RBA, 26 (1976), 10-18.

3333 Vietta, Susanne. "Zum Verhältnis von Subjektivität und
Zeitlichkeit im Werk von Ezra Pound und Charles Olson,"
Amst, 22, #1 (1977), 147-166.

3334 von Hallberg, Robert. "Olson, Whitehead, and the Objectivists," Boundary, 2 (1973-74), 85-111.

3335 _____. "Olson's Relation to Pound and Williams," CLit, 15
(Winter, 1974), 15-48.

3336 _____. "The Poets' Politics: A View from the Archives,"
ChR, 28, #1 (1976), 147-157.

3337 von Koppenfels, Werner. "Ezra Pound: Der Modernist als
Elegiker," Archiv, 212 (1975), 280-302.

3338   Vortriede, Werner. "Die Seefahrt zu den Herkünflen," Merkur,
       19 (1966), 487-491.

3339   Waggoner, Hyatt Howe. American Visionary Poetry. Baton
       Rouge, La.: Louisiana St. U. Pr., 1982, passim.

3340   _____. The Heel of Elohim: Science and Values in Modern
       American Poetry. Norman, Oklahoma: U. of Oklahoma Pr.,
       1950, pp. 90-99, passim.

3341   _____. "The Legend of Ezra Pound," UKCR, 10, #4 (Sum-
       mer, 1944), 275-285.

3342   Wagner, Geoffrey Atheling. Wyndham Lewis: A Portrait of
       the Artist as Enemy. New Haven: Yale U. Pr., 1957, passim.

3343   Wagner, Linda Welshimer, ed. "On Ezra Pound," Interviews
       with William Carlos Williams. New York: New Directions Pub.
       Corp., 1976, pp. 80-81, passim.

3344   _____. "The Poetry of Ezra Pound," JML, 1 (1970), 293-
       298.

3345   Wain, John. "Poetry," The Twentieth Century Mind: History,
       Ideas, and Literature in Britain. C. B. Cox and A. E. Dyson,
       eds. London: Oxford U. Pr., 1972, II, pp. 307-372.

3346   _____. "The Prophet Ezra v. 'The Egotistical Sublime,'"
       Encounter, 33 (August, 1969), 63-70.

3347   _____. "The Reputation of Ezra Pound," LonM, 2 (October,
       1955), 55-64.

3348   _____. "The Reputation of Ezra Pound," Preliminary Es-
       says. London: Macmillan; New York: St. Martin's Pr.,
       1957, pp. 157-169.

3349   Walkiewicz, E. P., and Hugh Witemeyer. "Ezra Pound's Con-
       tributions to New Mexican Periodicals and His Relationship with
       Senator Bronson Cutting," Paideuma, 9 (1980), 441-459.

3350   Wallace, Emily Mitchell. "Youthful Days and Costly Hours,"
       Ezra Pound and William Carlos Williams. Daniel Hoffman, ed.
       The University of Pennsylvania Conference Papers. Philadel-
       phia: U. of Pennsylvania Pr., 1983, pp. 14-58.

3351   Walsh, Chad. "The Postwar Revolt in England Against Mod-
       ern Poetry," BuR, 13, #3 (December, 1965), 97-105.

3352   Walsh, Ernest. "Ezra Pound," This Quarter, I, 1 (Spring,
       1925), 229-231.

3353 Walther, Ying Tai Shirley. "A Re-Examination of the Ideo-
      grammic Method of Ezra Pound," DAI, 44, #5 (Kansas St. U.:
      1983), 1456A.

3354 Wand, David Happell Hsin-Fu. "Cathay Revisited: The Chi-
      nese Tradition in the Poetry of Ezra Pound and Gary Snyder,"
      DAI, 33 (So. Calif.: 1972), 5205A-6A.

3355 Wang, John C. "Ezra Pound as a Translator of Classical
      Chinese Poetry," SR, 73, #3 (Summer, 1965), 345-357.

3356 Wasserstrom, William, ed. "Introduction," A Dial Miscellany.
      Syracuse, N.Y.: Syracuse U. Pr., 1963, pp. xi-xxx.

3357 Waugh, Arthur. "The New Poetry," QRL, 226 (October,
      1916), 365-368.

3358 _____. "Tradition and Change--the New Poetry," Tradi-
      tion and Change. Studies in Contemporary Literature. Free-
      port, New York: Books for Libraries Pr., 1919; repr., 1969,
      pp. 38-39, passim.

3359 Weatherhead, A. Kingsley. The Edge of the Image: Marianne
      Moore, William Carlos Williams, and Some Other Poets. Seattle
      and London: U. of Washington Pr., 1967, pp. 12-19, passim.

3360 Webb, Mark S. "Ezra Pound's Literary Criticism: The For-
      mation of a Modern Poet," DAI, 34 (Yale: 1973), 7252A.

3361 Weeks, Leroy Titus. "The New Beauty," Poetry, 6, #1
      (April, 1915), 48-50.

3362 Wees, William C. "England's Avant-Garde: The Futurist-
      Vorticist Phase," WHR, 21 (1967), 117-128.

3363 _____. "Our Little Gang," Vorticism and the English
      Avant-Garde. Toronto: Toronto U. Pr., 1972, pp. 119-155.

3364 _____. "Pound's Vorticism: Some New Evidence and
      Further Comments," WSCL, 7 (Summer, 1966), 211-216.

3365 Weintraub, Stanley. The London Yankees: Portraits of
      American Writers and Artists in England, 1894-1914. New
      York: Harcourt Brace Jovanovich, 1979, passim.

3366 Weinzinger, Anita. "Graves's Criticism of Contemporary
      Poets," On Poets and Poetry: Second Series. Salzburg
      Studies in English/Poetic Drama and Poetic Theory, No. 27
      (1980), pp. 49-101.

3367 Weiss, Theodore R. "The Blight of Modernism and Philip

Larkin's Antidote," The American Poetry Review, 6, #1
(January-February, 1977), 39-41.

3368 _____. "E. P.: The Man Who Cared Too Much," Parnassus, 5 (1977), 79-119; The Man from Porlock: Engagements,
1944-1981. Princeton U. Pr., 1982, pp. 17-57.

3369 _____. "The Many-Sidedness of Modernism," TLS, 1
(February, 1980), 124-125.

3370 Weisstein, Ulrich. "Vorticism: Expressionism English Style,"
Yearbook of Comparative and General Literature, 13 (1964),
28-40.

3371 Welke, Robert J. "Frobenius: Pound--Some Quick Notes,"
Paideuma, 2, #3 (Winter, 1973), 415-417.

3372 Wellek, Rene. "Cleanth Brooks, Critic of Critics," SoR, 10,
#1 (January, 1974), 125-152.

3373 _____. "Ezra Pound's Literary Criticism," UDQ, 11, #1
(1976), 1-20.

3374 Wells, Henry Willis. New Poets from Old: A Study in Literary Genetics. New York: Russell & Russell, 1964, passim.

3375 Welsh, Andrew. "'Melos' and 'Opsis,'" DA, 31 (Pittsburgh:
1970), 2407A.

3376 West, Ray B. "Ezra Pound and Contemporary Criticism,"
QRL, 5, #2 (1949), 192-200.

3377 _____. "Ezra Pound and Contemporary Criticism," Critics
on Ezra Pound: Readings in Literary Criticism. E. San
Juan, Jr., ed. Coral Gables, Fla.: Miami U. Pr., 1972,
pp. 36-37.

3378 West, Rebecca. "Imagisme," New Freewoman, I (August 15,
1913), 86-88.

3379 West, T. Wilson. "D. G. Rossetti and Ezra Pound," RES, 4,
#13 (January, 1953), 52-56.

3380 Westlake, Neda. "Ezra Pound: A Retrospective of an American Poet: An Exhibition at the University of Pennsylvania,
April-June, 1975," William Carlos Williams Newsletter, 1, #1
(1975), 6-7.

3381 Whicher, G. F. "Impressionists and Experimenters," Literature of the American Poeple: An Historical and Critical Survey. Arthur Hobson Quinn, ed. New York: Appleton-
Century-Crofts, 1951, pp. 857-864.

3382   Whigham, Peter. "William Carlos Williams," Agenda, 3, #2
       (October-November, 1963), 25-32.

3383   Whitehead, Cintra. "Essay I: Ezra Pound and James Legge.
       Essay II: Modern Personality Theory and Literary Criticism,"
       DAI, 38 (Toledo: 1977), 6698A-99A.

3384   Whittemore, Reed. "Literature as Persuasion," SR, 68, #4
       (October, 1960), 565-575.

3385   _____. "Little Magazines," UMPAW, #32, Minneapolis: U.
       of Minn. Pr., 1963.

3386   Wickes, George. "Hemingway's Arcadia," American Dialog, 3,
       #2 (Summer, 1966), 32-33.

3387   Widershien, Marc Alan. "The Presence of Modern French
       Literature in the Writings of Ezra Pound," DAI, 41, #5 (Bos-
       ton: 1979), 2099A-2100A.

3388   Wiggs, Sharon J. "Pound's 'Greek Epigram': Indictment and
       Sentence for Inconstancy," StHum, 7, #1 (December, 1978),
       48-51.

3389   Wildi, Max. "Pound and Eliot," NZZ, 12 (November, 1972),
       51.

3390   Wilhelm, James J. "Arnaut Daniel's Legacy to Dante and to
       Pound," Italian Literature: Roots and Branches: Essays in
       Honor of Thomas Goodard Begin. Giose Rimanelli and Kenneth
       John Archity, eds. New Haven: Yale U. Pr., 1976, pp. 67-
       83.

3391   _____. Dante and Pound: The Epic of Judgement.
       Orono: U. of Maine Pr., 1974.

3392   _____. "Ezra Pound's Dante," Punto de Contacto Point of
       Contact, (New York), 1, #2 (1976), 55-60.

3393   _____. "Pound and the Troubadours," Paideuma, 2, #2
       (1973), 133-137.

3394   _____. Seven Troubadours: The Creators of Modern Verse.
       London: University Park, 1977, pp. 145-172.

3395   _____. "The Troubadours as Guides to Poetry and Para-
       dise," UES, 15, #2 (1977), 35-40.

3396   Willard, Charles B. "Ezra Pound and the Whitman 'Message,'"
       RLC, 31 (January, 1957), 94-98.

3397 _____. "Ezra Pound's Appraisal of Walt Whitman," MLN, 72 (January, 1957), 19-26.

3398 _____. "Ezra Pound's Debt to Walt Whitman," SP, 54 (October, 1957), 573-581.

3399 Williams, Ellen. Harriet Monroe and the Poetry Renaissance: The First Ten Years of Poetry, 1912-1922. London; Chicago: U. of Illinois Pr., 1977, pp. 33-37, passim.

3400 Williams, Raymond. "A Changing Social History of English Writing," Audience, 8 (Winter, 1961), 76-82.

3401 Williams, William Carlos. "A 1 Pound/Stein (1935)," Selected Essays of William Carlos Williams. New York: New Directions, 1954, pp. 162-166.

3402 _____. "The American Language--again," Pound Newsletter, (October, 1955), 2-7.

3403 _____. "Ezra Pound," The Autobiography of William Carlos Williams. New York: Random House, 1951, pp. 56-66, passim.

3404 _____. "Ezra Pound," The Critical Heritage. Charles Doyle, ed. London; Boston: Routledge & Kegan Paul, 1980, passim.

3405 _____. "Ezra Pound: Lord Ga-Ga!" Decision, 2 (September, 1941), 16-24.

3406 _____. "A Letter to Babette Deutsch," Pound Newsletter, 8 (October, 1955), 22-23.

3407 _____. "Letter to Edgar I. Williams," (April 12, 1905), The Selected Letters of William Carlos Williams. New York: McDowell, Obolensky, 1957, pp. 8-10.

3408 _____. "On Ezra Pound," Interviews with William Carlos Williams. Ed., with Introd., by Linda Welshimer Wagner. New York: New Directions, 1976, pp. 80-81.

3409 _____. "Public Speech and Private Speech in Poetry," A Time to Speak. Cambridge, Mass.: The Riverside Pr., 1941, pp. 61ff.

3410 _____. "Reply to Pound," New Democracy, Vol. 2 (March 30-April 15, 1934). 5.

3411 _____. "T. S. Eliot, or Religion," Three on a Tower: The Lives and Works of Ezra Pound, T. S. Eliot and William

Carlos Williams. New York: William Morrow & Co., Inc.,
1975, pp. 93-191.

3412   Wilmer, Clive. "Definition and Flow: Thom Gunn in the
1970's," British Poetry Since 1970: A Critical Survey.
Peter Jones and Michael Schmidt, eds. New York: Persea
Books, c1980, pp. 64-74.

3413   Wilson, Edmund. Axel's Castle: A Study in the Imaginative
Literature of 1870-1930. New York: Scribner's, 1931, pp.
100, 109, 111, 113.

3414   _____. The Devils and Canon Barham: Ten Essays on
Poets, Novelists and Monsters. Foreword by Leon Edel.
New York: Farrar, Straus and Giroux, 1973, pp. 27, 109,
112-117.

3415   _____. "Ezra Pound's Patchwork," The Shores of Light:
A Literary Chronicle of the Twenties and Thirties. New
York: Farrar, Straus and Young, Inc., 1952, pp. 44-48.

3416   _____. "The First Waste Land," NYRB, 17 (November 18,
1971), 16-17.

3417   _____. "Marxism at the End of the Thirties," The Shores
of Light: A Literary Chronicle of the Twenties and Thirties.
New York: Vintage Books, 1961, pp. 732-743.

3418   _____. "Mr. Pound's Patchwork," NR, 30, #385 (April 19,
1922), 232-233.

3419   _____. "The Permanence of Yeats," Selected Criticism.
New York: Macmillan, 1950, pp. 22-23.

3420   _____. "T. S. Eliot," NR, 60, #780 (November 13, 1929),
345-346.

3421   Wilson, Suzanne M. "Emily Dickinson and Twentieth-Century
Poetry of Sensibility," AL, 36, #3 (November, 1964), 349-358.

3422   Wimsatt, W. K., and Cleanth Brooks. "Eliot and Pound: An
Impersonal Art," Literary Criticism: A Short History. New
York: Random House, 1967, pp. 657-680.

3423   Winterich, John T. "Ezra Pound," SatRL, 28 (December,
1945), 10.

3424   Winters, Lee Eugene, Jr. "The Relationship of Chinese
Poetry to British and American Poetry of the Twentieth Century," Diss. U. of California, Berkeley, 1956.

3425 Winters, Yvor. _Forms of Discovery: Critical and Historical_
      Essays on the Forms of the Short Poem in English. Denver:
      Alan Swallow Co., 1967, passim.

3426 Witemeyer, Hugh. "Ezra Pound," ConL, 14 (Spring, 1973),
      240-246.

3427 _____. "Ezra Pound's Poetry, 1908-1916," DAI, 28
      (Princeton: 1966), 2271A.

3428 _____. "Ezra Pound's Presence in Guy Davenport's
      Tatlin," Vort, 9 (1976), 57-61.

3429 _____. "Walter Savage Landor and Ezra Pound," _Romantic_
      and Modern: Revaluations of Literary Tradition. George
      Bornstein, ed. Pittsburgh: U. of Pittsburgh Pr., 1977,
      pp. 147-163.

3430 Wood, Michael. "Ezra Pound," NYRB, 20 (February 8, 1973),
      7-11.

3431 Wood, Tom. "The Value of a Pound," LGJ, 1, #i (1973),
      30-33.

3432 Woodard, Charles R. "Browning and Three Modern Poets:
      Ezra Pound, Yeats, and Eliot," Diss. Tennessee, 1953.

3433 Woodward, A. G. "Ezra Pound," UES, 15, #2 (1977), 1-7.

3434 _____. "Ezra Pound: From Enlightenment to Myth,"
      Standpunte, 146 (1980), 32-43.

3435 _____. "Pound and Santayana," SAQ, 83, #1 (Winter,
      1984), 80-90.

3436 Woodward, Anthony. "Ezra Pound, Mussolini and Fascism,"
      Standpunte, 36, #3 (June, 1983), 20-30.

3437 Woodward, Daniel H. "John Quinn and T. S. Eliot's First
      Book of Criticism," PBSA, 56 (2nd Qt., 1962), 259-265.

3438 Woodward, Kathleen. "The Poetry of Old Age: The Late
      Poems of Eliot, Pound, Stevens, and Williams," DAI, 37
      (Calif., San Diego: 1977), 5821A.

3439 Wright, Arthur F., (ed.) "Some Reflections on the Difficulty
      of Translation," _Studies in Chinese Thought._ Chicago: U.
      of Chicago Pr., 1953, passim.

3440 Wykes-Joyce, Max. "Some Considerations Arising from Ezra
      Pound's Conception of the Bank, [1949]," _An Examination of_

Ezra Pound: A Collection of Essays. Peter Russell, ed.,
Cf., #114, pp. 218-228.

3441   Yeats, William Butler. "Ezra Pound," Ezra Pound: A Collection of Critical Essays. Walter Sutton, ed. Cf., #2240,
pp. 9-10.

3442   _____. "Ezra Pound," Critics on Ezra Pound: Readings
in Literary Criticism. E. San Juan, Jr., ed., Cf., #535,
p. 16.

3443   _____. "Ezra Pound," Introduction, The Oxford Book of
Modern Verse. William Butler Yeats, ed. New York: Oxford
U. Pr., 1936, pp. xxiv-xxvi.

3444   _____. Interviews and Recollections. E. H. Mikhail, ed.
New York: Barnes & Noble, 1977, passim.

3445   _____. The King of the Great Clock Tower. New York:
Macmillan Co., 1935, pp. v-vii.

3446   _____. "Letter to Lady Gregory," (December 10, 1909),
The Letters of W. B. Yeats. Allan Wade, ed. London:
Hart-Davis, 1954, p. 543.

3447   _____. Letters on Poetry from W. B. Yeats to Dorothy
Wellesley. Dorothy Wellesley, ed. New York: Oxford U.
Pr., 1964, p. 23.

3448   _____. Memoirs of W. B. Yeats: Autobiography-First
Draft Journal. Trans. and Edited by Denis Donoghue. New
York: Macmillan, 1972.

3449   _____. A Packet for Ezra Pound. Dublin: The Cuala
Pr., 1929; repr., in A Vision (by Ezra Pound). London:
Macmillan, 1937; New York: Macmillan, 1936, 1956.

3450   _____. "Speaking to the Psaltery," Essays and Introduc-
tions. New York: Macmillan, 1961, pp. 13-27.

3451   Yip, Wai-Lim. "Classical Chinese and Modern Anglo-
American Poetry: Convergence of Languages and Poetry,"
CLS, 11, #1 (March, 1974), 21-47.

3452   Yoshino, Masaaki. "Luminous Eros: Ezra Pound and
Provencal Alba," SELL, 29 (1978), 21-43. (In Jap.; Eng.
sum., pp. 205-206.)

3453   _____. "Pound and His Method of Cognition--as Seen in
Terms of His Language," SELL, 24 (1974), 63-77.

3454   Young, Kenneth. "Poets without Readers--and Why," Daily
       Telegraph (London), (August 7, 1954).

3455   Zabel, Morton Dauwen, ed. "Introduction: Criticism in
       America," Literary Opinion in America. New York: Rev.
       Ed., Harper, (1937), 1951, pp. 22-24.

3456   _____. "Recent Magazines," Poetry, 44, #3 (June, 1934),
       173-174.

3457   _____. "Recent Magazines," Poetry, 46 (June, 1935), 172.

3458   Zach, Natan. "Imagism and Vorticism," Modernism, 1890-
       1930. (Pelican Guides to European Literature.) Malcolm
       Bradbury and James [Walter] McFarlane, eds. Hassocks,
       Eng.: Harvester; Atlantic Highlands, NJ: Humanities,
       1978, pp. 228-242.

3459   Zapatka, Francis Edward. "Ezra Pound and Francois Villon,"
       DAI, 34 (Catholic U. of America: 1973), 1262A.

3460   Zapponi, Niccolò. "Odi e amori futuristi di Ezra Pound,"
       ["Ezra Pound and Futurism,"], SA, 18 (1972), 299-312; re-
       vised in "Odi e amori futuristi di Ezra Pound," L'Italia di
       Ezra Pound (1976); ed., and trans. by Angela Jung and
       Guido Palandri, Images of Ezra Pound: Twelve Critical Es-
       says. Mei Ya Pubs., Inc., Taipei, Taiwan, 1979, pp. 128-
       139.

3461   Zardoya, Concha. "Espana en la poesia de Ezra Pound,"
       Insula, (Madrid) 8 (April, 1953), 1-3, 8.

3462   Zilczer, Judith. "The Noble Buyer": John Quinn, Patron of
       the Avant Garde. Washington: Pub. for the Hirshhorn Mu-
       seum and Sculpture Garden. Smithsonian Institution, by the
       Smithsonian Institution Pr., 1978.

3463   Zimmermann, Hans-Joachim. "Die Aphrodite mit dem goldenen
       Zweig des Argostöters: Betrachtungen zu Ezra Pound Canto
       I," Geschichte und Gesellschaft in der amerikanischen litera-
       ture. Karl Schubert and Ursula Müller-Richter, eds.,
       Heidelberg: Quelle & Meyer, 1975, pp. 166-174.

3464   _____. "'An Armour against Utter Consternation'
       Neuere Literatur zu Ezra Pound," Archiv, 217 (1980), 111-
       121.

3465   _____. "Ezra Pound," Englische Dichter der Moderne:
       Ihr Leben und Werk. Rudolf Sühnel and Dieter Riesner, eds.
       Berlin: Schmidt, 1971, pp. 230-251.

3466 _____. "Ezra Pound, 'A Song of the Degrees': Chinese Clarity versus Alchemical Confusion," Paideuma, 10 (1981), 225-241.

3467 Zinnes, Harriet, ed. Introduction. Ezra Pound and the Visual Arts. New York: New Directions Pub. Corp., 1980.

3468 Zukovsky, Louis. "Ezra Pound," Prepositions: The Collected Critical Essays of Louis Zukovsky. Expanded Ed., Cf., #1054, pp. 67-83.

3469 _____. An Objectivists Anthology. Le Beausset, France; New York: 1932, pp. 17-21.

3470 _____. "Objectivists, 1931," Poetry, 37, #5 (February, 1931), 268-272.

3471 _____. Louis Zukofsky: Man and Poet. Carroll F. Terrell, ed., with Introduction. National Poetry Foundation: U. of Maine, Orono, Maine, 1979, passim.

3472 Zverev, A. "Ezra Pound--literaturnaja teorija, poèzija, sud'ba," [Ezra Pound--literary theory, poetry, fate], VLit, 14, #6 (1970), 123-127.

3473 _____. "Der 'linke' Elitarismus und die Folgen: Ezra Pound," KuL, 4 (April 29, 1981), 427-444. [Tr. from Modernizm v literature, SShA, 1979.]

V. INTERVIEWS

3474 Bridson, D. G. "An Interview with Ezra Pound," New Directions, 17, (1961), 159-184.

3475 Dembo, L. S., and Cyrena N. Pondrom, eds. The Contemporary Writer: Interviews with Sixteen Novelists and Poets. Madison, Wis.: University of Wisconsin Pr., 1972, passim.

3476 Hall, Donald. "Ezra Pound: An Interview," ParisR, 7, #28 (Summer-Fall, 1962), 22-51; repr., in Ezra Pound: A Collection of Criticism. Grace Schulman, ed., Cf., #1084.

3477 _____. "The Paris Review Interviews with T. S. Eliot and Ezra Pound," Remembering Poets: Reminiscences and Opinions: Dylan Thomas, Robert Frost, T. S. Eliot, Ezra Pound. New York: Harper & Row, 1978, pp. 201-244.

3478 Henderson, Archie. "Pound's Stretlets Interview (1915)," Paideuma, 11, #3 (Winter, 1982), 473-486.

3479 Johnson, Edd. Interview with Ezra Pound. Philadelphia Record. (May 9, 1945).

3480 Kerblat-Blanchenay, Jeanne. "End to Torment: Etude de l'interrogation dans la memoire de H. D." in All Men Are Created Equal: Ideologies, Reves et realites. Martin, Jean-Pierre, ed. Aix-en-Provence: Pubs. Univ. de Provence, 1983, pp. 147-167.

3481 Pound, Homer L. [Father of Ezra Pound]. Interview. Evening Bulletin of Philadelphia (February 20, 1928), quoted in Imagism and the Imagists: A Study in Modern Poets by Glenn Hughes. New York: Humanities Pr., c1931, 1960, pp. 227-28.

3482 Reid, B. L. "Four Winds," SR, 87 (Spring, 1979), 273-288.

3483 Reid, David, and Mark Turner. "A Conversation with Hugh Kenner," Cf., #3063, pp. 18-48.

3484 Remnick, David. "An Interview with Charles Wright," PR, 50, #4 (1983), 567-575.

3485 Yoshikawa, Kojiro. "An Interview with Ezra Pound," EWR, 1 (1964), 212-217.

3486   Anceschi. Luciano. "Due lettere su Dante," NC, Nos. 5-6
       (1956), 58-69.

3487   _____. "Lettere di Pound," Aut-Aut, No. 2 (marzo 1951),
       157-159.

3488   _____. "Tre lettere di Ezra Pound al Dr. Rouse sul
       tradurre poesia, e una lettera di Joyce," LetM, I (September,
       1950), 220-226.

3489   Atkinson, F. G. "Ezra Pound's Reply to an 'Old-World'
       Letter," AL, 46, #3 (November, 1974), 357-359.

3490   Barnard, Mary. "Ezra Pound, Sappho, and My Assault on
       Mount Helicon," MHRev, 66 (October, 1983), 140-144.

3491   Bartlett, Lee, and Hugh Witemeyer. "Ezra Pound and James
       Dickey: A Correspondence and a Kinship," Paideuma, 11, #2
       (Fall, 1982), 290-312.

3492   Bergman, Petter. "Ezra Pounds brev," Dagstidningen
       Arbetaren. Stockholm: (November 9, 1954). (Review:
       Letters).

3493   Bodini, Vittorio. "Alcune lettere di Ezra Pound," SA, 4
       (1958), 421-423.

3494   Brown, Ray C. B. "The Ounce of Prevention," Voices, No.
       141 (1951), pp. 15-18.

3495   Bryer, Jackson R. "Pound to Joyce on Ulysses: A Correc-
       tion," AN&Q, 4 (April, 1966), 115-116.

3496   Carpenter, Humphrey. Ezra Pound and Dorothy Shakespear:
       Their Letters: 1909-1914. Omar Pound and A. Walton Litz,
       eds. New York: New Directions (1984).

3497   Casillo, Robert. "Letters of Ezra Pound to Clark Emery in
       the University of Miami Library," Carrell, 21 (1983), 24-35.

3498   Connolly, Cyril. "Nor Could the Muse Defend Her Son,"
       The Observer, (April 22, 1951). 7.

3499   Cowley, Malcolm. "Mad about Poetry; and Other Things,
       Too," New York Herald Tribune, Book Review (November 12,
       1950), 4. (Review: The Letters.)

3500   Creeley, Robert. "A Note Followed by a Selection of Letters
       from Ezra Pound," Agenda, 4, #2 (October-November, 1965),
       11-21.

3501   Cummings, E. E. "Letters to Ezra Pound," PaR, 39 (Fall,
       1966), 55-87.

3502   _____. "To Ezra Pound," Selected Letters of E. E. Cum-
       mings. F. W. Dupee and George Stade, eds. New York:
       Harcourt, Brace & World, Inc., 1969, passim.

3503   Curci, Lino. "Alcune letters," SA, 4 (1958), 421-430.

3504   Dudek, Louis. "Correspondence," Canadian Forum, 29
       (November, 1949), 185-186.

3505   _____, ed. Some Letters of Ezra Pound. Montreal:
       Dudek-Collins, 1974.

3506   Dupee, F. W., and George Stade. "Letters of E. E. Cum-
       mings to Ezra Pound," PaR, 10 (Fall, 1966), 55-87.

3507   _____, and _____, eds. Selected Letters of E. E.
       Cummings. New York: Harcourt, Brace & World, 1969,
       passim.

3508   Eliot, T. S. "Letter to Ezra Pound from T. S. Eliot," Ezra
       Pound: Perspectives. Cf., #125, pp. 110-111.

3509   _____. "Mr. Pound and His Poetry," Athenaeum, (Novem-
       ber 7, 1919), 1163. (Reply to Pound's Letter, Athenaeum
       [October 31, 1919], 1132.)

3510   Ellman, Richard, ed. "Joyce Letters," TriQ, 8 (Winter,
       1967), 166-176.

3511   Farmer, David. "The Bibliographical Potential of a 20th
       Century Literary Agent's Archive: The Pinker Papers,"
       LCUT, 2 (November, 1970), 26-35.

3512   _____. "An Unpublished Letter by Ezra Pound," TexQt,
       10 (Winter, 1967), 95-104.

3513   Fitts, Dudley. "O Dulce Convivium," Cf., #2316.

3514   Fitz Gerald, Mary. "Ezra Pound and Irish Politics: An Un-
       published Correspondence," Paideuma, 12, #2-3 (Fall-Winter,
       1983), 377-417.

3515   Ford, Ford Madox. "Letter," _Ezra Pound: Perspectives_.
       Cf., #125, p. 126.

3516   Fuller, Roy. [Review: _The Letters_], The London Magazine,
       I, #4 (May, 1954), 94-100.

3517   Gallup, Donald, ed. "Ezra Pound: Letters to Viola Baxter
       Jordan," Paideuma, 1 (Spring-Summer, 1972), 107-111.

3518   Gershman, Herbert S. "Ezra Pound to 'Littérature,' " MLN,
       74 (November, 1959), 608-609. Reprint of Pound's Letter to
       Littérature, #16 (1920), 48.

3519   Gillespie, Don C. "John Becker's Correspondence with Ezra
       Pound: The Origins of a Musical Crusader," BRH, 83 (1980),
       163-171.

3520   Hagemann, E. R. "Incoming Correspondence to Dorothy and
       Ezra Pound at the Lilly Library," Paideuma, 12, #1 (Spring,
       1983), 131-156.

3521   Helsztynski, Stanislaw, ed. "Ezra Pound's Letters to an
       Editor of His Anthology," KN, 20 (1973), 59-65.

3522   _____. "Ezra Pound's Letters to a Polish Scholar," KN,
       17 (1970), 299-323.

3523   Herdeck, Donald E. "A New Letter by Ezra Pound about
       T. S. Eliot," MassR, 12 (1971), 287-292.

3524   Hungiville, Maurice. "Ezra Pound, Educator: Two Uncol-
       lected Pound Letters," AL, 44, #3 (November, 1972), 462-
       469.

3525   _____. "Ezra Pound's Letters to Olivet," TexQt, 16, #2
       (Summer, 1973), 77-87.

3526   Hutchins, Patricia. "Letters from Ezra Pound," TC, 164
       (October, 1958), 355-363.

3527   _____. "Ezra Pound and Thomas Hardy," SoR, 4 (n.s.)
       #1 (January, 1968), 90-104.

3528   Izzo, Carlo. _Civiltà americana_. Vol. II: _impressioni e note_.
       Rome: Edizioni di Storia e Letteratura, 1967.

3529   _____. "Three Unpublished Letters by Ezra Pound," IQ,
       64 (1973), 117-118.

3530   _____. "23 lettere e 9 cartoline inedite," NC, Nos. 5-6
       (genn.-giugno, 1956), pp. 123-154.

3531 _____. "Twenty-three Unpublished Letters and Nine Post Cards of Ezra Pound," Italian Images of Ezra Pound: Twelve Critical Essays. Angela Jung and Guido Palandri, eds. Taipei, Taiwan: Mei Ya, 1979, pp. 139-159.

3532 Joyce, James. Ezra Pound: Perspectives: Essays in Honor of His Eightieth Birthday. Noel Stock, ed. Cf., #125, pp. 112-113, 115-116.

3533 Kenner, Hugh. "Praestantibusque Ingeniis," KR, 13, #2 (Spring, 1951), 342-345.

3534 Laughlin, James. "Gists and Piths: From the Letters of Pound and Williams," Cf., #2712, pp. 229-243.

3535 Lawton, Harry. "The Ezra Pound Correspondence: Letters of the Lost Legion," Sadakichi Hartmann N, 1 (Winter, 1970), 1-3.

3536 Leary, Lewis. "Book Reviews," SAQ, 50 (October, 1951), 595-596.

3537 _____. "Ezra Pound: A Letter to Jay Hubbell," Paideuma, 5, #3 (Winter, 1976), 417-418.

3538 _____. "Pound-Wise, Penny Foolish: Correspondence on Getting Together a Volume of Criticism," St. Andrews Rev, 1, #1 (Fall-Winter, 1970), 5-9. See also #772.

3539 Leavis, F. R. "Pound in His Letters," Scrutiny, 18, #1 (June, 1951), 74-77.

3540 Lewis, Wyndham. "The Rock Drill," NS&N, 41 (April, 1951), 398.

3541 Lilly Library, Indiana University, Bloomington, Indiana. Reception of more than 12,000 letters from Ezra Pound Estate, donated by Pound's widow, Dorothy Shakespear Pound.

3542 Lindberg-Seyersted, Brita, ed. "Letters from Ezra Pound to Joseph Brewer," Paideuma, 10, #2 (Fall, 1981), 369-382.

3543 _____. "A Note on Ezra Pound as Letter-Writer," Edda, 1 (1981), 59-60.

3544 _____, ed. Pound/Ford: The Story of a Literary Friendship: The Correspondence between Ezra Pound and Ford Madox Ford and Their Writings about Each Other. Cf., #2751.

3545 Lowe, Robert Liddell. "High Thought," Furioso, 6, #2 (Spring, 1951), 71-74.

3546 McShane, Frank, et al. "Letters: The Case for Pound,"
Cf., #357.

3547 Materer, Timothy. "Doppelganger: Ezra Pound in His Letters," Cf., #2833.

3548 _____. "A Letter by Ezra Pound," MissouriRev, 6, #1
(Fall, 1982), 117-135.

3549 Meacham, Harry M. "Illustrations and Facsimile Letters,"
The Caged Panther: Ezra Pound at St. Elizabeth's. Cf.,
#361, pp. 97-102.

3550 Mencken, H. L. Letters of H. L. Mencken. Selected and
Edited by Guy J. Forgue. New York: Alfred A. Knopf,
1961, passim.

3551 Meyer, George Previn. "The Sage of Rapallo," SatRL, 33
(December 2, 1950), 24-25.

3552 Meyerson, Edward L. "Letters, Essays, Poetry," The Seed
Is Man: A Collection of Poetry and an Essay on Ezra Pound.
New York: Wm. Frederick Pr., 1967, pp. 34ff.

3553 Mondolfo, Vittoria I., and Margaret Hurley. Introduction by
Walter Pilkington. Ezra Pound: Letters to Ibbotson, 1935-
1952. Orono, Maine: National Poetry Foundation, University
of Maine, 1979.

3554 Monroe, Harriet. "Poetry's Old Letters," Poetry, 47 (October, 1935), 38-39.

3555 Moore, Arthur V. Letter to Ronald Duncan, December 19,
1945; Letter to Ronald Duncan, February 20, 1946. Humanities Research Center, University of Texas.

3556 Moore, Marianne. Letters. Ezra Pound: Perspectives: Essays in Honor of His Eightieth Birthday. Cf., #125, pp.
116-120.

3557 Morgan, Frederick. "A Note on Ezra Pound," HudR, 4, #1
(Spring, 1951), 156-160.

3558 Namjoshi, S., ed. "Ezra Pound: Letters to John Buchan,
1934-1935," Paideuma, 8 (1979), 462-483.

3559 Nassivera, J. C. "Leaf is a Leaf: A Look at DK/Some Letters of Ezra Pound," Paideuma, 4, #1 (Spring, 1975), 175-178.

3560 Neame, Alan. "Ezra Pound Reconsidered," Blackfriars (May,
1951), Review: Money Pamphlets and The Letters.

3561 Newbolt, Henry. "A Bundle of Letters," Ezra Pound: Perspectives. Noel Stock, ed. Cf., #125, pp. 109-128.

3562 Oldani, Louis. "Two Unpublished Pound Letters: Pound's Aid to Dreiser," LC, 42 (1977), 67-70.

3563 Österling, Anders. "Ezra Pounds brev," Stockholms-Tidningen (January 24, 1951). Review: The Letters.

3564 Paige, D. D. "Letters of Ezra Pound," HudR, 3, #1 (Spring, 1950), 53-56.

3565 _____, ed. The Letters of Ezra Pound, 1907-1941. New York; London: Harcourt Brace, 1950; repr., Norfolk, Conn.: New Directions, 1950.

3566 _____, ed. The Selected Letters of Ezra Pound, 1907-1914. London: Faber, 1971; New York: New Directions Pub. Co., 1971.

3567 Pearlman, Daniel D. "Fighting the World: The Letters of Ezra Pound to Senator William E. Borah of Idaho," Paideuma, 12, #2-3 (Fall-Winter, 1983), 419-426.

3568 Perrine, Laurence. "Ezra Pound's Ideas," SWR, 36 (Winter, 1951), xvi-xix. (Review of Pound's Letters.)

3569 Peschman, Herman. Review: ABC of Reading and The Letters, PoetryRev, 42, #5 (September-October, 1951), 273-275.

3570 Porter, Katherine Anne. "Yours, Ezra Pound," NYT (October 29, 1950), 4.

3571 Pound, Dorothy Shakespear. Letter to Julian Cornell. The Trial of Ezra Pound, Cf., #291, pp. 59-60.

3572 _____. Letter to E. E. Cummings, November 4, 1945, Houghton Library, Harvard University.

3573 _____. Gift of letters from Ezra Pound Estate to Lilly Library. Cf., #3541.

3574 Pound, Ezra. E. P. to L. U.: Nine Letters Written to Louis Untermeyer. Bloomington: Univ. of Indiana Pr., 1963, pp. 46. Review by Marvin Magalaner, BA, 38, #3 (Summer, 1964), 317.

3575 _____. "A Letter by Ezra Pound," MissouriRev, 6, #1 (Fall, 1982), 117-135. Notes by Timothy Materer.

3576 _____. "A Letter to Jay Hubbell," (Lewis Leary, ed.) Paideuma, 5 (Winter, 1976), 417-418.

3577 _____. "Letters from Ezra Pound to Benito Mussolini," ed.
by C. D. Heymann; tr. by R. Connolly. Encounter, 46, #5
(May, 1976), 35-41.

3578 _____. "Letters to Elizabeth Winslow," Paideuma, 9 (Fall,
1980), 340-356.

3579 _____. Letters to Ibbotson, 1935-1952. Vittoria I. Mondolfo and Margaret Hurley, eds. Introduction by Walter
Pilkington. Orono: National Poetry Foundation, University
of Maine, 1979.

3580 _____. "Letters to John Buchan, 1934-1935," Paideuma, 8
(Winter, 1979), 461-483.

3581 _____. "Letters to Natalie Barney," Edited with Commentary by Richard Sieburth. Paideuma, 5 (Fall, 1976), 279-299.

3582 _____. "Letters to Viola Baxter Jordan," Paideuma, 1
(Spring-Summer, 1972), 107-112.

3583 _____. "Letters to a Young Poet from Ezra Pound,"
Poetry, 76 (September, 1950), 342-351.

3584 _____. "Letters to the Editor," SatRL, 32 (June, July,
1949), 21-24.

3585 _____. "A Prison Letter," PaR, 28 (Summer-Fall, 1962),
17.

3586 _____. "Tidings from Pound to Joyce: Letter," Esquire,
64 (December, 1965), 152ff.

3587 _____, and T. S. Eliot. "[An Exchange of Letters on The
Waste Land,]" Nine, 4 (Summer, 1950), 176-179.

3588 Pound, Omar, and A. Walton Litz, eds. Ezra Pound and
Dorothy Shakespear: Their Letters, 1909-1914. New York:
New Directions, 1984.

3589 Read, Forrest, ed. Pound/Joyce: The Letters of Ezra
Pound to James Joyce, with Pound's Essays on Joyce. New
York: New Directions, 1970.

3590 Robbins, J. Albert, ed. EP to LU: Nine Letters Written to
Louis Untermeyer by Ezra Pound. Bloomington: Indiana
University Pr., 1963.

3591 Sieburth, Richard. "Ezra Pound: 'Letters to Natalie Barney,'"
Paideuma, 5 (Fall, 1976), 279-299.

3592   Sinclair, Upton. "Ezra Pound," My Lifetime in Letters.
       Cf., #3175, pp. 368-376.

3593   Singh, G. "Ezra Pound as a Letter Writer," AJES, 2 (1977),
       167-193.

3594   Steele, John L. "Ezra at the DTC: A Correspondence be-
       tween Carroll F. Terrell and John L. Steele," Paideuma, 12,
       #2-3, (Fall-Winter, 1983), 293-303. [DTC: Disciplinary
       Training Center]

3595   Stein, Sol. Reviews: The Letters and An Examination of
       Ezra Pound, ArizQt, 7, #2 (Summer, 1951), 180-186.

3596   Stock, Noel, ed. "A Bundle of Letters," Ezra Pound: Per-
       spectives, Cf., #125, pp. 109-128.

3597   _____. "Ezra Pound and the Sense of Responsibility,"
       ModAge (Chicago), 5 (Spring, 1961), 173-178.

3598   _____. "Verse Is a Sword: Unpublished Letters of Ezra
       Pound," XQtRev, I, #4 (October, 1960), 258-265.

3599   Symington, R. T. K. "'I Like to Get Letters': Ezra Pound
       and a Canadian Correspondent," MHRev, 66 (October, 1983),
       129-139.

3600   Tanselle, G. Thomas. "Two Early Letters of Ezra Pound,"
       Cf., #1781, pp. 114-119.

3601   Terrell, Carroll F. "An Interlude: Creating and Sweeping
       Up: [Letters to Marcella Booth and Her Replies]," Paideuma,
       4, #1 (Spring, 1975), 189-195.

3602   _____. "Ezra Pound's Letters to William Butler Yeats,"
       Antaeus, 21 (1976), 34-49.

3603   Thirlwall, John C. "The Quality of Mercy was not strained:
       a Footnote Followed by a Letter," Pound Newsletter, 8 (Octo-
       ber, 1955), 22-23.

3604   Thompson, James H., ed. "Letters to Elizabeth Winslow,"
       Paideuma, 9 (1980), 341-356.

3605   Traverso, Leone. "Letture de Ezra Pound," Studi urbinati di
       storia, filosofia e letteratura, 45 (1971), 300-303.

3606   Tseng, Pao Swen. "Letter to Mr. and Mrs. Pound," YLM,
       127, #6 (January, 1959), 11.

3607   Van Doren, Mark. Preface. The Letters of Ezra Pound, 1907-
       1941. D. D. Paige, ed. Cf., #3565, pp. v-ix.

3608 Wade, Allan, ed. The Letters of W. B. Yeats. London:
      Rupert Hart-Davis; New York: Macmillan, 1954, passim.

3609 Weissman, David L., et al. "Correspondence," Cf., #252.

3610 West, Ray B., Jr. "Letters of an American," SR, 59 (Spring,
      1951), 342-347.

3611 Wigginton, Waller B. "A Homer Pound Letter," Cf., #149,
      pp. 27-29.

3612 Williams, William Carlos. "Letter," Ezra Pound: Perspectives.
      Noel Stock, ed. Cf., #125, pp. 124-125.

3613 Yeats, W. B. "A Packet for Ezra Pound," A Vision. New
      York: Macmillan, [c1938], 1956, pp. 26-30.

3614 Z[abell], M[orton]. "Recent Magazines," [Letters]. Cf.,
      #3456, pp. 173-174.

VII. BIBLIOGRAPHY

3615 Agenda, Ezra Pound Number, #2, IV (October-November, 1965); Nos. 3-4, VIII (1970), William Cookson, ed.

3616 Altieri, Charles, Comp. "Ezra Pound," Modern Poetry. AHM Pub. Co., Arlington Hts., Ill., 1979, pp. 76-79.

3617 The Analyst, ed. Robert Mayo. Evanston: Northwestern University, 1953- .

3618 Angus, Ian D. A List with Description of the Books of Ezra Pound. London: [Microfilm copy of typescript.], 1952.

3619 Arms, George, and Joseph Kuntz. Poetry Explication. New York: Swallow Press and William Morrow & Co., Inc., 1950.

3620 Bornstein, George. "Pound and Eliot," American Literary Scholarship: An Annual/1977. Durham, N.C.: Duke U. Pr., 1979, pp. 119-133.

3621 _____, and Stuart Y. McDougal. "Pound and Eliot," American Literary Scholarship: An Annual/1978. J. Albert Robbins, ed. Durham, N.C.: Duke U. Pr., 1980, pp. 111-125.

3622 _____, and Stuart Y. McDougal. "Pound and Eliot," American Literary Scholarship: An Annual/1979. James Woodress, ed. Durham, N.C.: Duke U. Pr., 1981, pp. 115-132.

3623 _____, and Stuart Y. McDougal. "Pound and Eliot," American Literary Scholarship: An Annual/1980. J. Albert Robbins, ed. Durham, N.C.: Duke U. Pr., 1982, pp. 121-141.

3624 _____, and Stuart Y. McDougal. "Pound and Eliot," American Literary Scholarship: An Annual/1981. James Woodress, ed. Durham, N.C.: Duke U. Pr., 1983, pp. 127-136.

3625 "A Checklist of Explications." Pound Newsletter, #5 (January, 1955), 20-21; #6 (April, 1955), 16-19, 24-30; #7 (July, 1955), 6-10; #8 (October, 1955), 33-35.

3626 Corrigan, Robert A. "An Annotated Checklist of Ezra Pound
      Criticism: Part I," Paideuma, 1 (Winter, 1972), 229-263;
      (supersedes author's "The First Quarter Century of Ezra
      Pound Criticism," RALS, 2, 157-207.

3627 Crosland, Andrew. "An Annotated Checklist of Criticism on
      Ezra Pound, 1961-1965," Paideuma, 8 (Winter, 1979), 523-538.

3628 Crowder, Richard. "Ezra Pound: Poetry, 1900 to the 1930's,"
      American Literary Scholarship: An Annual, 1969. J. Albert
      Robbins, ed. Durham, N.C.: Duke U. Pr., 1971, pp. 253-
      261.

3629 _____. "Ezra Pound: Poetry, 1900 to 1930's," American
      Literary Scholarship: An Annual, 1970. J. Albert Robbins,
      ed. Durham, N.C.: Duke U. Pr., 1972, pp. 280-288.

3630 _____. "Ezra Pound: Poetry: 1900 to the 1930's,"
      American Literary Scholarship: An Annual, 1971. J. Albert
      Robbins, ed. Durham, N.C.: Duke U. Pr., 1973, pp. 278-
      283.

3631 _____. "Ezra Pound: Poetry: 1900 to 1930's," American
      Literary Scholarship: An Annual, 1973. James Woodress, ed.
      Durham, N.C.: Duke U. Pr., 1975, pp. 305-311.

3632 Davis, Charles T. "Pound--Poetry: 1910-1930," American
      Literary Scholarship: An Annual, 1963. James Woodress, ed.
      Durham, N.C.: Duke U. Pr., 1965, pp. 173-177.

3633 Dilligan, Robert J., James W. Parins, and Todd K. Bender.
      A Concordance to Ezra Pound's Cantos. New York; London:
      Garland Pub., Inc., 1981.

3634 Edwards, John. A Preliminary Checklist of the Writings of
      Ezra Pound. New Haven: Kirgo-Books, 1953.

3635 _____, and W. W. Vasse. Annotated Index to the Cantos
      of Ezra Pound. Berkeley: U. of Calif. Pr., 1958.

3636 Espey, John. "Ezra Pound: Bibliography," Fifteen Modern
      American Authors. Jackson R. Bryer, ed. Durham, N.C.:
      Duke U. Pr., 1969, pp. 323-344.

3637 _____. "Ezra Pound: Bibliography," Sixteen Modern
      American Authors. Jackson R. Bryer, ed. Durham, N.C.:
      Duke U. Pr., 1974, pp. 445-471.

3638 Froula, Christine. A Guide to Ezra Pound's Selected Poems.
      New York: New Directions, 1983.

3639 Gallup, Donald Clifford. A Bibliography of Ezra Pound.
      London: Rupert Hart-Davis, 1963.

3640 _____. "Corrections and Additions to the Pound Bibliogra-
      phy (Part 3)," Paideuma, 1, #1 (Spring-Summer, 1972), 113-
      125; 2, #2 (Fall, 1973), 315-324; 3, #3 (Winter, 1974), 403-
      404.

3641 _____. On Contemporary Bibliography, with Particular
      Reference to Ezra Pound. Austin, Texas: Humanities Re-
      search Center, U. of Texas, 1970.

3642 Hatlen, Burton. "Work in Progress," Paideuma, 3, #2 (Fall,
      1974), 275-277.

3643 Havlice, Patricia Pate. "Ezra Pound," Index to American
      Author Bibliographies. Metuchen, N.J.: Scarecrow Pr.,
      Inc., 1971, pp. 132-133.

3644 Henault, Marie P. Guide to Ezra Pound. Merrill Guides.
      Columbus, Ohio: Charles E. Merrill, 1970.

3645 Jones, Howard Mumford, and Richard M. Ludwig. "The
      Thirties," and "The Poetic Renaissance," Guide to American
      Literature and Its Backgrounds Since 1890. 4th ed., Rev. &
      Enlarged. Cambridge, Mass.: Harvard U. Pr., 1972, pp. 174,
      198-199.

3646 Jung, Angela, and Guido Palandri, eds., and trs. Italian
      Images of Ezra Pound: Twelve Critical Essays. Taipei,
      Taiwan: Mei Ya, 1979, pp. 163-167.

3647 Koster, Donald N. "Ezra Pound (1885-1972)," American Lit-
      erature and Language: A Guide to Information Sources.
      Detroit, Mich.: Gale Research Co., 1982, pp. 224-232.

3648 Kunitz, Stanley J., ed. Twentieth Century Authors: A
      Bibliographical Dictionary of Modern Literature. New York:
      H. W. Wilson Co., 1955, pp. 1121-1123.

3649 Kuntz, Joseph M., and Nancy C. Martinez. "Ezra Pound,"
      Poetry Explication: A Checklist of Interpretation Since 1925
      of British and American Poems, Past and Present. Boston:
      G. K. Hall & Co., 1950; 1980, pp. 351-354.

3650 Lane, Gary. A Concordance to Personae: The Shorter
      Poems of Ezra Pound. New York: Haskell House Pubs.,
      1972.

3651 Leary, Lewis. "Ezra Pound," Articles on American Litera-
      ture, 1900-1950. Durham: Duke U. Pr., 1954, pp. 252-254.

3652 _____. "Ezra Pound," Articles on American Literature,
      1950-1967. Durham, N.C.: Duke U. Pr., 1970, pp. 450-561.

3653 _____, with John Auchard. "Ezra Pound," Articles on
      American Literature, 1968-1975. Durham, N.C.: Duke U.
      Pr., 1979, pp. 426-437.

3654 Libman, Valentina A., com. "Ezra Pound," Russian Studies
      in American Literature. Clarence Gohdes, ed. Chapel Hill:
      U. of North Carolina Pr., 1969, p. 155f.

3655 Little, Matthew. "Corrections to Gallup's Pound and Some
      History of Pound's Essays on the Jefferson-Adams Letters,"
      BSAP, 74 (1980), 200-272.

3656 Ludwig, Richard M. "Pound and Eliot," American Literary
      Scholarship: An Annual, 1974. James Woodress, ed.
      Durham, N.C.: Duke U. Pr., 1976, pp. 101-121.

3657 McDougal, S. Y. "Pound and Eliot," American Literary
      Scholarship: An Annual, 1975. James Woodress, ed.
      Durham, N.C.: Duke U. Pr., 1977, pp. 131-142.

3658 _____. "Pound and Eliot," American Literary Scholarship:
      An Annual, 1976. J. Albert Robbins, ed. Durham, N.C.:
      Duke U. Pr., 1978, pp. 109-118.

3659 Millett, Fred Benjamin. "Ezra Pound," Contemporary Ameri-
      can Authors. New York: AMS Pr., 1970, pp. 529-533.

3660 Mondolfo, Vittoria. "Annotated Bibliography of Criticism of
      Ezra Pound, 1918-1924," Paideuma, 5, #2 (Fall, 1976), 303-
      328.

3661 _____, and Helen Shuster. "Annotated Checklist of Criti-
      cism on Ezra Pound, 1930-1935," Paideuma, 5, #1 (Spring,
      1976), 155-184.

3662 Morrow, Bradford, and Bernard Lafourcade. With Introduc-
      tion by Hugh Kenner. A Bibliography of the Writings of
      Wyndham Lewis. Santa Barbara, Calif.: Black Sparrow Pr.,
      1978, Pound passim.

3663 Munson, Gorham. "Ezra Pound," American Literary Scholar-
      ship: An Annual, 1966. James Woodress, ed. Durham,
      N.C.: Duke U. Pr., 1968, pp. 193-196.

3664 _____, and Ann Stanford. "Ezra Pound--Poetry: 1900 to
      1930's," American Literary Scholarship: An Annual, 1968.
      Durham, N.C.: Duke U. Pr., 1970, pp. 228-232.

3665 Nilon, Charles H. "Ezra Pound," Bibliography of Bibliographies in American Literature. New York; London: R. R. Bowker Co., 1970, p. 232.

3666 O'Connor, William Van, and Edward Stone, eds. A Casebook on Ezra Pound. New York: Thomas Y. Crowell Co., 1959.

3667 Paideuma: A Journal Devoted to Ezra Pound Scholarship. Hugh Kenner and Eva Hesse, eds. U. of Maine, Orono, 1972.

3668 Pound Newsletter. John H. Edwards, ed. Berkeley, U. of Calif. 1954-1966.

3669 Quarterly Review of Literature. Ezra Pound Issue, 5, #2 (1949). Bard College, Annandale, N.Y.

3670 Richardson, Kenneth ed. "Ezra Pound," Twentieth Century Writing: A Reader's Guide to Contemporary Literature. Levittown, New York: Transatlantic Arts, Inc., 1971, pp. 499-501.

3671 Rizzardi, Alfredo, ed. "Studi e Opinioni su Ezra Pound," Nuova Corrente, Nos. 5-6 (January-June, 1956).

3672 Rooks, George. "An Annotated Checklist of Criticism on Ezra Pound, 1976," Paideuma, 8, (Fall, 1979), 303-316.

3673 Rosenfeld, Alvin H. "Ezra Pound--Poetry: 1900 to the 1930s," American Literary Scholarship: An Annual/1972. Durham, N.C.: Duke U. Pr., 1974, pp. 312-319, passim.

3674 Russell, Peter, ed. Ezra Pound: A Collection of Essays edited by Peter Russell to be Presented to Ezra Pound on His Sixty-fifth Birthday. Norfolk, Conn.: New Directions, 1950.

3675 San Juan, Jr., E[pifanio]. Critics on Ezra Pound: Readings in Literary Criticism. Coral Gables, Florida: U. of Miami Pr., 1972.

3676 Schneeman, Peter. "Pound in Romania," Paideuma, 10, #2 (Fall, 1981), 421-434.

3677 Schulman, Grace, ed. Ezra Pound: A Collection of Criticism. New York: McGraw-Hill, 1974.

3678 Schwartz, Joseph. "Books on Pound," Spirit, 37, #2 (1970), 42-46.

3679 Seymour-Smith, Martin. "Ezra Pound," Guide to Modern World Literature. New York: Funk & Wagnalls, 1973, pp. 67-73.

3680   Sickles, Hollis. "An Annotated Checklist of Pound Criticism,"
       Paideuma, 8 (Spring, 1979), 97-140.

3681   Slatin, Myles. "More by Ezra Pound," YULG, 30 (October,
       1955), 74-80.

3682   Somer, John, and Barbara E. Cooper. American and British
       Literature, 1945-1975: An Annotated Bibliography of Contem-
       porary Scholarship. Lawrence, Kansas: Regents Pr. of
       Kansas, 1980, passim.

3683   Spiller, Robert E., et al, eds. Literary History of the United
       States. Bibliography Supplement II. New York: Macmillan,
       1972, Vol. 3, pp. 240-244.

3684   Stanford, Ann. "Ezra Pound--Poetry 1910-1930," American
       Literary Scholarship: An Annual, 1964. James Woodress, ed.
       Durham, N.C.: Duke U. Pr., 1966, pp. 184-186.

3685   _____. "Ezra Pound--Poetry: 1900 to the 1930's," Ameri-
       can Literary Scholarship: An Annual, 1965. James Woodress,
       ed. Durham, N.C.: Duke U. Pr., 1967, pp. 204-208.

3686   Stock, Noel, ed. Ezra Pound: Essays in Honour of His
       Eightieth Birthday. Chicago: Henry Regnery Co., 1965.

3687   _____, Guest-ed. Helix. Special Issue Nos. 13 and 14
       (1983). (119 Maltravers Road, Ivanhoe, Australia 3079).

3688   Sutton, Walter, ed. Ezra Pound: A Collection of Critical Es-
       says. Englewood Cliffs, New Jersey: Prentice-Hall, 1963,
       Cf., #2240.

3689   Tate, Allen. "Ezra Pound," Essays of Four Decades. Chi-
       cago: The Swallow Pr., 1968, pp. 364-371, 509-513; Cf.,
       #240, #970.

3690   _____. Sixty American Poets, 1896-1944. Washington:
       Library of Congress and Biblio Division, 1954, Rev. ed.,
       pp. 93-101. Cf., #3262.

3691   Vasse, William. "Bibliography," The Pound Newsletter,
       [Ten issues], (January, 1954-April, 1956).

3692   _____. "A Checklist of Explications: I: The Pre-Canto
       Poetry," Pound Newsletter, 5 (January, 1955), 20-21.

3693   _____. "A Checklist of Explications: II: The Cantos,"
       Pound Newsletter, 6 (April, 1955), 16-19.

3694   Weber, Brom, and James Woodress. "Ezra Pound--Poetry:

1900 to the 1930's," American Literary Scholarship: An Annual,
1967. James Woodress, ed. Durham, N.C.: Duke U. Pr., 1969,
pp. 212-216.

3695   Wenzel, Gernot.   "Addenda to Robert A. Corrigan's Biblio-
       graphical Contributions on Pound," Paideuma, 5, #1 (Spring,
       1976), 214-215.

3696   Williams, William Carlos.   The William Carlos Williams Reader.
       Edited with Introduction by M. L. Rosenthal.   New York:
       New Directions Pub. Corp., 1966, pp. 308-318.   Cf., #423.

INDEX OF CRITICS

INDEX OF TOPICS